HOT DOG MONEY

GUY LAWSON

HOT DOG MONEY

Inside the Biggest Scandal
in the History of College Sports

Little
a

Published by Little A, New York

www.apub.com

Amazon, the Amazon logo, and Little A are trademarks of Amazon.com, Inc., or its
affiliates.

ISBN-13: 9781662519666 (hardcover)
ISBN-13: 9781662519642 (paperback)
ISBN-13: 9781662519659 (digital)

Cover design by Jack Smyth
Cover image: © peterspiro / Getty; © TokenPhoto / Getty

Printed in the United States of America

First edition

For Maya, always

CONTENTS

AUTHOR'S NOTE

Louis Martin "Marty" Blazer started talking to me in May 2020, as the COVID-19 pandemic was first spreading across the world. Blazer had recently been sentenced on multiple federal fraud charges, ending the threat of being exposed to further legal jeopardy if he spoke publicly about his story. I write about crime, and occasionally, convicted criminals who want to tell their stories approach me. Most often, these accounts couldn't carry a magazine article, let alone a book. But as I started to investigate the details of Blazer's incredible, multidimensional, and often truly unbelievable tale, it appeared to have real significance—if he was willing to be forthright. Blazer assured me that he wanted his story to be told fully, with no punches pulled or embarrassing events left out or downplayed, a real reckoning with all that had happened on his descent into criminality, which led to his becoming an undercover FBI cooperator in an infamous college basketball fraud-and-cheating investigation. Blazer agreed from the start that I would have editorial control, no matter where the truth and my reporting led.

In the press, Blazer had been likened to New York Police Department detective Frank Serpico, the renegade '70s cop who'd exposed epidemic corruption in law enforcement—a compelling comparison. But in Blazer's case, he had not been portrayed as heroic; to the contrary, he had been almost universally condemned and ridiculed in the media as both a con man and a dubious FBI informant. It had been reported that he'd helped ensnare multiple college basketball coaches in federal felonies in an attempt to avoid prison.

I had recently watched *The Scheme*, an HBO documentary on Christian Dawkins, who'd been convicted of bribery as a result of Blazer's work with the FBI. Dawkins's remarks seemed to accurately reflect the general attitude of those who had been targeted in the federal fraud case.

"Marty Blazer should probably go to prison," Dawkins said. Adding, for emphasis, "Fuck Marty Blazer."

Apart from the adverse portrait of Blazer in the press, there were good reasons to question Blazer's reliability. Before he'd gotten in trouble with the law, Blazer had long been convinced he was the smartest person in every room he entered, an overweening arrogance that had led him to ruination as a financial adviser to star players in the National Football League. He wanted me to know that he hadn't become a criminal in a single day—it had been an evolution, with cut corners and broken rules and self-justifications mounting for years. Blazer didn't see himself as just another white suburban father; he was the type of man who could be found hanging out in Las Vegas with Mike Tyson, or sipping single malt scotch in a club in Miami with rapper Lil Wayne, or pacing the sidelines at a Penn State football game near legendary coach Joe Paterno. Associating with young, wealthy athletes and adept at obtaining the finer things in life, at the height of his time as a financial adviser to sports celebrities, the middle-aged Blazer would dress in a hoodie and sneakers, accented by a Rolex on his wrist and reservations on his new iPhone for a private flight to an exclusive party on a private Florida island. His teenage daughter's friends loved him because he represented NFL players, Blazer was convinced, and had famous sports and rap affiliations and a devil-may-care attitude that had left him heedless to the consequences of his conduct.

Over more than two years of reporting, I went through thousands of pages of testimony from multiple trials as well as mountains of documentary evidence and recorded conversations to corroborate Blazer's tale. To help me understand his struggles, Blazer sent me his personal diaries recording his innermost thoughts. His stack of notebooks—pages he had shared with no one else—suffered from a helter-skelter chronological disorder and appeared to be a mishmash of events and emotions memorialized contemporaneously, along with later musings and margin notes written to add emphasis or jog his memory.

"I was devastated that I put my family into this situation," Blazer wrote in a cover letter. "I wear a lot of pain and frustration in these pages, so please excuse my rambling and disorganized thoughts. I'm probably overdramatic, I know, and a lot of people have gone through much worse, but I've always had trouble letting people in and allowing them to know the real me."

~

Twenty-first-century law enforcement operates in what could be called the Age of the Snitch. Performing duties once filled by trained and accountable undercover cops and federal agents, thousands upon thousands of untrained and largely unaccountable criminal-defendant cooperators are secretly working on behalf of the government, creating a parallel universe in law enforcement. The implications, paradoxes, and dangers of the government using cooperating informants and cooperating witnesses—CIs and CWs, as they are known—are fully understood by few, including the many agents and prosecutors in the country who haven't pondered the troubling aspects of unleashing operatives who are inherently devious and cunning—elements I will examine in new and shocking detail in these pages.

Blazer's work as a CI and the story he helped break held a mirror up to important American institutions, including the FBI and the NCAA—the National Collegiate Athletic Association—but also sneaker companies and television networks and prestigious colleges reaping huge profits on the backs of kids playing the sports they love.

Despite the importance of the case and the value of Blazer's cooperation, federal prosecutors and FBI investigators wouldn't cooperate with this book—for reasons that will become clear—and some evidence remained under seal. Part of his story was necessarily subjective, too, a product of his experiences and perceptions. But over time, it became apparent to me that Blazer did indeed want to tell the truth, urgently and fully.

The man you will encounter in these pages was not always admirable or even entirely likable, often doing things that were questionable, and he was occasionally prone to bouts of self-pity and excuse making, but in the end, he was a human being making mistakes and trying to atone for his crimes, driven by the desires to save his own skin and also do some good in the world. It seemed to me that Blazer personified the age-old contradiction at the heart of so many stories about crime and punishment: *Yes, I lied then, but now I'm telling the truth.*

The vast majority of the targets of the investigation were Black, while Blazer is white, as is this author. Race isn't a subtext of this story; like so much of American history up to the present moment, most every aspect of this tale is informed by racism—systemic, institutional, personal. It is widely known that big-time college sports are exploitative, broken, and hypocritical, but they are also hugely popular and entertaining and beloved, a paradox that lies at the center of Blazer's story. *How does the NCAA really work? What are the inner truths? Who are the winners and losers in this lucrative industry? How widespread are corruption and cheating?* What follows is a voyage into the most secretive sanctums of an underworld known to few—a shadowy, hidden quarter of American society that exposes the corrupt and corrupting reality of the NCAA's code of amateurism and an ongoing multibillion-dollar scam.

Guy Lawson

June 1, 2024

New York, New York

CHAPTER ONE

Takedown

The sense of bewilderment was complete.

At dawn on the morning of September 26, 2017, the FBI pulled a wealthy hedge fund manager from his shower—naked—in Princeton, New Jersey, while his wife and children watched in horror and confusion. A convoy of the bureau's armed vehicles rumbled through the upscale suburbs of Auburn, Alabama, toward the home of the associate head basketball coach of the Auburn Tigers. Across the country, in a leafy Portland, Oregon, neighborhood, FBI agents took Adidas's head of global marketing for basketball away in handcuffs. The day before, a young hustler had arrived at a luxury suite in the W Hotel in Manhattan's Times Square for a meeting with the investor in his nascent basketball player–management business with the ambitious name of Live Out Your Dreams, only to be placed under arrest, SWAT-style, the takedown shocking him so much he began to hyperventilate and peel off his clothes in panic and disbelief.

On the day of the takedown, the FBI also raided a nondescript low-slung office building in Englewood, New Jersey, where they seized records detailing a vast number of payments made to scores of the best college basketball players represented by ASM Sports, a leading NBA agency that operated out of the modest structure. Players from North Carolina, Duke, Texas, Michigan State, Alabama, Kentucky—the truly elite college basketball programs—had been implicated in a scheme to secretly provide them with money in apparently blatant contravention of the NCAA's amateur rules.

The sense of incredulity that the targets all displayed when they were busted was equaled by the reaction of the press and the public as the scale and sweep of the FBI's investigation emerged. The actions taken by the Department of Justice in the fall of 2017 seemed like a frontal attack on the multibillion-dollar collegiate sports–industrial complex. The coaches and executives and moneymen arrested all operated in the world of NCAA amateur sports, and they were all breaking the rules—*who wasn't?*—but suddenly the open secret of cheating in college basketball was exposed in the form of multiple criminal indictments on the federal level.

From the lowliest rungs of the enterprise, from whispered conversations about illicit payments with the parents of gangly kids on the sidelines of high school basketball courts, to millionaire-celebrity head coaches preening on national television, federal prosecutors claimed that the cases constituted the biggest scandal in the history of the NCAA.

"We have your playbook," warned a senior FBI official, live on ESPN at the press conference staged by the Southern District of New York, sending a shiver of dread throughout the world of college basketball.

The press conference looked like a display of the federal government at its most competent, vigilant, and powerful. The FBI had undertaken a masterful investigation, resulting in a triumphant series of arrests that personified the term for such events: *takedown.* Law enforcement had literally and figuratively taken down the power structure of college basketball, sending out shock waves that would resonate through all college sports and beyond, putting bad actors preying on the code of amateurism on notice.

Or so it seemed.

But watching from his home in Pittsburgh, former financial adviser and secret undercover FBI operative Marty Blazer knew the government hadn't actually exposed the nature and scope of college basketball's corruption, no matter what the officials said. The entire investigation of college basketball had been his brainchild. Far from being victims, Blazer knew the NCAA colleges were the predators, running a corrupt billion-dollar enterprise that hid behind a veil of amateurism by not compensating players, who generated vast fortunes for the schools. As an undercover cooperating FBI witness for three years, Blazer had covertly recorded thousands of hours of conversations that revealed an epidemic of cheating and bribery. But the government hadn't truly targeted the highest levels of the NCAA, or the head coaches, sneaker companies, agents, and financial managers who gorged themselves on the supposedly amateur sport. Blazer knew that no one in power wanted to confront the darker, larger truths. The reason he could see through the grandiose claims and self-righteous bluster was simple: he had been at the center of events, and you can't bullshit a bullshitter.

CHAPTER TWO

The Proffer

Marty Blazer's FBI saga started three years earlier, on the morning of May 21, 2014, when he finally decided he was going to tell the truth. For months, Blazer had been under investigation by the US Securities and Exchange Commission, a civil inquiry into his alleged misappropriation of millions of dollars from his NFL-player clients. In the weeks leading up to his decision, the legal pressure had escalated in an alarming way, with the SEC instructing Blazer's civil attorney that his client might want to retain a criminal attorney, and all intelligible signs pointed toward an impending federal indictment for fraud. Blazer was not only guilty of those crimes but also had no reasonable defense or plea of mitigation to offer. Blazer was, in short, cornered, with prosecutors of the Southern District of New York surrounding him and preparing a legal case that promised to result in multiple years in a federal prison. His "Spidey-Sense," as he described his instinct to anticipate imminent danger, told him it was time to come clean about all his activities and hope for the best with the federal government.

On that May morning, arranged on the far side of a long table in a windowless, fluorescent-lit conference room in a Lower Manhattan government building, were seven federal prosecutors and investigators from the Southern District and the SEC, skeptically eyeing Blazer and his criminal and civil attorneys. Blazer was *Queen for the Day*, the law enforcement nickname for the subject of an investigation who is confessing to all the crimes they've ever committed, with the proviso that, for that day—and that day alone, at least metaphorically—the confessor will have immunity. Prosecutors couldn't directly use evidence from the proffer session for future prosecutions, at least in theory, and the hope was that in return for his admission of guilt, Blazer would receive some consideration—a letter from the government recommending a judge grant him a lesser sentence.

"They probably already know the answer to most of their questions," Blazer's criminal lawyer had told him before the session. "If you think you're in trouble now, watch what happens if you lie to them."

The message was unmistakable and stark: do not prevaricate, hedge, or shade the truth. This might seem simple, but not for Blazer, who had been habitually lying for years.

Blazer was in his midforties, a businessman with a rapidly disappearing case of overconfidence. Until recent months, he had been a seemingly successful Pittsburgh-based financial adviser to professional football players, with an upscale suite of offices in a fashionable district of the city, and he had managed a roster of more than a dozen NFL clients, earning recurring fees for business management and concierge services of more than half a million dollars annually; he had also had a separate investment-advisory company to put more than $20 million of his players' money to work on their behalf in return for a 1 percent commission. Blazer had been steadily growing his business, but he was also an opportunist who'd secretly misappropriated more than $2 million from some of his clients to fund failed entertainment ventures—including an unwatchable mobster movie.

Wire fraud, aggravated identity theft, making false statements to federal officers . . . Blazer's yearslong run as a high-flying money manager was certain to end in multiple felony convictions, a reality that was only beginning to sink in as he gulped and stared at the large binders documenting his crimes in front of each official. Blazer had followed his attorney's instructions not to wear cologne or jewelry or loafers, and he was attempting to assume a mien of extreme humility instead of his usual glib-salesman attitude. He'd made a plan for what he was going to say, rehearsing in the hotel-room mirror that morning, but the words evaporated in terror when he felt the power he was confronting. *Everyone has a plan until they get punched in the mouth,* Blazer thought, recalling the Mike Tyson quote as he stared at the stone-faced authorities who obviously held him in disdain.

On the far side of the table from Blazer was Assistant United States Attorney Damian Williams, a Black prosecutor who looked to him exactly like Steve Urkel from *Family Matters*: skinny tie, skinny pants, suspenders, big glasses, tight shirt. A rising star in the Southern District of New York, Williams specialized in securities fraud and prosecuting high-profile cases. He would go on to become the United States attorney for the Southern District, making him one of the most powerful law enforcement figures in the nation. But Williams was still a line prosecutor when he slid a document across the table, telling Blazer that it was a bank transfer. Blazer inspected the document, recognizing it, well aware of what AUSA Williams wanted to know.

"Whose signature is that?" Williams asked.

This was a moment when Blazer would have reflexively lied or deflected; he'd been lying to the SEC for months. He desperately wanted to lie, or shade the truth in some way, even as he knew it would lead to disaster. The truth was that he had forged the signature of one of his players, something he had done many times.

Blazer sighed. "That's my signature," he said, a sense of relief flooding over him. He'd done what he wasn't sure he could: told the truth.

As Blazer began to tell the prosecutors the tale of his criminal behavior, he discovered that he actually liked telling the truth. It wasn't just liberating—it was exhilarating. *How did Blazer attract his player clients?*

AUSA Williams wanted to know. That, Blazer explained, required an understanding of the player–financial adviser relationship—and *that* required an understanding of how leading colleges recruited star college athletes. And *that*, in turn, required an appreciation of the nature and extent of corruption in the NCAA's amateur-sports system.

Blazer's narrative started moving in an unexpected direction. For hours, he told prosecutors how he'd given elite college football players large amounts of cash in return for them signing on as his clients when they turned pro, money usually disguised as loans that all concerned parties knew would never be repaid. The bribes were the gateway to an extremely lucrative business. These payments weren't an aberration or exception, Blazer said; it was how big-time NCAA sports functioned, with colleges, coaches, players, agents, financial advisers, runners, boosters, sneaker companies—the whole industry—in on the game.

As Blazer unburdened himself, he could see Williams's attitude shift. The prosecutor's eyes grew larger, and his jaw fell open as he stared in frank disbelief. All along the row of dour officials, the same expression began to form as Blazer gave them an insider's view of the reality of NCAA sports. Blazer was describing a complex, vast conspiracy that had huge implications for one of the most popular entertainment industries in the nation. This was potentially the kind of high-profile, headline-grabbing organized crime case that the Southern District had long reveled in.

Finally, one of Blazer's attorneys interrupted him, as if they'd all heard more than enough. Pin-drop silence descended. After a pause, AUSA Williams said he needed to confer privately with his colleagues, and with that, all seven federal officials disappeared, leaving Blazer and his two attorneys alone in the conference room. They sat quietly, the attorneys exchanging knowing looks. The information Blazer had provided made him an attractive prospect as a confidential informant—or CI, or snitch.

Ten minutes passed in silence, until the federal prosecutors solemnly reentered single file.

"We feel that you've been forthcoming today," AUSA Williams said. "We are going to postpone filing any charges at this time. We are wondering if you would be interested in discussing some other matters in depth and perhaps assisting us with looking into the things you've discussed."

Blazer swallowed, not quite sure he'd heard Williams correctly. Their eyes met, and Blazer could see that the prosecutor was serious. Inwardly, Blazer was thrilled.

"Yes," he said with composure. "Of course. I'd be more than happy to help in any way that I can."

The government wasn't going to move forward with his prosecution for the time being, AUSA Williams said. Blazer's fate now seemed to depend on the value of his cooperation, and if he played his cards right, he might get a reduced sentence or maybe even avoid prison entirely.

The truth, he realized, might set him free.

CHAPTER THREE

More, Always More

Before he landed in the Southern District's crosshairs, Blazer's career as a financial adviser had begun in the late nineties. He attended weekend warrior games of pickup basketball at the Pittsburgh Rivers Club, an athletic facility frequented by well-to-do businesspeople and professionals. Blazer had played football and basketball in high school, and Division III football at Carnegie Mellon University. He had an easy familiarity with jocks, could talk trash and take and deliver elbows as he fought for possession of the ball.

The games yielded twisted ankles and black eyes, and Blazer frequently had deep-tissue massages to treat his aches and pains. In one session, his massage therapist mentioned she had started working with a new client who played for the Pittsburgh Steelers, a former first-round-pick defensive back who'd recently signed as a free agent with the team—Donnell Woolford.

Soon after, Blazer was back for another appointment when Woolford turned up. Blazer had the gift of gab, and if he wanted to involve himself in someone's life, he had an uncanny knack for doing precisely that. Offering Woolford connections in Pittsburgh, Blazer employed flattery, self-deprecation, and locker-room language to become fast friends with the cornerback.

Thinking of Woolford as a potential client for his stockbroker business, Blazer took him out for lunch, only to discover that the player had blown through his money and was in such dire straits that he asked Blazer if he'd help try to negotiate an early payment on the next season's signing bonus from the Steelers. Blazer failed to convince the Steelers to make the prepayment, but representing a pro football player in talks with an NFL team was exciting. Blazer was a Steelers fan, and Woolford offered him free tickets. Blazer went to the games and got to work, trying to attract NFL players as brokerage clients.

At the time he met Woolford, Blazer was a thirty-year-old broker, bored with the humdrum existence of trading stocks and bonds and looking for a challenge in life. His looming future as a midlevel financial adviser in a sleepy Pittsburgh office filled Blazer with existential dread. His wife, Trish, had just stopped working after their first child had been born, and Blazer was getting serious about making money, but taking orders from middle-class clients for blue-chip stocks was deadly dull.

"I had graduated at the top of my class in high school," Blazer recalled. "I had been a good student at Carnegie Mellon, one of the most prestigious college business programs in the country. I felt that peddling securities to retirees was not intellectually stimulating. I wanted more."

Blazer had recently watched *Jerry Maguire*, and the glamour of professional sports management was alluring. It turned out that Woolford's agent, William "Tank" Black, had recently been indicted for money laundering and running a Ponzi scheme with a South Carolina attorney. They had been caught operating a high-interest loan scam offering 20 percent returns and conducting deals with bags of cash. Black's network of investors had included gangsters from a Detroit cocaine-distribution outfit, who had been laundering millions of dollars.

Black had lost more than $13 million of his clients' money. After he pleaded guilty to criminal charges and went to prison, the motley crew of schemers and hangers-on he had developed became the conduit through which Blazer received his entrée into professional sports management. It was not an auspicious beginning.

"Tank's recipe for building relationships was the norm for signing players, I discovered, and it was what I adopted," Blazer said. "Lure big-time college prospects by providing them with cash and gifts in the hope that the money I paid them would be enough to buy their business when they turned pro. For the drug dealers and organized crime figures Tank was running with, it was a genius way to launder money. By giving dirty cash to kids—lots of it—they could clean it through Black's agency with the cash payments."

Blazer saw a way into the business while working Black's former network. Woolford was then represented by an aspiring Chicago agent named Rick "Rocky" Scalzo. When Blazer and Scalzo met in Pittsburgh, through Woolford, they agreed that Blazer should try to recruit college players at local schools such as Pitt and Penn State, hotbeds for big-time college football players. Scalzo would then become the players' agent, while Blazer would become their financial adviser, a tandem arrangement that wasn't uncommon in pro sports.

Scalzo sent Blazer a list of players to recruit. The first one Blazer approached was a running back for the University of Pittsburgh named Kevan Barlow. Blazer read online that Barlow's uncle had recently been murdered. The uncle had been playing in a neighborhood Thanksgiving Day football game when an argument broke out between two strangers. It was a bit of personal information that Blazer hoped to use to bond with Barlow.

Blazer pulled up to Barlow's off-campus housing in his BMW 740i, wearing a custom suit and Rolex to demonstrate he had money. In the player's dive apartment, Barlow insisted they watch his highlight reel on a mattress he'd dragged from the bedroom to serve as a couch. The encounter, Blazer quickly realized, was about stroking Barlow's ego, so he pretended to be much more impressed by the highlights than he really was.

"I didn't mention Rocky Scalzo or agents. It was all about me and my services."

As Blazer was leaving, Barlow had a question for him, providing him with a nickname that would stick in the sports industry and a catchphrase that would encapsulate the essence of college sports.

"Hey, Blaze, you got any hot dog money for me?"

Fast on the uptake, Blazer didn't need to be told what "hot dog money" meant. He had a couple of hundred in cash in his pocket, so he palmed Barlow the notes.

"We'll keep talking," Blazer said, taking his first step into the hall of mirrors of NCAA sports.

Blazer was soon introduced to other University of Pittsburgh players, handing out more hot dog money and getting an elementary education on how the NCAA really worked. As the 2001 draft neared, Blazer knew that Barlow was taking money from all manner of agents and rival financial advisers, but he didn't mind.

"I told Barlow to lie to everyone else, just don't lie to me," Blazer said. He could see that college sports were populated by predators and prey—and he knew which he wanted to be. "I became the gatekeeper for Kevan, so suddenly the agents had to deal with me and keep me happy. Having a commodity like Barlow was a bargaining chip, and it brought people to the table to deal with me on my terms. Even if I knew the player had no intention of doing business with a certain agent, I became a master at leveraging my asset to get something in return."

Barlow had had a great senior year, but there were questions about his work ethic, and word that he was taking money from several shady operators traveled around the small circles of professional football. Instead of being picked in the first round as expected, Barlow was selected in the third, which was a disappointment to Blazer, who had only one player in the draft that year—but he was in the game.

Then Blazer got a lucky break. The wife of a Smith Barney colleague had a nephew who played football at Northwestern. The player wasn't NFL caliber, but he introduced Blazer to other players. In 2002 Blazer represented two first-round picks, including the Northwestern linebacker Napoleon Harris, who invited him to the Senior Bowl in Mobile, Alabama—one of the premier meat markets. The top one hundred draft prospects were there for a weeklong series of meetings with NFL management and agents, a feeding frenzy where college amateurism met the brutal commercial reality of kids who were multimillion-dollar carrion.

"Every big-name player was present, and so was every big-time agent, all of them accessible to anyone bold enough to approach—and I was bold enough," Blazer remembered.

By the 2003 draft, Blazer had players on his roster in multiple rounds of the draft, and he helped his clients pick agents who would complement his financial services. Blazer was convinced he needed to develop a pipeline of early talent. Confident he could handle high-level NFL prospects, he cold-called an assistant coach at Penn State, Larry Johnson. The coach's son, Larry Johnson Jr., was a star running back for Penn State, a lock first-round pick and a key player Blazer was targeting. Johnson Jr. went on to become a celebrity superstar NFL player, but his father was also a top target for Blazer.

Blazer visited Johnson Sr.'s Penn State office and made an earnest pitch to be his son's financial adviser when he turned pro. Blazer sold himself without making a pitch for the other elite Penn State players many agents and advisers were also chasing. Blazer wanted Johnson Sr. to know that he could trust him to make his son his top priority, believing that by signing Johnson Jr., he would forge a lasting relationship with a coach at a successful college program.

With Larry Johnson Jr. signed as his first future superstar client, Blazer developed a concierge-like range of services, including coordinating the purchase of home and car insurance and structuring spending budgets. In 2004 Kevan Barlow signed a five-year $28 million contract with the San Francisco 49ers, and by then, Blazer had players scattered all over the league. He decided to focus on fewer players with better prospects. As part of his role as financial adviser, Blazer tried to keep his young and frequently financially inexperienced clients from burning through their money; it wasn't unusual for a player to spend tens of thousands of dollars on luxury goods in a single day. Players like Barlow had grown up with little financial stability, and there were no guardrails on spending from the NFL teams or the league.

Using illicit payments in increasingly large amounts, Blazer was able to ink new talent who went on to play for NFL teams like the Oakland Raiders, Denver Broncos, Pittsburgh Steelers, and New York Giants. By 2006, Blazer had more than a dozen active NFL players on his roster, with four appearing in the Pro Bowl. He had multiple players from leading college programs on his hot dog–money payroll. He had connections in nightclubs around the country and could get VIP tables, and he was trying to keep his players out of career-ending trouble by developing an intelligence network to warn them about groupies with ulterior motives. Hot dog money came in myriad forms, like electric bills or mortgages for his college kids' parents; it was the way to ensure future business with college players who had no money but multimillion-dollar prospects.

Over the years, not every player Blazer paid off made the pros, and players not infrequently took his money and then signed with someone else. But signing a single talented player could far outweigh the downsides. Blazer was making an excellent living, so he could afford to take risks.

"It was what I wanted to do," Blazer said. "I was needed. Protecting my players from vultures and hangers-on was incredibly satisfying. I felt good, intellectually."

Along the way, Blazer made exceptions for the convenience of the high-maintenance players; assessing the merits of an investment in Jay-Z's Vegas nightclub wasn't in his job description as a Smith Barney financial adviser, but he did it to become indispensable to his clients. He felt invincible, even if all the wheeling and dealing was turning frenetic.

When Smith Barney's rigid compliance department questioned Blazer's advising on dicey investments in the bars and restaurants players had brought to him for review, his wife, Trish, got upset. It didn't escape her that he easily could have lost his trader's license and been fired for all the questionable tasks he did for his players.

The phrase "hot dog money" became Blazer's watchword as he built his business and roster of players, which ranged from New York Giant Hakeem Nicks to the now spendthrift superstar running back for Kansas City, Larry Johnson Jr. Over time, Blazer developed a shtick—cast as a big brother to his players, he did whatever they needed and had their backs whenever they screwed up. Like the night one of his clients was playfully wrestling with his date and one of her breast implants burst. Blazer had to find a doctor for the girl, lest her life be in jeopardy. From obtaining the drug Valtrex for sexually transmitted diseases to conducting what he called his "CSI cleanings" of apartments after a player had hooked up with a woman he wanted to hide from his regular girlfriend or wife, Blazer would do anything for his guys.

Trish didn't approve of his growing network of football players, believing they took advantage of his dedication, as she'd eavesdropped on their calls and heard the frequently onerous and borderline immoral demands. But Blazer strongly believed he was making friends with his new clients, treasuring the expensive watches and steak dinners that were becoming a lifestyle he was quickly getting used to. Blazer turned his connections with strip clubs and bars in NFL cities into a nationwide network. When he recruited college kids, he told them two things. The first thing: *If you sign with me, I will tell you exactly what's going to happen after you get drafted.* He said he came from the future, and he knew how the story would play out—the money, girlfriends, family demands, hangers-on, real estate, and investment opportunities. The second thing he told them: *Wherever you are picked in the draft—to whatever city—I have trusted connections.* High-end auto dealerships, restaurants, clothing stores, marketing opportunities . . . He could hook them up.

Blazer's business was booming, but Smith Barney's staid Pittsburgh office wasn't the ideal location to operate in such an unorthodox industry. At that time, Blazer's Kansas City star, running back Larry Johnson Jr., was hanging out with celebrities like Beyoncé and Jay-Z, and the player was burning through money flying private to New York and LA on exclusive NetJets planes. One of Blazer's marketing sources, who helped sell his clients' autographs, knew members of the Donahue family, who owned a company called Voyager Jet Center. If the marketer made the connection, Blazer could inexpensively charter flights on Johnson's behalf, saving his client a small fortune.

Blazer was soon introduced to Mike Dolan and Ben Barton, two grandsons of Jack Donahue, the billionaire founder of Federated Investors. In Pittsburgh, Donahue's story was legendary. He'd started out selling mutual fund shares door-to-door and turned that into a business with more than half a trillion under management. With thirteen kids and scores upon scores of grandchildren and great-grandchildren, Jack Donahue's clan was often referred to as the "Kennedys of Pittsburgh."

The two Donahue cousins, who were both in their twenties, quickly fell under the spell of Blazer's proximity to professional athletes. In Pittsburgh, establishing and nurturing relationships with the Donahue family came with the promise of access to huge amounts of money, but it also carried the mystique of generational wealth, allowing Blazer to bask in an aura of real success and excess.

In 2008, Dolan and Barton partnered with Blazer when he left Smith Barney. The pair of scions weren't particularly intelligent or capable, but they were rich and they were willing to fund hot dog money for players. Their presence would increase Blazer's ability to recruit players and expand his business. The cousins eagerly hung out with Blazer's players in bars and nightclubs. Putting out an air of easy entitlement, Dolan and Barton didn't ask uncomfortable questions about payments or insist on participating in clandestine meetings, instead contenting themselves with sideline tickets to Penn State games and entrée into parties where they might smoke weed with NFL players.

"Benny Barton was better looking than Mike Dolan," Blazer recalled. "But Mike was definitely the alpha dog. They were only in their late twenties, but Mike already had gout, so he limped around like a much older person, always carrying a fountain soda, crunching loudly on the ice. Mike had a bowl cut, and he was usually unshaven and badly dressed in a short-sleeve shirt, khaki shorts, and sneakers in summer. In winter, it was dirty jeans and the same sweater for weeks on end. Benny dressed a little better but still a few years out of fashion, and he was easily distracted. Benny was appointed as the cruise director for nights out with my clients, but he couldn't grasp the idea that the athletes' needs came first. Many times, I had to repair relationships with players because Benny saw nothing wrong in trying to compete for some random woman's attention in a bar.

"I was willing to put up with a lot from Mike and Benny because what they brought to the business was worth its weight in gold. It wasn't their money or ideas that had the biggest value—it was the perception of wealth that was key. They played the part of rich kids perfectly. They said they were members of the 'LSC—Lucky Sperm Club.' I would tell players stories about the perks that came from being associated with the Donahue family, and they would eat that shit up. The family wealth was very real, even if Mike and Benny had limited access to it, and I'd been in the business for nearly a decade by then, so I knew exactly what buttons to push to recruit an athlete. Everyone else in the business was doling out cash, but we had difference-making luxuries and connections. Like taking players to party on the Donahues' private island in Florida, in Keewaydin Island in Naples. It was one of the most expensive stretches of residential land in the country. Driving up to the house, there was a twenty-five-car garage with a Ferrari, a Viper, a Porsche. The boathouse was more like a villa, with dolphins swimming right up to the dock. The huge main house had an infinity pool, and tennis and basketball courts, and a helicopter pad, along with an elevator to move around the five floors.

"Then there were the private flights. Having a private-jet card loaded with flight hours was a status symbol for any successful athlete or entertainer. The jet card I could get my players with Voyager was deeply discounted, and we had the ability to jump on empty planes headed to private airports like Teterboro for New York City or Opa locka in Miami. We used the planes for shuttling around strippers to entertain the players, or picking up a player to come to Pittsburgh to officially sign on with me and then fly home."

Blazer accompanied his athletes to places like the exclusive third-floor executive suite at Tootsie's Cabaret in Miami, a vast strip club with hundreds of scantily clad women selling overpriced drinks and lap dances. Blazer took pride in knowing the owners of those clubs and in ensuring his players wouldn't be ripped off or rolled. He used his influence on athletes to sway which restaurants and clubs his players invested in to parlay first-class treatment for himself at the most exclusive places in the country.

A November 2009 game between the Pittsburgh Steelers and the Kansas City Chiefs was a typical day for the high-flying Blazer. More than eighty thousand fans attended the game at Arrowhead Stadium in Kansas City, including Blazer, who had clients on both teams, most notably Larry Johnson Jr., who was having a birthday. To celebrate, Johnson chartered a private jet and flew ten strippers from Tootsie's in Miami to Kansas City for a party that went until six in the morning, when the entertainers were flown back to Florida.

One of Blazer's clients got romantically attached to a stripper at Tootsie's, a woman who moonlighted as a prostitute. The manager of the club called Blazer and warned him that the woman had a pimp who had designs on extorting money from the player. Since his client was considering marrying the stripper, Blazer told the player that he was going to be threatened with a rape accusation or simply jumped when he left Tootsie's one night. The narrow escape cemented the bond between the adviser and the NFL star.

"Come to the club with me, and you were sitting with Lil Wayne and drinking his alcohol," Blazer recalled. "A trip to Miami with my connections was extremely seductive. You weren't paying twenty-five grand for a private table at LIV. I'd get my guys whatever they wanted, whatever they were willing to pay for. Weed, Louis XIII cognac, reservations at an exclusive restaurant, and a new custom Audemars Piguet watch from the high-end jeweler I had in Manhattan—the dude they made the movie *Uncut Gems* about."

But Blazer knew he had to be careful around his players, who were often suspicious of smooth-talking moneymen. If he had smoked weed or cheated on his wife—neither of which he did—they might fire him; if he was dishonest or unreliable in any way, they could think he'd do the same to them.

"I was always careful not to be too flashy or flaunt the wealth that was being generated by my young clients," Blazer said. "Nothing raises a red flag like pulling up in a Bentley, wearing a two-thousand-dollar suit. They didn't like to think that I was struggling or poor—that was just as bad. It was like the Goldilocks principle: not too hot, not too cold, just the right temperature. I had a nice house but not too nice. I tried to practice what I preached to my players by not going overboard on expensive indulgences. Balance was best. I'd wear a nice suit but no tie, and my Rolex Submariner was my only jewelry. For casual events, I'd wear a hoodie with cool sneakers, like a new pair of Nike Air Force 1s."

Personally, Blazer had developed a reputation among his Pittsburgh friends and neighbors as a businessman with insider access to incredibly attractive perks. Movie premieres, product launches, and restaurant openings—he was able to piggyback on the invitations his NFL players received to all kinds of events. If a party was in Pittsburgh, he'd take Trish, along with close friends, who couldn't help but be impressed by the way Blazer could get behind the red velvet ropes in places where even the wealthy couldn't manage entry. Blazer even had access to locker rooms at stadiums around the country.

"My friends joked that I had three different personas," Blazer said. "There was Martin, the stockbroker and suburban dad at soccer games. Then there was Marty, the guy who loved to party and have fun and travel and enjoy the finer things in life. But my third character was the one that everyone in the world of athletes knew me as. That was Blaze, the financial adviser. When I was Blaze, I was hanging in clubs or one of the best restaurants in Miami or Atlanta, throwing $10,000 dinners for my clients or having more than a hundred people over to my house for Fourth of July and New Year's Eve parties. Our friends would laugh when my worlds collided and my athletes called me Blaze—they'd joke and ask, *Who the hell is Blaze?*"

~

Snagging an invitation to one of Blazer's—or, more properly stated, *Blaze's*—parties meant getting the opportunity to mingle with a celebrity of some sort. Or there could be an invitation to Foxhole, a nightclub in Miami where Blazer dropped thousands on a celebrity-studded party in his own honor called "Just Blaze," with cocktails circulated by scantily clad waitresses. His older daughter had just started high school, but her friends all knew that her father had famous friends, adding a degree of cool in the eyes of his child that couldn't be bought.

"I'd get front-row seats to concerts and then backstage access afterwards," Blazer said. "I would get to hang out with people like Ed Sheeran and Tracy Morgan and Chris Rock. When Rock was testing new material for an upcoming comedy tour, Trish and I took a small group of our friends to the show in a small club where it was impossible to get tickets."

As Blazer embarked on his many adventures, he was always surrounded by a posse, which consisted of his players; his attorney; partners in various endeavors; and always, his sidekick, Roderick "Dodge" Danley, a former colleague at Smith Barney who acted as a fixer and facilitator, tending to the details of the constant demands of the clients Blazer had accumulated.

"My players were calling me night and day. I didn't mind getting their calls in the middle of the night. I felt needed. I felt like I was doing something worthwhile. I felt challenged. I loved it all.

"I did everything for my players. I had access and I controlled everything. It was blind trust. I'd send money to a member of their family and then catch up with the details later. If I put a piece of paper in front of my players, they signed. They didn't want to be bothered with the details. I loved my guys, and it was mutual.

"The exhilaration of the lifestyle was like a drug, extremely addictive. The feeling of being on the sidelines at a Penn State game with a hundred thousand people in the stands going nuts—and me, standing next to Joe Paterno, the legendary coach—was incredible. You couldn't buy those experiences. It was intoxicating, and in hindsight, I was basically drunk on the life I had come to inhabit. I didn't realize how deep I was getting into that existence, like a junkie who thinks he can manage his habit but has really lost control of his appetite and begins to believe he's smarter and above everyone else. It was a seductive phenomenon that I would come to understand was not just common, but universal."

CHAPTER FOUR

A Million Dollars from One Kid

By the end of the 2000s, Blazer was a successful entrepreneur, but he was also neck-deep in the corruption and intrigue that surrounded college football. He was routinely sending cash to college players, using Western Union and addressing the deliveries to girlfriends or family members to avoid a paper trail, fronting two or three thousand dollars a month to the best prospects.

By that time, he had two separate but related businesses with Mike Dolan and Ben Barton's financial backing: Blazer Capital Management and Blazer Investment Advisory. His new partners weren't overly concerned about returns on their investments in various players, and Blazer was able to keep them away from the more delicate negotiations and unseemly developments. Parents of college players frequently promised to sign with Blazer in return for up-front cash, then jilted him after an NFL team drafted their son.

Deception, double-dealing, and outright fraud were epidemic in NCAA football, but with the real transactions all occurring outside the law, there was no resorting to the courts or authorities. Over time, Blazer learned how to function in a system riddled with dishonesty, even as he practiced his own forms of extralegal maneuvering. There were so many different ways to make money from players through annuities, marketing fees, and endorsements that the business model was lucrative despite certain unavoidable losses.

In Blazer's tiered investment system, he put significant amounts of his young players' money in instruments that would generate income when they reached their midforties. Then there were the side investments the players pursued on their own that nearly always failed, like restaurants or music labels or bars or barbershops. Investing in stocks and bonds through hedge funds, Blazer regularly provided returns on stock portfolios that ranged as high as 20 percent, an incredibly good return that went largely unnoticed by the players because buying and selling equities wasn't sexy or fun. He often advised the purchase of variable universal life insurance policies—up to $20 million in value—and it was easy for the young players to pass the health tests, provided they heed Blazer's warning to avoid smoking weed for a few days. But the players rarely had long-term goals or thought much about their future.

Blazer viewed the investments as a way to get cash out of the players' hands and provide an income stream after they'd stopped playing. It was also good business for him. Blazer would receive 80 percent of the first-year premium on the deals, netting a tidy $160,000. From a purely legitimate point of view—as understood in professional sports— Blazer was prospering mightily, which was why the industry was so competitive.

"The fight to do business with young and wealthy professional athletes was insane," he recalled. "Like everyone in the business, I was constantly looking over my shoulder, expecting someone to try to steal my players. Before I got into the sports business, I made money from trading the funds of my existing clients. But in the athlete business, the trick was consistently generating new clients because the day I signed a client was the day I started to lose him. The business was recession proof, but I had to fight to maintain the interest and loyalty of my players because a competitor would review the investment strategy I had created and find a way to throw shade on it, creating doubts by picking it apart no matter how sound it was—claiming I was getting hidden fees or that the risk level was too high, to make it seem like I didn't know what I was doing. The players were young, impressionable, and prone to freak out. I knew how that worked because I was doing the exact same thing to other players to get them to dump their adviser and work with me."

By far the most attractive aspects of the professional athlete business came from exploiting the phenomenon of the "jock sniffer"—or fan-boy—dying to meet players and do business with Blazer's clients so they could drop the star's name to their other clients. The list of transactions Blazer commanded was astounding: houses, second homes, mortgages, private-jet flights, cars, electronics, clothing, jewelry, alcohol, travel, hotel, restaurants, casinos, clubs—the gamut of indulgences and luxuries . . . and anyone who wanted to conduct business with his players had to have Blazer's approval.

"I was the gatekeeper," Blazer recalled. "I could approve a transaction, making the deal run smoothly, or I could force them to lower their price or kill the business entirely if I wanted to. The question I had for anyone who wanted to do business with my clients was simple: 'If I bless this deal, are you willing to make a deposit in the relationship bank account?' Most people who did business with my guys knew how the system worked."

When an attorney in Pittsburgh begged Blazer to represent his clients, Blazer carefully detailed what was expected—pro bono services for the financial adviser, for a start. The same was true for Elevee suits, or jewelry from the Jewelers of Las Vegas. But no transaction exemplified the intricacies of the celebrity-athlete industry better than automobiles, the universal status symbol for young sports stars enjoying their first taste of the high life, never questioning the price tag or premiums charged, provided the vehicle was exactly—and it had to be exact—what they wanted to impress their teammates, their women, and themselves.

Blazer had a collaboration with a woman at a Dallas car dealership. She had reputedly been a finalist in a Miss Texas pageant, and wore short skirts or tight pants with low-cut tops, but Blazer believed her flirtatious, soft southern accent disguised the wolf within. By the early 2010s, Blazer and the car dealer were doing deals on as many as ten vehicles a month, as players wanted to swap out cars in much the same way they tossed a scuffed pair of Air Force 1s. New Escalades, Denalis, Range Rovers . . . The cars were generally prestige SUVs for a friend, a girlfriend, or a family member—or the player himself—with a price tag under $80,000. But these deals were supplemented by exotic vehicles like Lamborghinis, Porsches, Bentleys, Rolls-Royces, Mercedes, Maybachs—automobiles that could cost up to $400,000. The cars would come with extras like rims or trims, creating a lot of gray area for their mutual profit, with the dealer delivering what Blazer called "mansions on wheels" in person to add an extra level of service.

"I was offered cash all the time," Blazer remembered. "It was tempting, but I didn't want to run my relationship bank that way. I wanted the deposits to take different forms. My philosophy was that the ancillary money was all gravy I put back into my business or used to pay for expenses I would otherwise have to pay personally. For example, all my own cars were provided by my connection in Dallas. I would get all the bells and whistles, like tinted windows and an enhanced sound system. I had a mortgage representative from First Choice Bank working in a small corner of my office, but he paid the rent for the whole suite. My tax returns were done for free. I had carte blanche with free private jets. Word would go around locker rooms that I had access to private flights, that's for sure—and the players were hyperaware of those kinds of fringe benefits.

"Sami Jenks from Elevee or Joseph the Tailor made all my custom clothes without presenting a bill. Leor Yerushalmi satisfied my no-cost jewelry needs. I had all the Double Cross, Wódka, or Belvedere Vodka I could handle. A rep from Rémy Cointreau gave me a four-thousand-dollar bottle of Louis XIII cognac and cases of Macallan scotch, which would become a favorite of the FBI in time. Hotel rooms, restaurants, nightclubs—all were comped when I sent my players to spend money in Miami Beach or Vegas or Manhattan or LA. I had biweekly deliveries of Vitamin Water and Red Bull sent to my players for free, but I'd also get the drinks to put in my own Red Bull fridge.

"When the people from rapper T.I.'s clothing brand, Akoo, sent five boxes of their clothes to Darrelle Revis of the New York Jets, I made sure they sent me two. Sleep Number in Denver wanted to do a deal with Ashley Lelie of the Broncos, so I insisted on a king-size mattress for my bedroom. 50 Cent's company, SMS Audio, shipped dozens of boxes of premium headphones and earbuds, and I received my fair share after I got my players to take pictures of themselves wearing the gear on the field. I'd even reach out to organizations I liked to see if they were interested in partnering by having my players promote their product. I would get a college player a box of Rocawear from Jay-Z, and then I'd send them Tsovet watches or Beats headphones in a FedEx box with their hot dog money."

Blazer's son, Connor, loved the Manchester United soccer team. One afternoon, Blazer and his son were watching a game on TV, and Blazer saw a banner advertising Holler watches. The watches weren't super premium, but the designs were attractive, so he went online and discovered Holler was an English company run by a diamond and jewel dealer named Darren McCormick. Blazer wrote to McCormick, introducing himself as the financial adviser to prominent NFL players, and the two men hit it off.

Over the few years that followed, Blazer collected more than one hundred free watches from Holler, giving scores of them to players as a way to win their business while showing other players in the locker room they weren't getting the same kinds of freebies from their financial advisers—and thus potentially stealing *their* business. Inevitably, McCormick invited Blazer and his son to England, where the watch entrepreneur rolled out the red carpet to take them to a Manchester United match, bringing it all full circle.

"The feeding frenzy around representing players happened for a reason. The legitimate fees and commissions weren't worth the risk or expense or trouble of the hot dog–money payments. It was all the side deals and hustles. I told my players that their relationship with me was much more important than it was with their agent. I said that if they hired me, they couldn't try to duck my calls or blow me off like it was a fucking hassle. We had to like each other because we were talking every day or every other day. I knew I had to keep the players happy. When it was all put together, an agent or financial adviser could make millions off one kid."

∿

Business was humming along—until Blazer got caught up in one of the biggest scandals in NCAA history. It was at this time that Blazer became close with one of his clients, former Michigan Wolverine and later Pittsburgh Steelers star linebacker Larry Foote, providing an excellent example of how relationships in sports can build on each other in serpentine fashion—and can lead to catastrophe.

Foote believed the best judges of talent were often other players—"Nobody knows players the way players do," he frequently said—and he took it upon himself to recruit promising prospects for Blazer. Foote never asked for any compensation for this role, which was a generous gesture, given that finding players for Blazer was no small task. With so many advisers and agents hunting for elite prospects, finding a diamond in the rough was extremely difficult.

In 2004 Foote recommended an undrafted rookie running back named Willie Parker who had walked on to the Pittsburgh Steelers' camp. The previous year, Parker had been reduced to a backup role as a senior at the University of North Carolina, allegedly because he lacked the instinct to read plays and look for holes to exploit. But in the Steelers' camp, Parker's promise was obvious to Foote. Blazer wasn't interested in talking to an undrafted player, but Foote insisted, saying Parker was going to be a star in the NFL. Blazer met with Parker and liked him, and when he made the roster as a third-string running back, Blazer signed him as a client. The money involved initially had been tiny, but Blazer's belief in the player, at a time when no one else was interested, created a strong and enduring bond between them.

During Super Bowl XL in 2006, Parker had the longest touchdown run in the history of the event—a record that stands to this day—and he was a core element in the Steelers' victory. Parker later signed a four-year $13.6 million contract, richly rewarding Blazer, who could expect to earn easily more than $500,000 from him over the life of the deal. The contract made Parker financially secure; he provided for his family and gave his Super Bowl ring to his father as a sign of gratitude. With Blazer's guidance, Parker invested in a town house in Pittsburgh and a mansion in Durham, North Carolina, so he could be near his alma mater during the offseason.

As he rose in the NFL ranks, Parker remained close to a former UNC cornerback named Chris Hawkins, who ran errands for Parker and managed the affairs of his mansion in North Carolina. It was a familiar arrangement: players often surrounded themselves with people they knew and trusted before they became NFL celebrities. Hawkins was a particularly determined and crafty version of that kind of barnacle, firmly attaching himself to the network that had grown around Parker—including Marty Blazer.

"I loved Chris," Blazer said. "He was a hustler and a very likable one. His presence enabled Willie to focus one hundred percent on football, which was really what was needed when he became a starter for the Steelers. Chris was always looking for ways to expand his role with Willie, coordinating marketing and appearance opportunities for him as a way to earn a few bucks. When Chris and I got to know each other, he said he wanted to introduce me to players—pros but also kids in college. He was basically a runner on my behalf down in North Carolina while he was managing Willie's mansion. We became close, and I appreciated the chance to meet new players, but I knew all along I wasn't the only one Chris was doing business with. He had a string of agents and financial advisers that he was also working with, looking for opportunities to make a buck."

On rare occasions, the football equivalent of a genius cluster appeared. Like Vienna in the time of Mozart, or Florence in the age of the Medicis, the college football version sprang from the earth at the University of North Carolina in the late 2000s. The teams weren't particularly great—certainly not able to live up to the talent the school had boasted—but there were no fewer than eight potential first-round NFL picks playing for the Tar Heels during that time. The result was a gold rush for men like Marty Blazer; agents, financial advisers, runners, and hustlers descended upon Chapel Hill in unprecedented numbers.

As an ambitious runner, Chris Hawkins aimed to take advantage of this plethora of talent. Willie Parker's mansion had a swimming pool, as well as expansive and luxurious spaces to party—not to mention it was a convenient twenty-minute drive from the UNC campus. For Tar Heels players, it was the perfect retreat from the stifling atmosphere on campus, where they could relax away from prying eyes with complimentary liquor and pretty, pliant coeds. As a recent UNC graduate, Hawkins was ideally placed to exploit his free access to Parker's house for the players and, in turn, for the agents and financial advisers eager to create relationships. Blazer and Hawkins agreed to a negotiated fee for each player referral. Hawkins was willing to provide the hovering agents and businessmen introductions, as long as he was cut in on any future deals—a typical arrangement for runners in the NCAA.

Hawkins wanted to connect Blazer with star wide receiver Hakeem Nicks. Nicks came from a troubled background, and his scholarship allowance didn't cover his living expenses, so Nicks had fallen behind on rent for his modest apartment. Hawkins arranged for a conference call with Blazer and Nicks so the player could hear directly that the financial adviser was open to offering him assistance. Blazer sent Nicks $940 to cover his back rent, hoping the kindness wouldn't go unrewarded.

Blazer had a steel-trap mind when it came to keeping track of the names, power structures, tallies of favors and obligations, and maze-like connections that constituted his business life, but Nicks somehow slipped through the cracks until the 2009 draft approached and he was on a call with an agent. Blazer quickly recalled that Nicks was a stand-out receiver. Agents were involved in negotiating contracts, and then it was largely a hands-off situation. Over the years, Blazer had developed a policy of remaining neutral about the agents his players chose.

"Football agents, especially the good ones, were the worst of the worst," Blazer said. "They would do anything to steal another agent's players. They would cut your throat and not even think twice about it. They would use runners like Hawkins to ingratiate themselves with the players. They couldn't directly give cash to players because it was criminal in most states, including North Carolina, but agents would make sure the players got what they needed. It could get incredibly petty—with agents bad-mouthing each other and offering all kinds of perks—but they usually got up to three percent of the player's contracts. It wasn't unusual for a top prospect to make more than $30 million of guaranteed money on a single contract, which meant that player was worth nearly a million bucks to the agent—so it was money worth fighting over."

One agent Blazer dealt with often was Peter Schaffer, a jockish man nearly ten years older who dressed in ill-fitting sweats and scuffed sneakers. He was constantly spitting in an empty bottle of Gatorade because of the chaw wedged in his lower lip. Ultra competitive, often quick to lose his temper, socially awkward, and paranoid to the point of obsession, Schaffer was incapable of understanding why any player would ever want a different agent. Blazer and Schaffer often bickered and then reconciled after a time, provided both had a deal where they would make money.

After an all-star junior year, in which he broke fourteen receiving records at UNC, Hakeem Nicks declared for the draft in 2009 and hired Schaffer as his agent. Schaffer said he was willing to recommend Blazer to the player, provided the financial adviser took on all three of the UNC players the agent had signed. Blazer thought of the trio as the Three Little Pigs because of their constant demands, and he knew he would be expected to provide the players with hot dog money until they signed their NFL contracts—a period of six months. Blazer was really only interested in Nicks, who had superstar potential. Still, he covered the cost of the pre-draft training and travel expenses for the other two players as well.

While Nicks was training in South Florida, Blazer pulled out all the stops to pitch his services, inviting the wide receiver and his teammates to the private island, where Dolan and Barton had hired a famous DJ, stocked the bar with top-shelf liquor, and brought in a half a dozen naked women to play topless volleyball in the infinity pool. Nicks and his pals were greeted by the smoky scent of Shorty's BBQ wafting through the party.

The strategy worked on twenty-year-old Nicks. That year, Nicks was a first-round draft pick of the New York Giants. But he had a propensity to be too generous with his friends, especially his former college teammates, who were constantly hitting him up for cash. Blazer saw it as his duty to run interference for Nicks as much as possible—until Nicks asked him to send two hundred dollars from his account to UNC wide receiver Greg Little. Blazer knew Little wasn't just another player mooching a few bucks; he had serious NFL potential. Recognizing the opportunity, Blazer asked Nicks for his permission to take over the payments to Little, and then he repeated the same process that had led to his signing Barlow years earlier, going to the player's modest apartment in Chapel Hill and pitching a structured deal with monthly payments of hot dog money, which Blazer called a "stipend," for the rest of the season.

"Lie to everybody else, just don't lie to me," Blazer told Little, repeating the mantra he'd used on the many players who had been taking cash from other agents and hustlers, fully aware of the pressures on the most talented kids. "If for some reason you want to go in a different direction with your financial adviser, just pay me back. No hard feelings. I'm confident I can prove myself to you—but shit happens and I understand."

While sitting at the kitchen table with Little and making his pitch, Blazer sensed the player's roommates were listening through the wall. The wide receiver asked if Blazer wanted to talk to two of his teammates, then hollered for his friends to come out. Blazer was happy to acquaint himself with as many Tar Heels as possible, hoping he could replicate his hot dog money–business model at UNC as he'd done at Alabama and Penn State and the University of Pittsburgh. Both friends readily agreed to take money from Blazer, their alacrity convincing the financial adviser that the players had done this before and would do it again in the future. It was the potato chip rule: if you see someone eating a potato chip, chances are they've eaten a potato chip before and they will eat a potato chip again.

Little mentioned another player, who Blazer instantly knew could represent the proverbial jackpot. Robert Quinn was only a rising sophomore, and he had gained relatively little notice as a freshman, but Little referred to the linebacker as "the motherfucking best-kept-secret superstar." Little called Quinn on his cell, and the player appeared in his kitchen only minutes later.

"Robert Quinn was UNC's crown jewel," Blazer recollected. "I could tell just by looking at him that he was going to be a monster in the NFL. He was six four, two-fifty, chiseled. Still just a kid, but I could see the man who would make an All Pro multiple times. His ask was bigger than the other players', but that only confirmed he was a breed apart and he knew it. I figured they could see how good Quinn was—the players know best—and no great deal ever came easy, so I agreed to his terms. I left Chapel Hill a happy man."

Quinn would go on to play for more than a decade in the NFL, signing a five-year $70 million deal with the Chicago Bears in 2020 and setting the team's franchise record for the most sacks in a season the next season. But in 2009, Blazer's main concern was coordinating all the Western Union wires he'd have to send to the four UNC players, each getting up to $1,000 in cash per month, with Quinn sometimes commanding double that amount. To solidify his relationship with the players, Blazer wanted to establish a presence close by to serve as a constant reminder of his generosity and to make sure their needs were being met—and that they would sign with him when they turned pro. In Blazer's experience, there was nothing more satisfying and effective than directly putting cash in a college player's hands, the visceral experience creating a kind of emotional bond, so he needed someone to be his proxy in Chapel Hill.

Blazer turned to Chris Hawkins. Blazer introduced Hawkins to the UNC players he was paying, and soon they were partying poolside at Willie Parker's mansion, further embedding themselves in Blazer's network. Hawkins started a business paying the players for their game-worn gear—signed jerseys, pads, cleats—and selling it all online and to memorabilia merchants for a tidy profit.

The system was functioning, but instead of contenting himself with catering to Blazer's potential clients, Hawkins started to act as a broker for the leading agents crowding the Durham airport to cash in on the cache of future NFL'ers. Agents Joel Segal, Alvin Keels, Doug

Hendrickson, and Drew Rosenhaus—who alleged that he'd been the inspiration for the film *Jerry Maguire*[1]—were the biggest names in the business, and they were being courted by Hawkins as he attempted to play them against each other so he could expand his business.

"I knew that Hawk was playing a very dangerous game with those agents," Blazer remembered. "I warned Hawk repeatedly that he was playing with fire. The only thing agents despised more than each other was losing out on a player."

Meanwhile, Hawkins set up a spring break trip to Miami for the UNC players, with Blazer agreeing to pay for flights and providing free rooms at the five-star Fontainebleau—a blatant breach of NCAA rules but not an uncommon event for highly desirable prospects. Blazer didn't take the trip, but he sent a chaperone to try to keep everyone out of trouble. Greg Little and Robert Quinn went, using Blazer's VIP connections at velvet-rope nightclubs and strip clubs.

The entourage was also accompanied by a brazen UNC teammate, Marvin Austin, a three-hundred-pound defensive lineman whom Blazer loathed. While in Miami, the knuckleheaded Austin posted pictures of himself hanging out poolside with celebrities—introductions Blazer had engineered—on social media. Tweeting out photographs of a college player partying at LIV on Miami Beach, where bottle service for Grey Goose and Dom Pérignon ran to thousands of dollars, wasn't foolish or reckless—it was suicidal. Word of the incredibly dumb and dangerous posts spread rapidly at UNC and beyond.

"I didn't care what happened to Marvin Austin," Blazer said. "I figured he was going to get caught at some point because he was so blatantly taking money from lots of people and living excessively in a big house. Obvious luxuries I would never let my players indulge in. But Little and Quinn were in Miami with him, and they were at risk."

---

1   Rosenhaus had a small part in the film, but it was widely known that the true inspiration for the character was an agent named Leigh Steinberg.

But there was bad blood between agents competing for UNC players, and Blazer believes one of them went to the NCAA. After that, the whole program blew up.

As the Miami trip Blazer had sponsored exploded into a national scandal in the summer of 2010, it also emerged that a young woman who had been tutoring UNC football players had actually been writing their papers and ensuring they had to do minimal work to comply with NCAA standards. UNC quickly became the poster child for corruption in college sports, the two scandals merging into a rolling fiasco that revealed the substandard education many student-athletes were receiving.

As investigations multiplied, some of the true nature of the NCAA's system was evident, but the association determined six years later that the school had broken no rules. Students were taking classes in the African and Afro-American Studies department, which never met and required only one short paper to pass, and they rarely had any interaction with professors, but bad schooling wasn't a breach of the organization's rules, in a classic NCAA non-investigative investigation.

Eventually, an official from North Carolina's office of the secretary of state interrogated Blazer because agents paying players or acting on behalf of an agent was a crime in the state, so using Blazer as a proxy would be against the law. But Blazer was told up front that he wasn't a target of the investigation, so when he was asked if he'd paid players on behalf of agent Peter Schaffer, he truthfully replied that he hadn't. His answer was technically honest, even if it disguised the reality. Blazer didn't add that he had been paying players for his own benefit, providing funds to Robert Quinn's family for jewelry and parties in Miami Beach and to help save his father's modest farmstead, nor did he offer that he had financed the Miami trip that had been the genesis of the scandal.

In the end, UNC's head coach was fired, along with a number of assistant coaches. Thirteen players were suspended for the season opener the following year. Hakeem Nicks forfeited the fourteen receiving records he'd set at the school, and he and Robert Quinn were declared "permanently ineligible," symbolic punishment for the high-flying NFL stars. Unable to play in his junior year, Quinn fell to the fourteenth pick in the draft's first round, but the majority of the players sanctioned would be only marginal pros due to the scandal— in part, at least. The team vacated two years' worth of previous wins, and it was banned from the 2012 postseason. Fifteen scholarships were taken away and three years' probation was imposed.

But after months of blaring headlines, the appropriate front-page banner—Everyone Knows College Corruption Is a Huge Problem—never appeared. As always with the NCAA, by far the biggest truth was the most obvious: absolutely nothing had changed. The central reality of the case involved Blazer and the payments and luxuries he was providing to UNC's players, and the NCAA hadn't seriously addressed that fact. The most famous college head coaches expressed bewilderment that players would take money from agents and financial advisers, as if it were an aberration, and the billions kept rolling in to college football.

In the aftermath, none of the UNC players became Blazer's long-term clients or repaid the money he'd "lent" them, apart from linebacker Bruce Carter, who returned $12,000. By then, Blazer had three players making more than $10 million per season, so with annual fees of 1 to 2 percent, he was back to a lucrative business, where he had mastered ways to maximize the returns from his players. He should have been content to escape this close brush with fate.

CHAPTER FIVE

Mafia: The Movie

In many ways, Blazer had become a prototypical American success story: a financial adviser who had used his wits to parlay access to the locker rooms, exclusive clubs, and private jets reserved for celebrities and their innermost circles. But Blazer also resembled Icarus, flying ever closer to the sun, impervious to how his greed and constant maneuvering were escalating at an alarming rate. What had started with the desire to be involved in professional sports had mutated into something more dangerous and frantic, a yearning that was becoming insatiable. Blazer had it all, but he was still burning with ambition—more, always more—and he was recklessly searching for a way to expand his roster of clients. With two dozen players scattered throughout the NFL and a business with substantial sums of hot dog money in circulation, Blazer was looking for a way to retain his clients and sign true superstars and future Hall of Famers. To attract higher-end clients, he reasoned that he had to find a trademark form of investment his competitors didn't offer.

"I had been in the business for ten years," Blazer remembered. "I didn't invent the system. You had to pay players. You had to work side deals. You had to be creative and even cutthroat. I had a formula that was working. It was like a drug for me—there was a high. In hindsight,

I had the absolute worst personality for that business. I was the type of person who was susceptible to that kind of addiction. I had an ego. I liked to brag. It was a combustible situation."

Mike Dolan, one of the Donahue scions, had indulged another of his various rich-kid fantasies by purchasing a run-down industrial building in a rough section of Pittsburgh and converting it into a movie studio. In 2009, he'd produced a film aptly titled *The Bridge to Nowhere*, starring Ving Rhames. Attending the premiere in Pittsburgh, Blazer sat next to Rhames, who whispered that he could do much better on his own, and with a lower budget.

"The movie was about human trafficking, and it was terrible," Blazer said. "The story was really bad, but the premiere was a great event. Ving was exactly like the characters he played in movies. Every word that came out of his mouth commanded attention. His look was intense and authentic."

Blazer and Rhames went out for drinks after the premiere, and the actor clearly knew he had a potential investor on his hands, as he bragged about the crime feature he was going to make with a budget of "only" $1 million—a sum that guaranteed it would make a profit, the celebrity declared. Rhames suggested that Blazer's players could invest in his production of *Mafia*. Blazer had accomplished so much, he reflected, and movies didn't seem like a particularly strange or challenging business to enter. *How hard could it be?* Blazer thought, taking a sip of his single malt whiskey and smiling as he listened to the charismatic Rhames hold forth.

"Ving said his movie wouldn't be a piece of shit like *The Bridge to Nowhere*," Blazer recalled. "There was no doubt in my mind I was going to use him and his movie to catapult my athlete-management business into the stratosphere."

The next day, Blazer took Rhames to the Steelers' training camp in Latrobe, Pennsylvania, to meet his players. The practice grounds teemed with thousands of fans, creating a carnival atmosphere that Rhames glorified in. At the sight of the movie star, head coach Mike Tomlin stopped practice so the Steelers could meet Rhames. The team gathered around Rhames, making jokes about his famous lines from *Pulp Fiction* and *Baby Boy*. Even the star players were impressed as they posed for photos with the actor. Watching Rhames at work, Blazer figured if he could come up with a system for investing in feature films, he wouldn't have to try to sell himself so hard.

"I was determined to reap the benefits of the movie business, no matter the cost," Blazer recalled. "But when I told Mike Dolan that I was going to work with Ving on his *Mafia* project, he cast doubts on any dealings with Rhames. He said that I couldn't trust Ving, and he said he was incredibly difficult to work with. At the very least, to protect myself, Mike said I should work with his producer from *Bridge to Nowhere*, a man named Brian Hartman, who I already knew and liked."

Hartman was a laid-back man in his forties with strawberry-blond hair, a beard, and very fair skin. After reading the script for *Mafia*, Blazer thought it seemed good enough, failing to detect warning signals like lack of plot or character development. It was the first script he'd ever read, and he didn't care about the quality of the work. The point was to offer an exclusive investment that his competitors couldn't match.

"Hartman explained the finances to me, and it looked like a no-brainer," Blazer recalled. "Hartman was in business with Dolan, so he was the partner of my partner and I didn't think he'd screw that up. There were generous tax credits in Pennsylvania, and Hartman said that Ving Rhames's name alone was worth a million dollars in foreign sales. It was sold to me like I couldn't lose."

Blazer told Rhames the movie would have to be made Hartman's way, and the star grudgingly agreed, taking a $300,000 acting fee and recruiting *Jackie Brown* star Pam Grier and *Terminator 2: Judgment Day* villain Robert Patrick to costar. Hartman hired a young producer named Phillip Glasser, whose sole claim to fame was his voiceover role as Fievel Mousekewitz in the 1980s animated comedy *An American Tail*. Blazer was told that Glasser's older brother David was the chief operating officer of the Weinstein Company, which created the false assumption that there was no need to worry about distribution of the film.

When Blazer took Trish to the set of *Mafia* one evening, she was appalled by the quality of the performances. She was no expert on moviemaking, but the actors were obviously terrible. Blazer was heedless, reasoning that the movie didn't have to be any good—it just had to break even and provide his players entrée to Hollywood in the form of producer credits, bit parts, red-carpet premieres, and dates with actresses. In his experience, pro athletes wanted to put their money in ventures that were cool or fun. And what was more glamorous than cinema?

But only a few players had agreed to invest, and the amounts they were willing to risk had constituted a fraction of the million-dollar budget. As Blazer was trying to convince more players to come on board, Hartman wanted to continue production without waiting. Blazer agreed, thinking the budget was firm and that he would get other clients involved. When the production blew through $400,000 in less than a month, Hartman told Blazer they would then need $1.3 million and that all would be lost if they failed to raise the full amount. Blazer was convinced he was in an impossible situation. Still, with the filming of *Mafia* underway, he wanted to complete the movie no matter what.

Blazer knew he was at a crossroads: he was signing big clients and generating substantial fees, and he had more than enough hot dog money—but he didn't have the kind of cash to fund the movie himself, as he believed Hartman knew. The implication was obvious to Blazer, even as it was supremely risky: Blazer should just help himself to the needed funds from his players and figure out how to deal with his actions down the road.

"I was arrogant," Blazer recalled. "I felt like I could work my way out of this situation. I wanted it to work out so badly. I thought if I stopped the movie and said I wasn't going to fund it anymore—and tell my players their money was lost—I was absolutely convinced it would be the end of my business.

"The first time I stepped over the line was the hardest. I told my assistant to send a wire to Fidelity authorizing the transfer of another $100,000 from Shawntae Spencer's account to the account for *Mafia*. She looked uncertain, so I told her I'd just spoken with Shawntae, which was a lie, and she knew it but didn't say anything. I'd done this countless times—taken money from the accounts of my players without their prior approval. I'd just circle back and make it right if they asked, but none of them ever did. They were kids. They cared about having enough money on the credit cards to do what they wanted. The players didn't examine their statements or question what I was doing, and I was making good on things like payments to their girlfriend or mother, payments I knew they would approve of.

"The difference was that this wasn't for an honest purpose—and I knew it. So did my assistant. The same was true for the lawyer who worked in the office as I continued to move money from players' accounts to the movie. It was like I had become a kind of financial serial killer at stealing the money, and it got easier and easier the more I did it. I had a spiel I was going to use if any of the players asked me about the transfers, but none ever did."

Soon, Blazer had taken funds from his five most liquid players' accounts and wired large sums to the production account of *Mafia*, with no consent from his players—not just a breach of trust but also criminal conduct, as he well knew. Blazer didn't attempt to disguise the transactions; if the players had bothered to look at their accounts, they would have seen the large transfers. Each had more than $5 million in cash entrusted to Blazer Capital Management, with most depositing more than $250,000 every week during the season— up to $1 million a week from All Pro Rashean Mathis of the Jacksonville Jaguars, a particular favorite of Blazer's.

In his mind, Blazer said he didn't actively deceive his players in the sense of convincing them to engage in fraudulent or fake activity; he'd simply misappropriated their money and then tried to hide his criminal deeds. The others involved in the production pressed Blazer to dip into the large amount of money at his disposal, likely knowing he didn't have his players' approval.

Consciously harming others and giving himself the moral permission to do so tested Blazer's interior monologue; he wasn't a sociopath, and his mother hadn't raised a liar and a cheat, but he'd developed a toxic unwillingness to admit failure. The blend of arrogance and ease of deception, coupled with Blazer's knowledge of his players' lack of financial sophistication, proved too much to resist.

For Blazer, what distinguished him from run-of-the-mill criminals was that he never personally took a dime from his players for his own use. Under immense pressure, Blazer kept wiring tranches of $100,000 and more to the production, taking the money from players' accounts, doubling down on the fraud when Hartman urged him to help fund a horror movie called *Sibling*, later renamed *A Resurrection*, a production that was dead on arrival at the box office, taking in a paltry $10,000.

In the midst of the chaotic production, Blazer continued doing business in a frantic manner that bordered on maniacal. The fast-paced lifestyle caught up with him in late October 2010, on one of his regular private flights to Miami. On this trip, which mixed business and pleasure, Blazer was accompanied by his acolyte Tony Johnson, the younger brother of Larry Johnson Jr. Blazer had long figured out that it was difficult—if not impossible—to get players and various business associates to travel to Pittsburgh, particularly during the colder months. Miami had thus become a place to conduct business and easily get his clients to visit, using his connections to grant complimentary hotel suites and access to the most exclusive restaurants and clubs. Blazer believed that once a player he was trying to recruit experienced his triple-luxury Miami hospitality, they would be changed forever.

On this occasion, Blazer intended to visit the Donahue compound in Naples and then whip across town for a dinner of truffle-lobster macaroni and cheese, Kobe steak, and oysters at Prime 112. It was impossible to get a reservation, but Blazer was friendly with the owner, so he could sweep in unannounced. This was followed by an indulgent evening in the executive suite at Tootsie's, followed by Blazer and Johnson going to the throbbing nightclub LIV in the Fontainebleau Hotel. Stumbling up to his complimentary suite in the hotel at six a.m., Blazer managed to stay awake until seven so he could call his wife and children to wish them a good day at school.

"I would try to mask all the alcohol and exhaustion by sounding as foggy as possible so it would sound like I had just woken up and that I was tired because of the travel," Blazer recalled.

After a couple of hours' sleep, Blazer went to the poolside cabana he'd been granted for free due to his relationship with the manager of LIV. The scene at the sunshine-splashed Fontainebleau pool was sensual, with beautiful people in tiny swimsuits taking in the sun and scanning for celebrities. It was Blazer's habit to travel to the cabana twice a month for meetings with players and brand ambassadors so he could score deals for his clients to promote attractive luxury items on social media.

By this time, incredibly, Blazer had also veered into the world of music promotion—yet another extremely risky but glamorous industry—working as a financial adviser to a growing roster of rappers and producers. All afternoon, Blazer met with a cavalcade of musicians and fast-talking hustlers. Operating on only a few hours' sleep, along with a surplus of premium alcohol from the cabana, he was exhausted but jubilant in his role as an aspiring impresario.

"What I loved most about Miami was the diversity," Blazer recalled. "The women were from Europe and South America, and they had to be reminded that bikini tops weren't optional. The action was nonstop. There were dozens of cabanas, but I was sure everyone around the pool was most interested in what we had going on in ours. I loved the attention. I was on the level of a celebrity, only I wasn't famous. I loved watching people trying to figure out who I was and what I was doing. I told folks who had never experienced my kind of Miami that their feet were never going to touch the ground. The entire atmosphere was intoxicating."

Blazer hadn't eaten much all day, and he was highly stressed, but he was convinced it was the good variety of stress as he pursued these increasingly jumbled and high-stakes enterprises. Then, that night, while Blazer stood at a bar on Miami Beach, Ketel One in hand, the lights started to throb and blur as his heart began to race and his breath grew short. Blazer excused himself, making his way back to his room, where he fell to his knees, then crawled to the bathroom and vomited. Convinced he was experiencing an allergic reaction to the granola bar he had just eaten, he called the concierge and said he needed an ambulance. After being wheeled out of the hotel on a stretcher, past nightclub-goers at the place he'd intended to spend the evening, Blazer was told at the hospital that he'd had a heart attack. The cardiologist said that Blazer needed stents inserted in his heart immediately. He was lucky to be alive—he should have died.

When once again it seemed like things couldn't get worse, instead of chasing Blazer for more money, Hartman ghosted him, offering excuse after excuse as time passed and domestic and foreign distribution deals failed to materialize. Finally, Blazer refused to continue to play the shell game. By the end of 2010, as he learned that other investors had suffered a similar fate with Hartman, Blazer knew that the movie projects were doomed, and the money was gone forever.

"I was like the frog in a pot of water, unaware as it is slowly brought to a boil," Blazer recalled. "I was trying to figure the whole mess out on my own, and I wasn't willing to give Hartman any more money. I didn't know what had been happening until the water was boiling and I was cooked."

The shoot for *Mafia* wrapped in early 2011, and the film was in postproduction when Ving Rhames told Blazer he didn't like what he was seeing in the editing suite—another ominous sign. As Blazer recovered from his heart attack, convinced he was still on death's doorstep, he gradually began to doubt the film was going to be released or that he was going to be able to make whole the money he'd stolen from the players. Unable to get straight answers from Hartman and with the film still incomplete, Blazer realized he was never going to get the money he'd invested back and that the project was going nowhere.

In the end, the unwatchable film never had a theatrical release, going straight to DVD and complete obscurity. *Mafia*, in fact, was a stream of gratuitous violence populated by characters with no motivations or consistency, coupled with a plot that made no sense and had no arc or narrative coherence. The story could be summed up as consisting of a series of disjointed scenes with Ving Rhames hamming it up while pumping random people with bullets and snarling instantly forgettable one-liners.

In a matter of three months—October to December 2010—Blazer had blown up his life. But he was remarkably undeterred by the experience of both the movie fraud and the heart attack. By the time *Mafia* vanished into thin air, the alleged good intentions he had started with were hardening into evasions and rationalizations. For months his crimes had been hiding in plain sight and he hoped he might avoid catastrophe; perhaps no one would ever notice the missing money. By then, Blazer had a half dozen employees and was leasing an office in Pittsburgh's upscale SouthSide Works, which was a stone's throw from the Steelers' training facility and had a steady stream of players coming and going. The mortgage broker for First Choice, a small regional bank, was subletting a space in the suite, so Blazer effectively had an in-house lender to establish a revolving line of credit of $250,000. He used these funds to give cash to his college football players during the bridge period between the NFL draft and receipt of their first professional payments—a time when serious hot dog money was in high demand, with the riches of the NFL just around the corner and expensive cars and fashionable trips beckoning.

As Blazer seemed to be thriving, and with the fraud undetected, tales of his famous clients attracted the attention of a hedge fund manager named Munish Sood. Sood was in his forties, a New Jersey resident of Indian descent with a comb-over and a tall, thin, slope-shouldered body. As a former chairman of the board of First Choice Bank, Sood could provide connections that would enable him to cut corners and get approval for all manner of transactions and arrange for lines of credit or mortgages for Blazer's clients with checkered credit histories.

Or, as Blazer put it, "Fuck the regulations."

Sood had a significant business of his own, running a hedge fund with hundreds of millions from institutional investors and wealthy individuals, but the glamour of a night at Tootsie's, in the exclusive third-floor suite with NFL players and rap stars, was intoxicating for the nerdy moneyman. Blazer kept Blazer Capital, but he and Sood formed a new investment advisory company called Princeton Blazer Capital, which managed less than $20 million at its peak but had an outsize impact on Sood, as he imagined he'd transformed himself into what he'd never been: a cool insider, partying at the best clubs, trading stories with sports stars and celebrities, and cutting to the front of the line at red-carpet events.

As Blazer continued to argue with Brian Hartman, demanding accountability for the failed film, other investors started to get agitated as well. It turned out that Dolan and Barton had also lost a lot of money, investing in a cavalcade of terrible, instantly vanished movies—from the never-completed *Hollywood and Wine* to *Mob Priest* and *Gearheads*—squandering a slice of their family's vast wealth on Hartman's projects that had caused other less wealthy investors to lose large sums, including Marty Blazer.

"I don't know if any one of you have had a chance to review this utter disaster of a 'film,' but my suggestion is that we lose the hard drive and collect the insurance money somehow," one investor wrote of another Hartman production.

By October 2012, with recriminations growing more and more bitter, Blazer's former in-house attorney left Blazer Capital. But the lawyer maintained a relationship with Shawntae Spencer of the San Francisco 49ers, who had agreed to invest $100,000 in *Mafia*. The attorney knew that Blazer had taken an additional $450,000 from the player's account to fund movies—without his permission or knowledge. Now that attorney told Spencer that Blazer had actually invested nearly half a million more than the agreed-upon amount.

Blazer was in a Halloween-costume shop with his kids when he received a call from an irate Spencer. Spencer threatened to send someone to confront Blazer about getting his money back, and this threw the adviser into a panic attack. Spencer had been raised in one of the most violent sections of Pittsburgh, so it was a credible threat. Agitated, Spencer said he was going to contact the NFL and then call law enforcement as well. In a follow-up call, Spencer's football agent, Peter Schaffer, attempted to mediate the situation, saying that if Blazer could get the money back into the player's account quickly, the problem would go away—but it had to happen within thirty days.

Just before Thanksgiving 2012, Blazer woke up to a text from Schaffer saying the player had decided he wanted the money immediately . . . or else. Blazer was convinced the "or else" alluded to the terrifying prospect of Spencer going to the NFL and triggering an investigation. His back to the wall—panicked again—Blazer made a decision that would define his life from that moment forward. As his money manager, Blazer knew that Seattle Seahawks offensive tackle, Pro Bowl player Russell Okung, had $20 million in cash with Blazer Capital Management. The financial adviser had power of attorney for two of his accounts. So he withdrew $200,000 from each of those accounts, and then he took another $200,000 from a third account, forging Okung's signature on the withdrawals from First Choice Bank, the same document he would be shown during his proffer with the Southern District two years later.

As if that weren't bad enough, since the production of *Mafia* had burned through so much money, Blazer had taken large sums from multiple players, and those problems weren't going away either. For a time, the fast-talking Blazer was able to keep the scheme afloat, relying on his NFL players' trust. Then, in the summer of 2013, the SEC conducted a supposedly routine audit of the investment advisory business, which operated out of Sood's office in Princeton, New Jersey. When Blazer was told the government regulators wanted to ask him some questions, he defiantly claimed he didn't have to answer to government regulation because he'd dropped his stockbroker license when he left Smith Barney—hardly a wise course of conduct.

"You can't touch me," Blazer provocatively told the SEC auditor. "I don't answer to you."

Still outwardly consumed by arrogance, in July 2013, Blazer took a call from the SEC while he was on vacation with his family at Rehoboth Beach, Delaware. As the SEC detailed their concerns regarding Blazer's expenditures—a line of questioning that would have alarmed most any sentient being—the cocksure financial adviser sighed. "Hurry up. You're cutting into my beach time," he said, then added defiantly, "Why do I need to answer your questions?"

With the regulators turning up the heat in September 2013, the SEC asked about the specific withdrawal of $200,000 from one of Okung's accounts. Blazer told them the Okung withdrawal had been to take another player out of the movie investment—which was true, strictly speaking—but he made no mention of Okung's lack of consent and knowledge, and the SEC didn't follow up with questions.

In the end, the SEC contacted Okung to ask if he'd known about Blazer's various movie investments on his behalf. Okung immediately called Blazer, not to express outrage about the misuse of his funds but because he was confused about the SEC harassing him with false accusations. Surely the authorities were mistaken, because his financial adviser would never take advantage of his friend and client . . . right? This amount of deception proved too much for Blazer; he couldn't keep up the fight. Heartbroken at betraying the generous and kind giant of a man, imagining himself a good person lost in a maze of his own design and seeking some way out, Blazer confessed to Okung. He knew Okung was a trusting soul, careful about whom he let into his inner circle, and Blazer prized his friendship, a connection he'd squandered by misappropriating the player's money.

"I knew there was no way I was going to be able to repay $600,000 to Russell unless it was from another player," Blazer said. "I told him I would make it up to him, but that was an empty promise. I was exhausted with the whole charade. My son was in the car when Russell called, so he went into the house. I sat in my car in the driveway at home, and I told him that I took the money to cover Shawntae. The cracking of Russell's voice was too much. I could have taken money from another player, but the SEC was on my tail and that would have only compounded my troubles. I was done. I thought about the other players I had taken money from and what was about to unravel. Then I walked into the house and went straight to my bedroom and just sat in a chair, totally lost. Trish came in and asked if I was okay. I told her I was not. I told her that I didn't even know where to start or the extent of what I had done, but it was bad. I told her about Russell and the SEC and how I'd taken the money because I didn't know what else to do. She had never seen me like that before, and she was scared. She took my hand and wouldn't let go. We both knew what I was thinking about and that I was serious. I didn't think anyone could figure out the full extent of what I had done if I wasn't there to tell it. If I had died three years earlier in Miami, when I'd had the heart attack, none of this would have happened. I thought Trish and the kids would be better off without me. She pleaded with me, said that whatever it was we had to go through, we would go through it together and we would get through it. She wasn't going to leave my side that night."

Blazer minimized the details and extent of his criminal activity at first so Trish wouldn't be too horrified, but she had never seen her husband in such a state. He was usually so strong and confident, not the broken and despondent man sitting in a chair, relating a hard-to-grasp story about committing fraud.

"It was an out-of-body experience," Trish remembered. "I couldn't believe this was happening to me and our family. I felt sad that our lives might never be the same. I felt helpless because I couldn't fix this for him. He was so upset. He said we'd be better off without him, and hearing that scared me. But I didn't cry, and I wasn't even mad. I firmly told him that I was there for him and the kids would be too, and no matter what, it would be the Blazer five. There are moments in your life when you are tested, and this was one of them for sure."

Through the winter of 2013 and into the following year, Blazer continued to provide documents to the SEC to buy time. Agent Peter Schaffer represented both Shawntae Spencer and Russell Okung, and he attempted to reconcile them without success. Okung had evidently talked to the SEC, as had Spencer, so it seemed it was only a matter of time before the walls closed in on Blazer. But to Blazer's surprise, the players who knew about his fraud didn't tell his other clients—largely, he calculated, because they didn't want to look foolish financially. In the unspoken code of professional sports, being cheated by an agent or financial manager was humiliating; players wanted to think of themselves as capable of handling their business, so they shared only their successes, not the failures and scams they encountered. The same was true for Peter Schaffer, who had to have known that if Blazer's misdeeds were widely circulated among players, it would reflect poorly on him, as he'd advised his clients to use the adviser. Competitive agents would use that as ammunition to steal away his roster of players and harm his future recruiting.

"Peter could have shut me down if he wanted to," Blazer said. "He was as cutthroat as you could be, but he was discreet because he had to be. This all meant I was able to continue to work with some clients, though there was natural attrition, as players left the NFL and I'd stopped recruiting because I'd run out of hot dog money. There was a code of silence. They were too embarrassed to admit they had made a mistake or had been fooled."

Early in 2014, Blazer was barely staying afloat, depleting his savings and collecting the scant fees he was still able to command. Then, on April 18, 2014, he was in the bathroom when the civil lawyer he'd retained called and told him that the SEC had referred the case to the Department of Justice. The SEC had informed the attorney that Blazer might want to get a criminal attorney. Under this pressure, Blazer decided to confess to the government to get ahead of the charges; he was convinced the feds would break down his door and take him away in handcuffs at any minute. Dark thoughts coursed through his mind again: ending it all, the condemnation of his three beautiful children, his humiliated wife, shame, outrage, bankruptcy, arrest, prison, his life a shambles. He stared down the specter of ruin, his ability to maneuver, delay, and obfuscate having failed him, but he decided he wasn't going to go down without a fight, whatever that might mean in the coming weeks and months and years.

Girding for the coming battle, Blazer hired a local criminal attorney, a hard-boiled litigator with experience in organized crime and drug cases, who had many war stories about gangbangers but less experience with white-collar matters and federal offenses.

Thus, after interminable legal and scheduling delays, Blazer traveled to New York City with his criminal and civil attorneys as Queen for a Day, to confess to federal prosecutors in that drab Lower Manhattan conference room on the morning of Friday, June 13, 2014. After his proffer, Blazer returned to Pittsburgh relieved and half convinced that he was in the clear after his confession, taking his family to the beach in August. But weeks and then months passed as he waited for direction, not knowing how the Southern District would proceed—or even if it would.

In the fall of 2014, Blazer's lawyer finally received a shocking call from AUSA Damian Williams of the DOJ saying that the potential cooperation deal was off. They were going to proceed with his prosecution because they weren't sure it made sense to pursue any of the areas discussed in the proffer after all. Blazer freaked out, pleading, cajoling, and expressing dismay and bewilderment to his attorney.

I realize that they are completely in control of any decision regarding the nature of any help I could potentially provide and how that would benefit my situation, Blazer wrote to his attorney, referring to the Southern District. *But I feel extremely surprised that if indeed there is a desire for someone to shed more light on these areas, I wouldn't get a chance to provide more details.*

In October 2014, Blazer wrote an email for his criminal attorney to send to the Southern District that the client called a Hail Mary. Promising to expose crimes at the biggest colleges in the country— LSU, Alabama, Penn State, North Carolina—the notice from the lawyer said his client was uniquely qualified to prove to law enforcement that there was widespread cheating in college football recruiting.

Mr. Blazer presents a unique set of qualifications and contacts that can proactively introduce law enforcement elements to the obvious and ongoing corruption of college athletics, the email read.

The email pointed out that in recent weeks, the scandal at the University of North Carolina had been back in the news, and Blazer's name was linked to the investigation. Days earlier, a *Wall Street Journal* reporter had approached Blazer for comment about his alleged connections to the specific UNC players and agents involved, the email said. Blazer hadn't spoken with the journalist, but the lawyer mentioned the reporter to tease the idea that Blazer was considered a valuable source, emphasizing his bona fide status and also hinting at the publicity attached to high-profile NCAA corruption scandals— always a motivating force for the Southern District.

I simply point this out to hopefully open your mind to meeting with my client again to explore what he can offer, the attorney wrote.

The attorney then named eight sports agents Blazer alleged were paying college players through a system of family members and runners, a term used in the industry for the lower-level operatives who did dirty work on behalf of the official representatives trying to find new recruits. The email added that Blazer could also name half a dozen runners, as well as a list of schools with players involved, from Penn State and UNC to Florida, Ole Miss, and LSU.

"A great wrong can be exposed with the help of my client," the attorney said at Blazer's urging.

Still, there was no indication of change in the government's intentions. Blazer didn't know it, but the Southern District was struggling internally with a simple but essential question: Cheating by secretly paying players as Blazer had described was against NCAA rules, of course— but was it a crime? Who were the victims? What law was being broken? What would be the legal theory of a prosecution?

There was a precedent for the situation. In the 1980s, a former nightclub owner named Norby Walters got into the sports-agent business. A fringe character in organized crime, Walters saw through the pretense of NCAA amateurism and started paying the leading college football players cash, executing secret, illegal, backdated agreements that committed them to his representation when they went pro. The twist was that Walters had consulted with a leading white-shoe law firm about the legality of his proposed business model beforehand, and he had been advised that he would be breaking the NCAA's rules, but no crimes would be involved.

Guy Lawson

But only two of the fifty-eight players Walters initially signed actually stayed with him after the draft, with nearly all refusing to repay the money he'd advanced, a development that didn't please the Mob-connected aspiring agent. With no way to enforce the illegal contracts, threats of violence were attributed to Walters, and the NCAA and reporters began to circle. Ultimately, the FBI investigated, and a grand jury indicted Walters for racketeering, wire fraud, and extortion, among other crimes. The legal theory used by the government was novel, an approach that perversely inverted the reality of college sports and claimed the schools were the victims of the scheme. By paying for scholarships for the players, it was alleged, Walter's conspiracy to pay players was fraudulent because the players had lied about being amateurs and thus were defrauding the schools. So the *players* were in the wrong as unindicted coconspirators of Walters's, according to this reasoning, reducing to the absurd the reality of amateurism. The vast majority of the players who had taken money from Walters and then gone pro simply repaid the scholarship money. Walters was convicted and given an extended prison sentence. But the conviction was reversed on appeal, twice.

"Many scholars understand the NCAA as a cartel," court of appeals judge Frank Easterbrook wrote, allowing that Walters was a "nasty and untrustworthy fellow" but pointing out that reality didn't exempt college sports from legal scrutiny. "The NCAA depresses athletes' income—restricting payments to the value of tuition, room, and board, while receiving services of substantially greater worth. The NCAA treats this as desirable preservation of amateur sports; a more jaundiced eye would see it as the use of monopsony power to obtain athletes' services for less than their competitive value."

The word *monopsony* said it all: the term describes monopoly powers on the buyer side of the market. In this case, the NCAA was the lone competitor for the purchase of the players' services, contriving to leave young athletes—many of them Black—like sharecroppers on a

58

plantation, only able to sell their yields to the landowner and compensated in goods sold at the landowner's store in the form of scholarships.

Back in Pittsburgh, trying to keep his family afloat and maintain his sanity, Blazer waited for word from the Southern District. The Hail Mary email had bought him some time, and he still hadn't been arrested or indicted or forced to spend so much as one night behind bars, despite misappropriating more than $2 million. To Blazer's relief, he then learned that AUSA Williams had called his attorney and said that he had referred the case from the financial-crimes section to the public-corruption section of the Southern District, so a second proffer would be held the next month in New York City. The prosecutors might now be open to the idea of pursuing a criminal case with Blazer, if they could be convinced that one existed.

Late in the fall of 2014, Blazer gave an eight-hour proffer to a prosecutor from the public-corruption section of the Southern District. AUSA Robert Boone was a tall, young Black man with an intelligent face and no-nonsense attitude. He listened to Blazer explain how he had funneled hot dog money to college football players. Boone took notes, writing furiously in his yellow legal pad.

"Boone wanted to know the exact nature of the payments," Blazer recalled. "He was particularly interested to know if I had paid family members or coaches, so I told him a story about an assistant coach at a major college football program who had had a really good player ready to go for the draft. Tony Johnson was a close friend, so telling Boone about him was proof to me that I was willing to commit to the investigation—I was crossing a bridge. Coach Johnson had called me and said he needed my help. I went to see him and the player's father and found out that the family was short on payments for their mortgage. In return for a loan of $10,000, the father said he'd encourage his son to sit down with me. Coach Johnson rightfully believed it was in the player's best interest to play another year because he wouldn't have to leave college and he could develop his skills to an NFL-superstar level.

The family could have lost their home, and their superstar kid couldn't be paid a penny by the college. But it was more complicated. The father ultimately thought the coach was trying to persuade the kid for selfish reasons, so the team could take a run at a national championship. The thought crossed my mind that there was also the chance Coach Johnson and the father were hustling me to get ten grand and there was no mortgage. There were all these crosscurrents and hidden motives, even with your close friends.[2]

"I was selling hard when I saw that Boone was interested. I sold like my life depended on it—because it did. I could tell Boone was seeing the story from the different points of view, including through a prosecutor's eyes. But I also sensed he was young and inexperienced, dressed in an inexpensive suit, and he wasn't manicured and smooth looking like I imagined the top prosecutors at the DOJ. I didn't feel like he had the power to really make a case happen. I knew a lot of attorneys, and he looked like a junior associate, not a partner—the guy the senior attorneys give the grunt work they don't want to do to. I figured the Southern District was just checking a box, not taking the possibility seriously."

The session at an end, Blazer exited exhausted and downhearted. He walked dejectedly through the frigid streets of Manhattan with his attorney and then went to the airport for a direct flight to Miami—the city where, four years earlier, he'd had a near-fatal heart attack. Now, reeling from the stress of what seemed like a doomed attempt to avoid years behind bars, Blazer faced his cardiologist, who was convinced there were more blockages in his heart. After a battery of tests, the cardiologist cleared Blazer—one small victory he clung to on the way back to Pittsburgh.

Then, in December 2014, after two excruciating weeks of waiting, a DOJ investigator named Lavale Jackson called Blazer. Jackson said that the government wanted Blazer to act as a cooperating informant, or CI.

---

2   Coach Johnson denies the exchange ever occurred.

Blazer was going to focus his efforts on two targets from his narrative: Atlanta-based sports agent and lawyer Safarrah Lawson—or "Law," as he was known—and Tony Johnson, the little brother of Kansas City Chiefs running back Larry Johnson Jr. The younger Johnson still worked for Blazer, while his father, Larry Johnson Sr., had moved on from assistant football coach at Penn State to associate head coach at Ohio State. Since Larry Sr. had grown more powerful in the NCAA, Blazer instantly suspected he was the government's real target.

In those first moments of Blazer's covert cooperation with the DOJ, a difficult but essential truth was revealed to him: to save himself, he might have to take down someone he liked. Blazer didn't mind triggering an investigation on Lawson, whom he thought of as a hustler who played the game with sharp elbows. On the other hand, Tony Johnson was like a little brother to Blazer, a good person and mentee whom he had no intention of luring into legal jeopardy. He hoped he could make sure the Johnson family wasn't swept up in the firestorm he wanted to unleash.

"The government never asked me how I felt personally about the targets," Blazer recalled, a hint of wonder in his voice. "Of course, I was going to deflect attention away from Tony and the Johnson family. I didn't want to hurt them."

The DOJ investigator, Jackson, explained how the operation would work. When making contact with one of the targets, Blazer would call a specific number provided by the government to register the communication, and after a beep, he would dial the number of the person he was trying to expose. This meant he could only record outgoing calls, and, they told him, the system worked only intermittently.

From the beginning of his cooperation, Blazer's investigation was largely self-directed and self-financed. He began trying to lure Lawson into his scheme, laying the groundwork for relationships he hoped would eventually pay off. Dozens of recorded calls turned into hundreds and then thousands as Blazer roamed the world of college football, looking for an opening to exploit. With Lawson, the few leads Blazer developed were for football players looking for some hot dog money. Fifteen-hundred-dollar payments to cover the needs of college cornerbacks and offensive guards likely to go in the middle rounds of the NFL draft weren't going to excite AUSA Boone, Blazer reasoned.

With Lawson, Blazer had spent years building up trust and rapport—or what passed for it in the sly world of college sports. In the 2009 NFL draft, an offensive tackle and future NFL star had been courted by Lawson, who wanted to represent him as an agent in return for a cut of the fees that would be generated when the player was inevitably drafted high in the first round. Lawson had assured Blazer he could get the player to sign with him as his financial adviser in return for $12,000 in cash the player's mother had requested. Blazer had believed that the player was taking money from other agents and runners, so it was a risky investment. In the end, the player had been selected early in the 2009 draft, as expected. But Blazer had never got so much as a meeting with him, squandering the seed investment.

"When that deal went nowhere, I didn't panic or go crazy on Law," Blazer recalled. "There was trust of a certain kind. We had an understanding that when things didn't go well, I wouldn't cut and run. Things didn't happen in a linear way in the athlete business. Sometimes the best outcomes came from a horribly wrong set of events. That was how long-term relationships were patiently constructed."

Under the logic of the NCAA's amateur system of college football, Lawson had been indebted to Blazer, and the agent had aimed to repay his obligation in the form of an Alabama player named Terrence "Mount" Cody. In 2010, Lawson had introduced Blazer to Cody, an amazingly agile and athletic 345-pound player with size eighteen feet. Lawson had represented Cody, and with the agent's endorsement, Cody had signed with Blazer to be his financial adviser at their first meeting, barely glancing at the document. The player had no idea he was being brokered under the unspoken rules of obligation between Blazer and Lawson, nor did he ask any questions.

In the months leading up to the draft, Blazer and Cody had developed a close relationship, Blazer helping with everything from deflecting demanding girlfriends to getting a custom Escalade built to fit the player's body. Bama had gone on to win a national championship that year, and Cody had played a key role. Over time, Cody had also introduced Blazer to a runner who could help sign other players and the owner of a local memorabilia store who'd pay star recruits and players "marketing guarantees" to sign products—a practice endorsed by the coaching staff and, in effect, a precursor to the Name Image Likeness policy that would come into existence more than a decade later.

"I would point out the future NFL stars I wanted to meet, and Cody would make it happen," Blazer recalled. "Everyone loved Mount Cody for his authenticity, his kindness, and his humility. He was my ticket into the Alabama gold mine, reeking with corruption but also overflowing with riches. It was yet another of the worst-kept secrets of college football, how massive the corruption was in Alabama. Not only were players taking money from boosters and financial advisers and agents, but they were doing so in many instances with the blessing of the university and the football program. The debt that Lawson repaid was Terrence Cody."

After scratching each other's backs for years, Blazer intended to rely on his relationship with Lawson to command the federal government's attention.

Cooperating with law enforcement meant Blazer needed to change his behavior in some conspicuous ways. He could record only outgoing calls, so he stopped picking up his incoming calls, as he'd always done as a twenty-four seven concierge service to his players. If he couldn't avoid a call, he'd pick up and have to invent a reason to call right back. He started to travel to Atlanta on his own dime to see Lawson, and he tried to shine enough light on the corrupt Alabama football program that the federal government would hopefully take his leads seriously and fund his endeavors. He might have still been working for deals, but he wasn't going to be able to profit from his endeavors. Blazer started to meet with Alabama's strength coach Scott Cochran, recording their conversations on a portable device supplied by federal agent Jackson. For months, Blazer tried to put the pieces together for a deal in Alabama, involving coaches and boosters and Lawson.

Thus, Blazer arrived in Atlanta on the morning of September 10, 2015, intending to travel on to Tuscaloosa that day to meet with Coach Cochran. When Cochran postponed to the following day, Blazer checked in with Lawson. The agent had a friend who owned a custom-suit store and wanted to meet with Blazer about potentially doing business with his basketball connections. Blazer was intrigued; he was known as a source of hot dog money in football circles, and it appeared word had spread to the basketball world. He went to a small shop on the north side of the city, where customers could sip complimentary single malt scotch and champagne while they browsed through swatches of silks and other fabrics that could be fashioned into slick suits suitable for NBA coaches and players.

The proprietor of the store was a former NBA referee named Rashan Michel. Tall and extremely fit, Michel had a commanding air and was always impeccably dressed, a look starkly at odds with his hyper, nonstop profane personality. As they introduced themselves, Michel brought up Blazer's adventures in filmmaking, but Blazer deflected much of the blame, claiming that the fiasco had really been little more than a business venture gone sour.

Offering Blazer a pour of Hennessy or Johnnie Walker Red Label, Michel talked about his basketball connections at the University of Alabama, a traditional source for many professionals in both football and basketball. Michel claimed he was "brothers" with the head coach of the basketball team, Avery Johnson. Name-dropping was a common practice in the sports business, even if exaggeration and outright lying were expected. Blazer knew little about college basketball—he didn't even watch games on television—and Michel talked at a hundred miles an hour, making it impossible to understand what exactly he wanted from Blazer apart from money.

"Rashan said he wanted to introduce me to a friend of his who worked for a basketball agent named Andy Miller," Blazer recalled. "I was a football guy, so the name meant nothing to me, but Rashan explained that Miller was the main competitor for the top basketball agent Bill Duffy, who represented players like Yao Ming and Steve Nash. Rashan told me his friend was looking for cash to help with the college basketball players he was recruiting for Miller.

"Rashan asked if we could drive over to the W Hotel in Buckhead to meet his friend, and I had time to kill, so we went to his car. It was a new Toyota Camry. But when I opened the door, the passenger seat was littered with documents and trash, and the floor was filled with burger wrappers and cups from fast-food joints. He told me he was addicted to fast food, which was weird because he was in fantastic shape. I almost didn't want to get in, it was so filthy, but I just swept the garbage out of the way and took a seat. In hindsight, the car was a perfect metaphor for the man: immaculate on the outside—gleaming and perfect—but a complete mess on the inside."

Blazer was skeptical, but being passed along among hustlers was typical. Everyone was on the hunt for a deal. The hustler in question, Christian Dawkins, was waiting at the W's nearly deserted bar. Dawkins was a Black man with thick glasses, dressed sharply in a short-sleeved shirt buttoned to the top, designer jeans, and fashionable sneakers. He had a strong hipster vibe and was in his early twenties. Dawkins claimed he was an agent with ASM, but Blazer sensed he was little more than a runner. The distinction was important in both basketball and football, where a runner was just an unlicensed freelance opportunist looking to make money from their connections.

"I knew who Christian Dawkins really was the minute we met," Blazer recalled. "I'd dealt with people just like him a million times in the football business. My first feeling was that Dawkins wasn't worth it."

Blazer and Dawkins quickly commenced name-dropping and discovered shared connections. The conversation turned to money, with Dawkins claiming that ASM gave him a budget to recruit players, which was entirely plausible, as was the claim that he wasn't getting enough money from them to sign the elite players he was targeting. It may not have been said aloud, but it had to have been understood that the money from ASM was to pay college players, in contravention of NCAA rules. The runner did the dirty work to protect the agents, in the same manner as college assistant coaches who made corrupt payments to players to protect the famous and highly paid head coaches. Dawkins proposed that in return for a monthly stipend, he'd pass the kids who signed on with ASM to Blazer as clients.

Blazer knew that agents who actually oversaw contracts had to be registered with the NFL or NBA and most were lawyers who understood the business. But those agents commonly relied on young men like Dawkins to act as conduits to the teenagers they wanted to represent, injecting a kid-like unpredictability and risk level into the enterprise. But the most obvious reason Dawkins wasn't an agent was simple: no real agent with half a brain would openly discuss paying money to college players with someone they were meeting for the first time, especially a stranger with the sole endorsement of a figure as temperamental as Rashan Michel.

The encounter lasted only half an hour, leaving Blazer uncertain. It was what bottom-feeding looked like: starting at the lowest level with a kid like Dawkins to try to move up the food chain to an agent like Andy Miller.

~

On a follow-up call a week later, with Michel coordinating to make sure he got a cut of any deal, Dawkins named his price: $7,500 a month for illicit payments to college players and their families. After some bargaining, they arrived at $6,000. Blazer didn't actually have the money, but he pretended he did. For all the wealth Blazer feigned, he was an expert at buying time and deflecting demands for cash. And he knew that giving money to a runner like Dawkins would almost certainly pay for nightclubs and hotel room service, but nothing would come of the initiative.

～

In that same recorded conversation with Dawkins, Blazer pushed to understand the role agent Andy Miller played in these transactions, asking who actually signed the contracts. Dawkins acted dumb and avoided the question, though he must have assumed someone with Blazer's experience would know perfectly well that a registered agent would have to be the signatory. This was college basketball Kabuki theater, a ritualistic dance with both sides intuitively adding layers of deception, both needing something from the other. But Dawkins had no clue what Blazer's true intentions were, while Blazer understood the desires of the ASM runner: free money.

Then Blazer switched gears and turned his questions to the role of coaches. In football, he'd seen the power that many college coaches wielded over their players, and he wanted to know if Dawkins had a strategy to ensure they wouldn't interfere with his deals. Dawkins assured Blazer he had good relations with many coaches and that they would bless his involvement, an intriguing development that would prove crucial. In the end, Blazer agreed to Dawkins's proposal, and the start date for monthly payments was set for the first of October.

Afterward, Blazer called Lavale Jackson to download the Dawkins conversations. Blazer was concerned that moving from football to basketball might make it appear that he was flailing, and he didn't tell Jackson about the need for money, lest he send the wrong message up the chain of command to AUSA Boone. But he also needed to show progress. Blazer was upbeat with Jackson, trying to create the impression that he could incite a real investigation. He was focused on making inroads at Alabama, not Dawkins, and he had a feeling he was running out of time with the government.

The October deadline with Dawkins came and went, and Blazer ghosted the runner. On his regular calls with Jackson, Blazer was still positive and filled with details that any insider would know didn't amount to true progress. But Jackson didn't understand the nuances of college sports, so Blazer's cajoling seemed to work. Every day, Blazer expected the Southern District to call and say the deal was off, and every day, he made scores of calls, reporting back to the DOJ on dead-end leads, convinced Jackson was no longer even listening to his calls but hoping his efforts would maintain their interest.

Blazer had also stopped returning Rashan Michel's calls. When Michel finally tracked him down, Blazer told him that the deal with Dawkins was too vague, with no specific actionable returns on investment. Michel tried to convince him to get the payments started anyway.

Playing hard to get with Dawkins turned out to be an effective—if unintentional—strategy. By going silent, Blazer had given Dawkins time to scheme and develop ideas to lure Blazer into funding him. Displaying indifference had ironically strengthened Blazer's hand, likely making Dawkins work harder to do business with him.

Blazer's phone pinged with a text from Dawkins in the middle of the afternoon on December 4, 2015. Sent directly to Blazer, the message cut Michel out of the deal.

Marty, the text said. This is Christian Dawkins from ASM sports. We sat down briefly in Atlanta. I wanted to reach out to see if you had any interest in working together on a few prospects. Let me know if you have any time to talk.

Blazer pretended to be surprised and suggested they talk the following week. He wanted to move slowly to keep Dawkins dangling and uncertain, and also to buy more time with Robert Boone and the DOJ. Every day was precious to Blazer in a way he'd never anticipated, as he spent the weekend taking his children to their sporting events and keeping the truth about the dire nature of the peril he faced hidden from Trish, who was now working to help support the family. Taking a job had never been part of Trish's plans, as she enjoyed being a stay-at-home mother focused on her kids and volunteering at their schools, but her husband's plight had put the family under financial and emotional strain. Trish focused on not letting their three children see the stress she was feeling as she strove to maintain their usual routine at home.

Fearing he would be sent to prison for multiple years, Marty agreed that the kids could have a dog, an Italian greyhound named Newt that didn't excite his allergies, and in many ways the little dog ruling the house provided distracted relief for the family. Blazer also cherished his connection with the small group of male friends who attended their sons' soccer practices and games. The men knew about Blazer's woes with the SEC, but they didn't seem to judge him, and the fact that they treated him the same as they always had was a treasure for a man certain he was on the brink of ruin.

Then Blazer's phone pinged again. It was another text from Dawkins, this one replete with spelling and grammatical errors, likely betraying increased anxiety. In the text, Dawkins sent a list of names, which included multiple future NBA players: Thomas Bryant (Washington Wizards), Mohamed "Mo" Bamba (Orlando Magic), Danuel House Jr. (Houston Rockets), Jonathan Isaac (Orlando Magic), and PJ Dozier (Denver Nuggets). They were still college players, but the harvest of talent would have been astounding . . . if Blazer had known a thing about basketball. Trying to educate Blazer, Dawkins urged him to research the PSA Cardinals, the shorthand name for Pro Scholar Athletics, a grassroots basketball organization with an excellent record in developing professional players.

If Dawkins could deliver those players, the opportunity would be attractive to the DOJ, Blazer hoped. Three days later, on December 7, 2015, Blazer and Dawkins spoke, with the DOJ's recording device turned on. Blazer personally recorded the call as well, a habit he'd developed to hedge against the government's system malfunctioning or officials not monitoring the calls. After niceties with Dawkins were exchanged, the runner said he was concerned that Blazer had gotten cold feet on their previous deal or didn't understand the proposed way of doing business together. Blazer and Dawkins both circled around the mutual decision that it was best to cut Rashan Michel out of their deal.

"I just wanted to reach out directly just to see what your thoughts were on everything because there's a lot of shit that has transpired," Dawkins said.

"To be honest, I was worried about the return," Blazer replied. "I think the structure was too loose. Rashan was saying I should send money and trust you, and that was kind of tough to swallow."

Blazer made it clear that his preferred structure for their deal did not include Rashan Michel as the middleman. Andy Miller had the name recognition and experience to command respect in the marketplace, Blazer said, flattering Dawkins. Instead of Blazer blindly sending Dawkins $5,000 tranches and hoping that players would sign with him, Blazer wanted to team up to go after specific players.

Dawkins claimed that ASM was in the position to be the preeminent agency for basketball, particularly by way of recruiting new players—provided he had sufficient funds. Dawkins said he needed the "resources," pointing out that Blazer had worked with football players for years, so he knew the score. Then Dawkins addressed the implicit peril of hustlers promising college players and then failing to deliver after the seed money had been squandered.

"One thing about me—if I tell you something is going to happen, it ain't me that's fucking it up," Dawkins said. "I'm going to do everything in my power to deliver. With ASM's record, averaging five or six dudes in the draft for the past ten years, we're going to get dudes. That ain't the issue. The issue for me is that in my position, I have to have the resources. I don't want to go to Andy for anything. If we're just getting shit done, it makes myself look better, and the people I'm dealing with on the financial side look better."

Dawkins said he had kids lined up for the draft that year and the next, and high school kids for the years ahead. When Dawkins asked Blazer how many NBA players he had worked with, Blazer hesitated for a moment, the waver in his voice audible; then he improvised—just a couple of players who went overseas, he said. Going overseas was a common path for prospects who didn't make the NBA. They could make a good living in Turkey or Greece or one of the many global basketball markets. Blazer had actually done business with a couple of basketball players from the University of Pittsburgh over the years, but it really hadn't amounted to much. Dawkins said that over the next few years, he wanted to sign fifty NBA players for ASM and Blazer—an obtainable goal, he claimed.

"Here's the thing for me," Blazer said. "I've transitioned my business so that there are a variety of ways I can make money. If it's not this but it's that, we can discuss what I can do to benefit from these relationships. It doesn't have to be—and I would prefer it not be—financial adviser."

Blazer talked about offering financial organization for players, adapting his services to whatever suited the particular individual, from insurance and annuities to concierge offerings like negotiating to buy high-end cars and jewelry. Dawkins said Blazer could be like an angel investor, putting money into kids to get a piece of the action on their contracts with NBA teams. Blazer heartily agreed, eager to reinforce Dawkins at every opportunity.

Blazer claimed he wanted to be done working with football players because they were fickle and blew their money too quickly. Basketball had larger rewards and more stability.

"On the basketball side, I want to build a relationship with someone like you, who has the experience and the momentum, like you said," Blazer said, now laying it on thick. "I want to be somewhat cautious. I want to put my foot in the water. To give towards the cause and see what I can get for it."

"That's the best approach," Dawkins said. "Let me ask you this: What would you say you're completely comfortable with?"

Baby steps, was Blazer's reply, lowering Dawkins's expectations to line up with his potential financial wherewithal. In addition to the laundry list of players from his prior text, Dawkins mentioned two specific players he was trying to land for ASM: Malik Beasley of Florida State and PJ Dozier of South Carolina—both future first-round picks, Dawkins claimed. Dawkins said he was also "taking care" of one of Dozier's coaches, a fact that would come to have enormous implications. Beasley was about to enter the draft, so he would represent a short-term opportunity, Blazer thought. Meanwhile, Dozier was going to play at least one more year in college before going to the NBA, so paying him and his coach represented a more attractive way of getting the attention of AUSA Boone and the Southern District.

If one or two players from that year's draft worked out, Blazer said, then they could start thinking about a long-term relationship and putting larger amounts of money to work. Agreeing to meet in Atlanta on December 10, Blazer waited a few beats after Dawkins hung up, before adding the time and date and nature of the conversation to the recording and FedExing the tape to the Department of Justice, information that would lie in wait until the appropriate time.

"I knew paying players was low-level activity at best," Blazer recalled. "The names Dawkins was dropping really didn't mean anything to me. My hope was to find a way to connect to Andy Miller and get someone with real power and importance in basketball involved. The hourglass in my head was running out. I was focused one hundred percent on finding a way out of the mess I had created."

CHAPTER SIX

Coaches

Later in December, Christian Dawkins followed up with a description of an intriguing connection to a coach. Dawkins told Blazer he had a relationship with Lamont Evans, an assistant coach at the University of South Carolina who would steer star player PJ Dozier in his direction, provided the coach received $2,000 a month—fifteen hundred for Evans and five hundred for the player. Dawkins said he had been paying Evans $2,500 a month but was behind by three monthly installments. If Blazer would take over the ongoing obligation, it would preserve Dawkins's chance to land Dozier as a client and strengthen the relationship with the assistant coach—to Blazer's benefit, if the player signed on as a financial client.

"I jumped at it," Blazer recalled. "Christian had a lot of hot dog money out and a lot of different irons in the fire. I was optimistic—at least a little. I had his list of players, and now I had a lead on a specific coach for the first time. The DOJ didn't even know about this possibility of paying coaches at the time. I was still talking to the DOJ about football, mostly. But I didn't have the kind of money needed to fund these basketball deals. I was digging into my savings. My wife and I kept our money separate, so she didn't know what was going on and she wasn't asking any questions. I was really struggling, and I was freaking out because I had to make it look like I could really help Christian or find someone else who had access to the funds."

After the movie debacle, among other things, Blazer had fallen out with the wealthy Dolan kids. There was one last person Blazer knew who might get involved in the Dawkins deal. His former partner, Munish Sood, had bought Blazer out of their partnership for one dollar, but he continued to manage money for a handful of Blazer's NFL clients, and Blazer knew that Sood was always interested in easy money.

After the SEC investigation, the odds that a sophisticated, licensed, successful hedge fund manager like Sood would continue to do business with Blazer seemed long. But Sood had been drawn to pro football's glamour like a moth to the flame, so Blazer decided to play up his access to college basketball and drop the name of big-time agent Andy Miller and his roster of famous players. Blazer also knew that beneath the veneer of sophistication, Sood was naive to the ways of professional sports, and he wouldn't be deterred by persnickety technicalities like the NCAA's code of amateurism.

Blazer was right: Sood couldn't resist the prospect of mingling with more celebrity athletes at strip clubs and bars.

"I knew from experience that Munish would want someone else to fund the business," Blazer said. "He never liked to use his own money. But I sold him to Christian as the chairman of a bank who also ran a successful and highly sophisticated hedge fund. Christian didn't think I had all the money he needed, but he thought I had access to the resources, and that kept him engaged. So I was pitching Munish to Christian just like I was pitching Christian to Munish, with the promise of big money in basketball. I was playing both sides against the middle. Both storylines were bullshit, but I was keeping the balls in the air.

"I told Munish that it was all or nothing with the Dawkins deal, so he'd need to front the money for Beasley and Dozier and the coach. He was more interested in a quick return on investment and Dozier was going in that year's draft, but I explained that the South Carolina situation with PJ Dozier had more long-term potential. I said he could put my cut of the deal in escrow until I'd figured out the financial part of the investigation by the SEC, which made it seem more real too. He knew that there would be some kind of restitution required by the government for the movie money, and he knew that I was involved in a civil dispute with the SEC, but that didn't deter him.

"In the past, he had always been taking from me—connections, opportunities, leads. I would introduce him to a player or an agent or one of my potential business partners, like Safarrah Lawson, and a few weeks later, Munish would suggest that he introduce me to the same person. Munish wasn't stupid. He knew what he was doing. He was using my business contacts and cutting me out of deals. At the time, it pissed me off, but it also gave me motivation to deal with him once I had the government involved. In the beginning, I didn't intend to bring Munish into the investigation, and he could have walked away at any time, but he couldn't help himself. He didn't deserve any mercy from me, that was for sure. Nor did Christian. They were both out for themselves, plain and simple, and greed was their Achilles' heel."

Putting Sood and Dawkins together, Blazer was starting to get somewhere in his self-styled investigation. In Lamont Evans, he had a lead on a Division I assistant coach, and in PJ Dozier and Malik Beasley, potential first-round players, with Sood established as the money behind any deals, so his prospects with the tangled web he was weaving seemed promising. But he still had no funds, and skinflint Sood was reluctant to risk money on Dawkins without more assurances.

"I think I can get Munish to fund this," Blazer wrote to Jackson about the Dawkins opportunity. "I have Dawkins on tape, as well as a text chain saying the same thing."

Dawkins set a meeting with South Carolina assistant coach Lamont Evans for March 3, 2016. Blazer flew to Atlanta at his own expense, with Sood coming along. The only thing he got from the DOJ was a recording device that best resembled a hotel-room key card. Blazer hoped it was an indication of increased interest. The pair met Dawkins at the airport and they made the three-hour trip up to Columbia, South Carolina. Blazer and Sood told the hustler about their glory days with private jets and parties in Miami clubs.

"Christian was full of questions about Munish's asset-management business and his position on the board of First Choice Bank," Blazer recalled. "Christian seemed genuinely excited and impressed. Sood stressed that Christian had to be careful—but that he understood corners had to be cut to do deals."

In Columbia, Lamont Evans was waiting for them in the lobby of the downtown Hilton. He had just come from a shootaround in preparation for a game that night, and he was dressed in sweats and sneakers.

"Lamont was tall, athletic, very confident and smooth talking," Blazer recalled. "He hugged me right off the bat. Christian had made it known that I was his guy, and that was enough for Lamont. It was clear to me from the start that I could work with Lamont. He was smart, and it was obvious he had the qualities to mentor younger men—like an easy manner and smile and the sophistication that comes from years of playing college and professional basketball. I could see why he was such a tremendous recruiter."

All the participants were at least partially aware of the peril involved with the type of conspiracy they were discussing, but none of the others suspected that Blazer had a recording device in his pocket.

The Ruth's Chris Steak House off the lobby of the Hilton was deserted in the middle of the afternoon, but Blazer asked for a private table, and they were shown to a back corner. Blazer then excused himself and went to the bathroom, where he pushed record on the device. A red light started flashing as he put the card back in his pocket and joined Coach Evans, Dawkins, and Sood at the table.

Evans described the recruits he was chasing—from Estonia, Germany, and North Carolina—some of the planet's leading young seven-footers. While the University of South Carolina was 23–6 and a long-shot contender in March Madness, it was having its best season ever, Evans said, and it was evident that the recruiting he had done was a key reason. The competition for talent was intense in the region, with Duke, North Carolina, and Wake Forest chasing the same leading players. Evans added that a single prospect like PJ Dozier could change the fate for South Carolina's program.

Lamenting the complexity of commanding the attention of teenagers and their parents, Evans readily agreed with Dawkins, emphasizing that "the job" was difficult; Blazer realized the coach wasn't referring to guiding players on the court or winning games so much as recruiting elite prospects.

Taking the opportunity to sell Blazer and Sood, Dawkins said that Evans illustrated the importance of having coaches help with recruiting for a financial-advisory business. The value of a coach like Lamont Evans, Dawkins said, came from the fact that the truly elite talents—players who were going to play one season in college and then enter the draft—were in college for only a few months. Thus, having a relationship with them in high school was vital. The earlier, the better. That was how the interests of college coaches recruiting high school prospects dovetailed with agents and financial advisers: they all had to convince eleventh- and twelfth-grade kids to select them from myriad suitors.

Keeping silent, Blazer was playing a complicated shell game. He wanted to convince Dawkins and Evans that Sood represented serious hedge fund money, even though he almost certainly wouldn't invest any substantial sum. Likewise, Dawkins and Evans were trying to sell Sood on the idea of paying college coaches to recruit players for his financial-service business. Playing his role, Blazer pretended to be skeptical about Dawkins and Evans's pitch, when he was only worried about capturing some criminal activity on the device recording in his pocket.

PJ Dozier was just the beginning of a relationship with a star recruiter like Evans, Dawkins said. "But shit, it's going to be like five PJs," he added.

"For sure," said Evans.

"It's going to be like this every step of the way," Dawkins said. "And that's the good thing about working with a college coach. Good players every year, buddy."

"Yeah, yeah," said Blazer.

Dawkins said the investment they needed was small. "Like a fucking phone bill paid, stuff like that. Phone bill paid, fucking probably totaled up to five grand for the whole fucking year, and [then you get a] dude who's a seven-footer, you know what I'm saying?"

Dawkins smiled.

They were just "coming out of high school," Dawkins said. "Those [are] the kind of times to get involved with them. Because they haven't been—"

"No guidance," Evans said.

"They haven't been—what's the word for it?" Dawkins said. "They haven't been spoiled, they haven't been, like, around enough to know, like, what their value really is."

"Listen, I always tell people—when you start traveling, you fly coach, right?" Sood said, offering an analogy.

"Oh, for sure," Evans agreed.

"You're in the back of the plane," Sood continued. "You fly and they give you some drinks, and then one time you get upgraded."

"First class," said Dawkins. "You can never ride coach again."

"You're like, 'Holy shit, I can't go back there,'" Sood said triumphantly.

"We talked about that when we hit the jet," Blazer agreed, referring to his many private flights in the past.

"Total difference," Dawkins said.

"You're right—that's the next leap," Sood said.

"That's why I'm involved with the coaches too," Dawkins said, then mentioned a few kids in the tenth grade whom Evans was recruiting. Dawkins could provide funds to the coach to entice the players to go to South Carolina. In return, the coach would smooth the path for Dawkins to become the players' agent and then select their financial adviser—and that was when Blazer and Sood entered the picture.

For more than a decade, Blazer had practiced good old-fashioned NCAA corruption, making under-the-table cash payments to players. Now he was being introduced to a new opportunity to successfully circumvent college amateurism.

"Paying an assistant coach at a major college basketball program with a seemingly bright career trajectory made all the sense in the world to me," Blazer recalled. "I knew landing basketball players was more complicated than getting football players, so the buy-in was a concept I could understand. There were fewer players on a basketball team, and big-time recruits could have a big impact on a program in basketball. I knew from experience that Lamont Evans wasn't going to take money from just anyone. Just like I knew it was likely that Christian Dawkins wasn't the only runner the coach was doing deals with. When I gave hot dog money to my football recruits, I was showing them that I believed in them and that I had skin in the game with them. Christian's approach seemed more transactional. He wasn't building a bond with the kids, but going after the coaches, and he wanted to get in early, before the players understood their real value."

Lamont Evans was the perfect candidate to pay off because he was a rising star assistant and a gifted recruiter, Dawkins explained. They could get to him before he was elevated to be the head coach of a Division I team. Head coaches at the leading programs made millions, so they weren't willing to risk losing their jobs trying to recruit a five-star kid by personally breaking the NCAA's rules. The burden fell on assistant coaches, in the same way capos and street thugs did the dirty work for Mafia dons.

"When they got their money, things the head coaches ain't willing to do 'cause they're making too much money," Dawkins said. "It's too risky."

Blazer nodded in agreement.

"And I told somebody," Evans added. "I say, we should go back and look at every coach's wife in ten years, just the fucking media guide picture, and if they're still head coach, look at how their wife changed."

Plastic surgery, shopping trips for clothes in Paris, pampered spa days—according to Evans, the luxuries available to the wives of wealthy head coaches strutting on the sidelines on national television were limitless and comically changed the appearance of their spouses. Evans gave the example of head coach South Carolina's Frank Martin and his very pretty and shapely spouse, Anya.

"Look at Coach's wife," Evans said. "Coach's wife looks like she's twenty-five, but she's fifty. Her clothes are nicer, her hair and nails always perfect, the plastic surgery—you look at her picture in the program now, and you know she just fucking looks better since he became head coach."

"Those spa treatments help," Sood said.

"That's the thing where it's, like, man, that's the grind you have to go through to become a head coach," Dawkins explained. "You got to shoulder that burden and take it on the chin. Because that's the kind of thing you've got to do until you make a million, or two million dollars."

"That's why I really wanted to meet you face-to-face, to look you in the eye and get to know each other," Blazer said to Evans.

"I appreciate you," Evans said.

"We have a lot of trust in you," Sood said to Evans.

"We can look up in five years from now, and ten of our dudes are in the NBA," Dawkins said.

"I want to be there for those resources, to help you recruit," Blazer said to Evans. "To get you where you need to be."

Evans asserted that he would deliver on the players he promised, not offer excuses. "It won't be like, 'I got blown out of the water,' or a Dear John letter apologizing."

"It's basically time to get some shit done," Dawkins said, then added, in reference to Evans, "He knows what it takes to get it done."

"The best part is the real relationship, like me and Christian," Evans explained. "It's not fly by—like fucking-drunk-in-the-club-we-meet-one-time bullshit. People say, 'Oh, that's my guy.' But you don't know the fucking guy."

"Because we met drunk at a club," Blazer said.

"Like I told you the first time we talked, I don't believe in fucking people over, man," Dawkins said earnestly to Blazer and Sood, addressing the possibility that he would take their money and not follow through on landing players as clients.

"Right," Blazer agreed.

"I'm either going to say I can help you, or I can't," Dawkins said. "I'm not in a position where I need to shit on people."

"And we're not either," Blazer agreed.

The collaboration between agents and financial advisers was important, Dawkins pointed out, but it wasn't enough to be effective with young players.

"Agents obviously have influence," Dawkins said. "But you got to get the college coaches too. Because if I'm coming to talk about PJ [Dozier], well fuck, you need to be talking to Lamont."

"Absolutely," Blazer said.

"It's almost like you're skipping a step if you just deal with agents," Dawkins said.

"Right," Evans agreed.

"That first meeting was very important for what followed," Blazer recalled. "Skipping a step by not paying coaches would prove a critical insight. Christian was motivated to take action. I had engaged Lamont Evans, and I had gotten Munish involved. And I'd done it all on my own, with no direction or support from the government. I was still strapped for cash. I was still probably dead in the water. But I had portrayed myself as having the ability to make a deal happen. I was flying by the seat of my pants, but at least I'd taken off and not crashed. Hell, I didn't even know for sure if the recording device was working."

The session at an end, Sood pulled out his black American Express Centurion card to pick up the tab, underscoring his role as the money. Driving back to Atlanta that afternoon, white-knuckled through slanting sleet, Blazer let the recorder run as Dawkins excitedly described how they could expand their collaboration. Lamont Evans was only the beginning, Dawkins said, a first step on the long voyage that lay ahead. Dawkins said he had another coach he wanted Blazer and Sood to meet: Tony Bland, the associate head coach at the University of Southern California.

"He's another of my close, close friends," Dawkins said. "Because I'll only introduce you to people I'm family with. If he takes you out with him in LA, you going to be like, 'Who the fuck are you, Denzel Washington or something?'"

"It's like that?" Blazer asked.

"He's the king up in that bitch."

"That's crazy," Blazer said.

"He was LA city player of the year and stuff," Dawkins said. "He went to Syracuse to play. He was at San Diego State, got them rolling. He's the highest-paid assistant on the West Coast."

"Wow," said Sood.

"What you think he makes?" Blazer asked.

"A lot of money," Dawkins said. "About four hundred grand. I got so many coaches, man."

Dawkins told Blazer and Sood how he'd grown up around many of the leading coaches who'd recruited players from his father's high school team in Saginaw, Michigan. His father had coached NBA star Draymond Green of the Golden State Warriors. The competition for the best prospects, Dawkins knew, wasn't just intense—it was insane. Dawkins said that Evans would block other financial advisers from gaining access to South Carolina's players, and he'd provide exclusive access for Blazer and Sood to the parents and others in the players' inner circles. It was vital to the coaches that no one get caught, Dawkins said, because they would lose their jobs under NCAA rules. Acting covertly, they would work with Evans to recruit elite players for their mutual benefit, and the price would be low. When Dawkins discussed the players and their families, it was like they were chattel subject to the machinations of this newly hatched conspiracy.

"If he's on a kid that's looking like a potential two-and-done or one-and-done, you talking about five grand or pay their mom's little rent in fucking Florence, South Carolina," Dawkins said of Lamont Evans and the assistance he needed. "That's going to be $550 a month. I mean, you got a first-round pick before the shit got crazy at the end, when people are talking about real money."

Blazer asked how much was needed to secure Evans, and Dawkins again said that he'd been paying the coach $2,500 a month. To make the payments, Dawkins said he would travel to Atlanta to meet Evans when the coach was recruiting in the basketball-mad city. They would provide funds when kids first turned up on campus.

The relatively paltry sums involved seemed unbelievable to the uninitiated. As a successful and rising assistant coach, Evans was making hundreds of thousands of dollars, so it was a mystery to Blazer why he'd risk a lucrative and promising career for a few thousand dollars a month.

"His job is on the line," Dawkins told Blazer. "If shit doesn't go right—what [Evans] did is wrong by the NCAA rules, so he's not going to let it not go right. Or if it doesn't go right, you better fucking believe he didn't try to fuck you. When the time is right, everything will be lined up because that's his job too. That's what, like—you almost got him by the balls, so to speak."

The final thought captured a reality Blazer could see; once a coach like Lamont Evans started to take money from Blazer and Sood, the simple threat of exposure would cement the bond that tied the coach to the conspiracy. The ingenuity of the scheme impressed Blazer.

"I called Lavale Jackson of the DOJ as soon as I got to my hotel room that night," Blazer remembered. "I hadn't received any specific instructions from the government to focus on coaches, but I could feel something special had happened in the meeting. If Dawkins really did have a bunch of coaches, I figured that could develop a pattern that would interest the Southern District. Maybe Christian wasn't the only path to coaches, but my first priority was to make sure I kept Lamont Evans happy, and that meant taking over the payments from Dawkins."

Blazer had no money from the government or help from Sood. So in the following weeks, he was able to slip Lamont Evans only five hundred dollars from his own funds to buy time.

Meanwhile, Dawkins had introduced star college prospect Malik Beasley to Blazer one week after the meeting with Evans. Blazer was certain that Sood couldn't resist a deal with Beasley, thanks to the promise of a near-term benefit since the player was going in the first round of that year's draft. But Blazer made it clear to Sood that he couldn't work only with Beasley—he had to back the transaction with Dozier through Lamont Evans the following year as well.

For all the extravagant contracts and high-profile celebrity clients, penny-pinching was a common trait among agents. Those who spread large amounts of hot dog money to attract clients kept careful tabs on their expenditures and wanted to be recompensed in a timely fashion, by whatever means. Partnering with a savvy financial adviser who understood the business enabled the agents to ensure they'd be reimbursed so that it didn't attract the notice or resentment of players. For the players, it was generally assumed that money provided to them in college had been a gratuity instead of a debt—only one of countless ways athletes were misled about the true nature of their relationships with their representatives.

With Blazer still playing for time, Dawkins finally sent an email to him and Sood that couldn't have been more explicit in the ways it proposed breaking NCAA rules and quite possibly the law. Fittingly, the April 10, 2016, email from Dawkins was titled "*Plans.*"

Moving forward I need confirmation on certain things to know how I will be able to operate, Dawkins wrote. *It can't be much gray area anymore, the business is non-stop and I have to be able to sustain things and have a clear picture if I can do things with you guys or take these opportunities elsewhere.*

The rest of the email provided a detailed bullet point analysis of the players he claimed he could sign to ASM—and thus to Blazer and Sood. It was an impressive group of names, including Malik Beasley.

Malik's trainer—I need to pay him an additional $30K, Dawkins wrote. *He helped to get me involved with the kid, and he also has his hands on Wendell Carter who could be a #1 pick in two years. So, it would be 2 for 1 here. I need help with this situation ASAP.*

The notion that a player would automatically engage the agent and financial adviser selected by his trainer was dubious at best. But that was beside the point for Blazer. The other payments weren't lump sums, Dawkins said, but monthly retainers. One player was Edmond Sumner, a point guard at Xavier who was trying to decide whether to declare for the June 2016 draft or risk injury by spending another year in college.

I will pick his business manager and financial advisor, Dawkins confidently wrote of Sumner. *If he returns to school, I need to get an insurance policy completed and financed, and I need a monthly stipend for the family. The kid will stay with me this summer and train and I have to cover those costs. This project will be worth about $75K over the course of the year. It is a lot of cash but for a top 10 pick the money could basically be made back in the first year.*

After years of listening to runners exaggerate their leads, Blazer read the email skeptically. He figured that paying players wasn't on the same level of criminality as paying coaches, and it likely wouldn't grab the Southern District's attention.

Next on the list was future overall number one pick for the Philadelphia 76ers Markelle Fultz—then playing for the University of Washington—with Dawkins claiming he'd had the player "locked" for the past year since he'd connected with the coach of the DC Blue Devils AAU team, alleging that the head of the grassroots program would listen to Dawkins "to a certain extent."

Michigan State's Miles Bridges was listed next. Dawkins said he was likely to play only one year of college basketball before entering the draft. His family needed $1,500 a month.

Reviewing the lists of potential clients, Blazer tried to figure out how he could attract more coaches like Lamont Evans. Dawkins introduced Blazer to an agent who claimed to know that coaches at Syracuse, Seton Hall, and Indiana would be willing to take money, just as Evans had, in order to facilitate recruiting players. Blazer now had the recorded digital and verifiable portal into NCAA corruption he'd hoped might save him years behind bars. In Evans, he had a coach at a major college program taking bribes. But weeks were ticking by, he knew, and his lack of money—or "resources," as it was referred to in the business—made it impossible for him to actually bribe people.

Then Blazer's world came to a shuddering halt. On May 6, 2016, just as Blazer was starting to build a real case for the DOJ, the SEC announced a public civil action against him for more than $2 million, alleging in a press release that he'd misappropriated the money in the movie fraud. The story was covered on ESPN, giving the report a devastatingly massive platform.

"The SEC alleges that Blazer, who founded Blazer Capital Management as a 'concierge' firm targeting professional athletes and other high–net worth individuals as clients, took approximately $2.35 million from five clients without their authorization," the press release said.

It went on to say that Blazer had settled the charges without admitting or denying the allegations, but the headline—which would live forever online—was more than damning: "SEC Charges Financial Adviser with Defrauding Pro Athletes and Alleges Lies to SEC Examiners."

The SEC's sixteen-page complaint detailed Blazer's offenses in grim specificity, relating how he had surreptitiously taken money from his clients and made a Ponzi-like payment to a player who'd demanded the return of their money after discovering the misappropriated funds. "The SEC seeks a permanent injunction against Blazer, enjoining him from engaging in the transactions, practices, and courses of business alleged in this Complaint," it was written in the indelible ink of an officially filed court document. The idea that the SEC had acted without notifying the DOJ, thus harming the investigation Blazer was pursuing, seemed incredibly incompetent.

"It was ridiculous," Blazer recalled. "It made no sense. I was just beginning to understand what it was like to work with the government—something I would come to learn a lot about."

To Blazer, it felt like the SEC was deliberately trying to end his cooperation with the Department of Justice, and that effort was likely to succeed in short order. He was at his son Connor's middle school track meet when the SEC press release broke, and he realized he had to try to get ahead of the news with his children. In the drive-through at Wendy's after the meet, Blazer tried to explain that, if anyone asked, it was simply a problem with an investment that had gone astray and that he was trying to fix it. His son appeared unfazed, relying on his father's word.

"I hated myself for putting that on my son," Blazer recalled. "The idea that I would leave Trish alone to raise the children kept me awake every night. I felt okay physically, but I had stents in my heart, and the stress wasn't good for me. I'd wake every morning and pray to be able to make it back to bed that night without a disaster happening to me. I knew I was going to wreck other people's lives with the investigation.

I had a conscience, but I was good at being duplicitous and I compartmentalized. I started to wonder if there was something wrong with me. I found myself growing closer to my children every day. I needed to be around them every day. I wanted to put them on the school bus in the morning. I lived for the little conversations I would have with my kids as I drove them to practice or school events. I knew what I was fighting for."

One evening, Blazer's youngest child, Ari, claimed to be feeling ill when she was obviously upset, and it quickly emerged that she had been playing a game with a friend by googling names. Ari had googled her father's name and discovered the SEC headlines. Ari didn't understand what she was reading, but it was clear that her father was in trouble and that was terrifying.

"She was crying hysterically," Trish recalled. "She thought Marty was keeping things from me. I had to explain it to her in a way that a ten-year-old could understand."

With the SEC publicly outing him, Blazer felt the need to preempt every conversation by disclosing and justifying the fiasco of his forays into the entertainment industry.

"I had to pretend that I had money and the potential to land clients," Blazer recalled. "Any of the players and agents that had dealt with me in the past could have warned the folks I was dealing with by saying, 'Marty is done and likely heading to prison.' But they didn't. I had to create the impression that I was still a successful businessman. I couldn't moonlight as a real estate agent or warehouse supervisor because everyone I was dealing with would have run for the hills if they detected the slightest whiff that I was struggling or not one hundred percent committed to signing and managing players. I had no time for anything else.

"I told people that it was just a civil matter. I said it was complicated. I said I didn't take any money; I just didn't paper the deal properly. I said it wasn't criminal and that I settled the matter with the SEC just to get past it and move on."

Blazer figured it was a lack of communication within the government that had resulted in the SEC press release, and he decided he had no choice other than to soldier on, relying on deflection and his gift of gab. He told Lamont Evans that the movie investment was more complex than it was being portrayed in the press and that he hadn't admitted guilt. To Blazer's amazement, Evans wasn't dissuaded, even if Dawkins had stopped dealing with Blazer.

A month after the press release, Blazer started to circulate the idea that he had a new, anonymous business partner willing to fund payments to college coaches in return for referring future NBA players to his financial-advisory company. In reality, this "business partner" was an acquaintance named Rick,[3] a business associate from Pittsburgh who was interested in opening a store to trade autographed sports memorabilia. But he was an invaluable decoy for Blazer to dangle in front of Sood, Lawson, and Evans.

Introduced by a mutual friend, Rick was a common sort in professional sports: a big fan—or hanger-on—who ran a small company providing armed security guards to the oil and gas industry. Blazer took to whispering to Sood on a nearly daily basis that Rick had big money and was interested in investing in his deals. Blazer knew that Sood wasn't happy about funding Christian Dawkins's efforts on his own, with any potential return months or even years away.

Blazer mentioned Rick to agent Safarrah "Law" Lawson, adding that his relationship with Lamont Evans remained strong. Lawson knew Blazer was implying that he was making payments to the coach, and he replied that he didn't agree with the business structure. But Blazer insisted that he and his "investor" were committed to the model of paying coaches, hoping that it would just be a matter of time before word circulated in the gossipy network of hustlers and runners that Blazer had a connection with deep pockets.

---

3   Not his real name.

To create credibility, Blazer invited Rick to accompany him to Miami to meet with Lamont Evans, who by then had taken a new position as the associate head coach at Oklahoma State, a measure of his rising prospects in college basketball. Blazer and Sood were each supposed to deliver their monthly cash deposits to Evans in person, though Rick knew nothing about the payments. Rick was a muscular blue-collar man in his early forties, a chain-smoker with a pinkie ring, a roll of hundreds in his pocket, a neck draped in gold chains, and a gut bulging over expensive designer jeans. With his red mullet and snakeskin cowboy boots, Rick gave off the aura of a somewhat dimwitted gangster. The most notable aspect of his personality, apart from his eagerness to please and his odd combination of unquestioning naivete and physical intimidation, was the way he threw money around; he was a successful businessman and clearly not to be trifled with, but he was also a potential sucker if he got excited—and nothing excited Rick more than the proximity to the celebrity and glamour of big-time sports that Blazer offered up.

In his inimitable manner, Blazer was simultaneously misleading Rick and Evans, playing them against each other. After a meal in a steakhouse, Blazer and Evans went to the lobby of his hotel, and Blazer handed him an envelope containing $1,500 in cash as had been agreed, hoping the hotel security camera would capture the handoff.[4]

Convening again the next day, Evans said he needed a favor: his wife had found a bunch of woman's effects in his rental car—panties, lipstick, a hotel matchbox . . . extremely compromising evidence of a tryst—and the coach wanted Blazer to cover for him. He wanted Blazer to tell his wife all the items in the car—"all the shit," he said—belonged to Blazer, not him. Blazer eagerly agreed, taking the request as a sign of the closeness of their connection. He'd routinely done this sort of favor for his clients before.

---

4   The recording device wasn't working that day.

Sood arrived in Miami to also meet with Evans and to supposedly deliver another $1,500 in cash. Blazer had been given another recording device by Lavale Jackson, so he went to the hotel bathroom and turned on the machine. Blazer, Sood, Evans, and Rick sat in the hotel lounge. Evans, with his promotion at Oklahoma State, was now making more than half a million dollars, but that didn't stop him from trafficking in cash bribes. Rick sat listening and smiling, chewing on a cocktail straw, oblivious to the subtext of Blazer's comments about what a high roller and big-time gambler Rick was. Despite repeated heavy hints from Blazer, Sood hadn't produced any money for Evans, with Blazer privately reassuring the coach he could collect the following day.

"Then I took Rick out for the night to show him what I had going on in Miami Beach," Blazer recalled. "I had an interest in a restaurant called the Drunken Dragon, a Korean-barbecue joint with great lobster rolls that I'd put some of my athletes into as investors. After dinner, I acted like a big shot with the hot female bartenders at the nightclub Foxhole while Rick and I had cocktails, and then it was on to round out the night at Tootsie's, all on the house. Rick was wowed—and he was hammered. Driving back to the hotel, he drunkenly asked the Uber driver to pull over on I-95. I thought he was going to be sick, but instead he went to the front of the car, pulled down his pants, squatted, and defecated—to put it politely—right there on the freeway with the headlights whipping by. He was that out of it.

"It was obvious that Rick wanted to get a piece of whatever I had going on in Miami. But he had no clue what I had been actually saying about him to Munish and Lamont. I was making him out to be an angel investor who was coming in to save the day . . . I said Rick had serious money, in cash, no questions asked—the kind of wealth earned by a tough-looking but unsophisticated hombre wearing a pinkie ring and a thick gold necklace, which suggested his cash wasn't clean, so he wouldn't ask too many questions."

While Blazer headed to the airport with Rick the next morning, bleary-eyed from the night's reveries, Evans drove back to Miami from his home in Fort Lauderdale for the promised cash payment from Sood that matched the $1,500 from Blazer. But Sood failed to produce an envelope with cash for some unknown reason.

Blazer was nearing the airport when his phone lit up with a call from Evans. Blazer couldn't record incoming calls, so he let it go to voicemail, and when he'd reached his terminal, he called Evans back, using the DOJ system to capture the conversation after he found a quiet place to talk out of Rick's earshot. The coach was incandescent about Sood stiffing him for the expected payment, not only wasting his time but also endangering the whole relationship. Blazer immediately began to backpedal, claiming it had been a misunderstanding and saying that he would catch up on overdue payments, by then theoretically up to seven or eight thousand dollars.

"Don't lose faith in what I'm trying to do," Blazer said to Evans. "I know what I can do with the seven right now—the eight, whatever—because I need it. Because I'm trying to lock in two guys, not for the future but right now."

"And that's no money," Evans said in exasperation, comparing the relatively paltry investment required to land a player to the major returns that would result.

Evans said he had other suitors lined up who were desperate to do business with him. He wanted Blazer to know that he was loyal but that such fealty came at a price.

In cryptic language, Evans delivered a not-very-veiled warning that he would abandon Blazer and Sood. Agents and financial advisers were offering him large sums for his players, the coach said.

"I got guys want to give me fifty grand," Evans said of his other alleged suitors. "I'm like, 'No, I'm not taking fifty grand,' because you all, you all gonna take it, think it's like that every time. And you all can buy people . . . *You got to develop a relationship. This shit gotta be right,* you know what I'm saying?"

Blazer did. Evans was saying that if Blazer continued to provide him with money—and not jerk his chain like Sood just had—he could have exclusive access to Oklahoma State's bounty of prospects for years to come. Evans then expounded on the value he brought to the table, speaking the language the two men understood.

"No, no, no," Evans said. "That's why I'm like two grand a month, that's what you guys going to get from me, that's, like, what, like, the guys that I recruit, even if you don't know them, they're going to be locked in regardless. That's what I'm saying, like, I'm, no, you guys, you guys are in the recruitment pack. You know what I mean, like?"

~

Evans assured Blazer that his players wouldn't have extravagant demands—ten suits, a coterie of minions to help assist with their draft-preparation workouts—because Evans had them under control and managed their expectations. If funded with $7,000, Evans would keep two thousand for future recruiting payments, while the remaining five thousand sealed the deal for the specific player—the catchphrase "five and two," as Blazer would explain to the Southern District. The coach claimed he controlled every aspect of his players' development, from start to finish, both on and off the court—including their future financial affairs.

"Okay, Marty, I might be like, *I need five grand at the end of the day for delivering this situation and keeping everyone out,*" Evans said. "And that's seven grand. You know what I mean? And that kid's a first-round pick. Boom. You know what I'm saying? Like, so for me and I'm like, *Okay, Marty I need five grand. Thank you, I appreciate it.* Boom, boom, boom."

Blazer knew that what he was hearing was a big deal, at long last. "Boom, boom, boom" meant that the process could be repeated. The conversation was being conducted in a little-known and difficult-to-master language. In this argot, in the context of illicit phone calls that could be recorded, as all its fluent speakers understood—though Evans evidently didn't imagine he actually was being recorded—the language consisted of indirection and euphemism and shorthand to address the actual subject being discussed. Often halting and circular and difficult to understand for the uninitiated, the language married ungrammatical street slang and the coded talk of mobsters and drug dealers, with the peculiar twist imposed by NCAA rules and the law.

To Blazer's giddy delight, Evans had explained in digitally recorded detail precisely how he manipulated players and their families—all in return for $2,000 a month to the coach and the occasional supplemental payment to close the deals for first-round picks. With Blazer acting as translator for the lawyers and investigators in the Southern District, providing an exegesis of the finer details and the hidden meanings of the conversation, the authorities would have to understand that associate head coach Lamont Evans of OSU was offering a guide to the way recruiting in college basketball really operated. Blazer fervently hoped that the government wouldn't turn its back on such blatant corruption.

~

In September, the seeds Blazer had carefully sown with agent Safarrah Lawson began to sprout again. Lawson called to say he'd heard of a coach at Auburn who was in need of cash. Lawson didn't agree with Blazer's strategy of paying coaches, but there was no personal benefit in pushing back, so Lawson was content to go with the flow of cash— standard operating procedure in college sports. Lawson said that Rashan Michel had brought him the opportunity to engage with the coach from Auburn who might be interested in taking cash to steer players in his direction. Days later, Michel called Blazer directly, a call Blazer once again returned immediately through the government's recording system. Sitting attentively at the desk in his home office, monitoring his devices, Blazer also recorded on his iPad to be doubly sure he captured this call.

"What you got going on, Marty?" Michel asked Blazer. "Law told me you got some good shit going on."

The pair lamented over how Sood and Christian Dawkins had "fucked us over," in Michel's words, by cutting them out of their deals, with Blazer adding that he was moving on from all his hassles with the SEC. Blazer said he had a new investor: the mysterious Mobbed-up Rick. The prospect of money instantly triggered Michel's hustler banter, with most every assertion made really meaning exactly the opposite of what was being said.

"This is how we gotta run it, Marty—you want to roll with me," Michel said. "I got to show you what I'm about. I'm about integrity, and nobody out here can say I owe them a single fucking red cent. I don't take nobody money, but this the way we can really make this shit work, if you really wanna make it work."

It appeared Michel had been convinced by Lawson that Blazer was indeed serious about funding coaches who could assist in signing basketball players.

"We know how we can make all this money, it's easy for all of us to eat off the pot," Michel said, the food analogy inelegantly stated but literally true in the predatory world of college basketball. "You know what I'm saying? And the good thing about it is, I got all the college coaches right now, because guess what? I'm the one who's watching them. I'm the one making they suits. So I got access to the locker room; I got access to the kids and everything. That basketball money about to become stupid too. We can get us goddamn ten basketball players in the next five years, and we actually sit back and do absolutely nothing."

Blazer readily agreed, saying that having a college coach in "our back pocket" was critical. The key concept was control, as Michel knew—as did Christian Dawkins and Munish Sood and Safarrah Lawson and every active (which is to say, opportunistic) agent, financial adviser, runner, and hanger-on in the realm of celebrity sports stars.

Blazer brought up the coach at Auburn who might be interested in taking cash to steer players in his direction. For years Auburn had rarely managed to attract players with NBA-level talent, but the arrival of head coach Bruce Pearl in 2014 had signaled the beginning of an era when the team would rise to national prominence and develop a steady stream of pro prospects. The obliging Michel explained how this particular deal would work.

"Well, my guy's going to have three or four pros coming out of there," he said. "Now, he's got one, two—that's gonna be pretty high picks. My guy needs like sixty thousand dollars. He's willing to pay you back over a twenty-four-month period, and, um, with that he'll give us two or three kids that's coming out of their program."

Michel was suggesting a forgivable loan structure, without explicitly saying so, and equally artfully eliding the meaning of the word *repayment*. Michel didn't mean the money would actually be repaid, but rather the sum would be "repaid" in the form of teenage players manipulated and cajoled by their coach to sign on for Marty Blazer's financial services—whatever the level of his honesty, competence, or constancy.

"Who's the coach?" Blazer asked. "Who's your guy?"

"Who—who's the coach?" Michel stammered, ducking the question.

Blazer didn't push, knowing that if he was too keen, he'd look suspiciously overeager. In the language they were using, what wasn't said was often just as important—or even more important—than what *was* said. Instead, Blazer pushed back on the sum, saying that $60,000 was a little rich for his blood; he offered $50,000. This was another aspect of the secret *lingua fraudster* they were speaking. If Blazer agreed to Michel's first bid without negotiating, it would look like he was foolish with his money and that would be suspect.

Michel explained that the coach had issues with the Internal Revenue Service, and he needed the money to catch up on taxes and get out of debt. The coach made $375,000 at Auburn, Michel said, but he'd been out of work for three years before he landed the job, so he was trying to get his finances back in order.

"Marty, Marty, Marty, listen to me—I'm just telling what it is, man," Michel said. "I know you get hungry; your eyes get big and all that. Fuck all that, Marty! Just concentrate on three situations, find those three situations, let them motherfuckers pay us our money back, let's get clients, and we'll just build it that way. I'm just telling you like it is, you know—I'ma be straight with you, I'm your boy."

With the bread crumbs Michel had sprinkled on the call, it took only a Google search for Blazer to figure out that the coach he had been referring to was none other than Chuck "Rifleman" Person. Blazer had never heard of Person but learned he had been the fourth overall pick in the 1986 NBA draft, after a storied college career playing with Hall of Famer Charles Barkley at Auburn and leaving as the school's all-time leading scorer. Person had played fourteen distinguished seasons in the NBA and then coached Kobe Bryant for the Los Angeles Lakers when Phil Jackson was the head coach. Person was, in sum, a legend at Auburn and basketball royalty, with connections to people at the absolute highest levels of the game.

Blazer texted Michel to ask if Person was the coach in question. Michel was hesitant, but real money was on the line, Blazer knew, and that would likely be irresistible. Blazer and Michel were relying on the invaluable commodity of trust—or what passed for it in college sports—and the coach's name had to be revealed at some point.

Michel confirmed the name, and Blazer contacted Lavale Jackson at the DOJ to tell him about this new development, certain the government would know that Blazer couldn't fund such a large payment to Person out of his own pocket.

"Once I had the name of the coach, I just wanted to establish his willingness to follow the model I had established with Lamont Evans," Blazer remembered. "But I was never going to be able to come up with $60,000. The rest would be up to the Department of Justice. They had to choose to engage with Rashan or walk away. At the time, I can't say that I had a lot of faith in the Southern District's ability to pursue a case. Like so many times in the past two years, I felt like I was going to have to scratch and claw to make something out of nothing in order to stay out of prison and protect my family."

~

At long last, the scattershot approach Blazer had taken in his quest to avoid prison was starting to build momentum. After the trip to Miami with fake investor Rick, Sood initiated a call with Blazer and Christian Dawkins to see if he could reignite a spark and discuss getting funding from Rick. Blazer was sure that Dawkins was getting money from the tightfisted Sood, but it wasn't clear how much might be involved. Whatever the amount, Sood remarked how nice it was to bring them all together again.

"How you doin' today, man?" Dawkins said to Blazer, his voice captured on the government's recording system. "I haven't heard from you. You fucking left me at the altar with Munish, Marty. What the fuck is up with that?"

This was patent nonsense, Blazer knew; the opposite was true: Dawkins had ghosted Blazer after the SEC press release. Blazer resisted the urge to upbraid the young Dawkins, certain that Sood had instructed him to be agreeable since there was another potential investor on the line.

Instead, Blazer said he didn't blame Dawkins for backing away. Blazer said he would have done the same thing, and indeed, in the past, he might well have avoided deals that appeared to have legal or regulatory complications.

"You can be sitting with me in a meeting and somebody googles my name," Blazer admitted to Dawkins, knowing that the only relevant matter was the promise of money. "It would be the kiss of death."

But Blazer assured Dawkins he didn't have to worry about future business associates looking him up online, because his name would not be in any of the contracts. Blazer would strictly be in the background, quietly brokering whatever deals Dawkins brought to the table, a suggestion that would come to play a large role in what would unfold in the coming months. Blazer would be present for conspiratorial meetings in hotel suites and restaurants all over the country. Though his compensation and stakes were left unclear, it was understood that his role was to protect the interests of the investors—like Rick—whom he brought to the business.

"Marty has cleaned up his stuff now and moved forward with a new team," Sood assured Dawkins.

Blazer told Dawkins about the trip to Miami and how impressed Rick had been at the meeting with Lamont Evans. Of course, Rick didn't know *what* had been discussed with Evans. Blazer added that Rick had asked him to come up with a budget for both football and basketball, and the financial adviser had done so, with the projections on the football side of the business already covered. Because of his existing relationship with Sood, Blazer said, he would commit Rick's money to the deals Dawkins was able to generate in the basketball space.

～

Dawkins wasn't fully buying the plan, Blazer sensed. But Blazer figured that Dawkins was back in play—at least a little.

"I was confident on the outside, acting like I was in control and had my shit together—but inwardly, I could feel the walls closing in," he recalled.

Blazer's day of reckoning arrived on October 24, 2016, on a call with Lavale Jackson and an Assistant United States Attorney named Noah Solowiejczyk. For unexplained reasons, senior prosecutor AUSA Boone was absent, which turned out to be a blessing in disguise.

Blazer asked Jackson and Solowiejczyk if the Southern District had the funds to bring the investigation to the next level. Then Blazer played a rapt Jackson and Solowiejczyk the recording of his recent conversation with Rashan Michel about Chuck Person at Auburn. After stopping the tape, he provided a breakdown of what had actually been discussed, translated from the original lingua fraudster, highlighting how Michel had indicated that Person wanted $60,000 but that he'd countered with $50,000 and that it was time to make a decision: do the deal or walk.

Blazer had thought about little else other than this moment for months on end. "I'd spent countless hours on the phone with Rashan, trying to make sure this wasn't just another hustle to get money from me," he recalled. "I told Rashan I needed to be one hundred percent certain about Chuck Person before I went to my investor. He kept telling me that Person was about to become the head coach at a major college, so the relationship was way too important to fuck up. Rashan had been very nervous about the details, insisting that the money for the loan go through him. I had insisted that it had to be crystal clear that payment was tied to specific players. Rashan had wanted to get on a call with my investor. I was really playing out the string, hoping that the government would see the opportunity."

AUSA Solowiejczyk was more malleable than Boone, and he expressed the view that the investigation couldn't succeed without proper funding, but he was concerned about the consequences of putting cash directly into the hands of men like Dawkins and Michel. Blazer shouldn't have to go it alone, the prosecutor concluded, but he was instructed to keep the case "warm" while Solowiejczyk went up the ladder in the Southern District and explained the potential to his superiors.

"I was told that the DOJ bosses in New York were going to meet to discuss how to finance the leads I'd developed," Blazer recalled. "I was told that they recognized how promising the leads were but that the DOJ higher-ups had to approve the funds for that kind of investigation. I was happy about the meeting, but I could also see that if my leads weren't approved, my cooperation was going to be toast."

On November 8, 2016—the momentous Trump–Clinton Election Day—Blazer traveled to Manhattan to discuss a possible plan with the DOJ. Blazer was forty-six, and he'd never voted in his life, but he figured he was almost certainly going to be a felon by the time the next presidential vote rolled around. He rose early that morning and voted for what he figured would be his first and only time.

Pacing outside the DOJ building in New York around noon as he waited to meet Lavale Jackson and AUSA Solowiejczyk, Blazer knew that it was do-or-die time for him. When the prosecutor and investigator greeted him on the sidewalk, they were in good spirits.

"We don't have the money to deal with these people," Solowiejczyk said, guiding Blazer away from the DOJ building. "But the FBI does. We're going to introduce you to our partners in the FBI."

As they walked across the busy Federal Plaza in Lower Manhattan toward FBI headquarters, Blazer was told that nothing in his life would change now that he was going to work with the bureau.

"You don't have anything to worry about," Solowiejczyk said. "Everything is going to remain pretty much the same with the FBI involved. You'll still mostly deal with Lavale."

Blazer was reminded of his mother dropping him off at his first day of kindergarten and how she'd assured him nothing was going to change, though everything had been transformed.

Inside, the FBI headquarters was quiet, corporate, the walls decorated with memorabilia from prior investigative triumphs, like gangster John Dillinger's machine gun and WANTED mug shots of Bonnie and Clyde. In a small nondescript conference room with bolts on the floors and walls for handcuffs and leg irons, Jackson introduced Blazer to the two special agents assigned to the case. Both were white and in their thirties—a decade younger than Blazer—and attempting to present themselves as the personifications of the bureau's incorruptible, relentless, fearless, and all-knowing self-image.

Special Agent Scott Carpenter was a cocky, short, bearded, and muscle-bound ex-military investigator who looked and acted like a smaller version of Captain America. The other agent was SA Jason Wake, a tall man with dark hair and a big nose; obviously the junior, he was the less intimidating of the pair.

"I could see right away that Jason was Scott's toady," Blazer recalled. "Scott was the alpha dog, and he was all business. Pissing off Special Agent Carpenter or getting on his bad side was definitely not a good idea. Jason was Robin to Scott's Batman—an awkward and skinny, subservient guy who looked like he'd joined the bureau after college graduation. Jason didn't say much, but I could see he was afraid of saying something wrong in front of Scott because he would get his head torn off, so he sneaked glances at Scott as he talked."

A tall, blonde agent named SA Jill Bailey entered. She would work on the case as well, Blazer was told, though her role wasn't defined. SA Carpenter told Blazer that they wanted to focus on Chuck Person initially while putting Christian Dawkins and Lamont Evans on the back burner.

Carpenter remarked on what a shame it was that Person was in this corruptible position after such a prolific NBA career, wondering aloud, "What the hell did he do with all his fucking money?" Blazer explained that Person was entirely typical of retired professional athletes, who often squandered their money on bad business ideas and high living long after they were able to afford such luxuries. Carpenter noted that Auburn was playing in New York on December 12, an ideal day to run a sting operation in the city. Blazer said that his son had a long-planned soccer tournament in Florida that weekend, but with one look from Carpenter, he understood his reality in no uncertain terms: there was a new sheriff in town, and the cooperator would do as he was told—period.

While Blazer cooled his heels, Jackson and the FBI agents left the room to strategize, then returned with paperwork for him to sign providing acknowledgment that all his electronic devices would be monitored and he would commit only crimes that the bureau had authorized. Carpenter expressed no interest in Blazer personally, nor did he reveal anything about his own life, instead focusing, laser-like, on the operation and improving his new cooperator's skills in getting the targets to incriminate themselves—when to talk, and when to shut up and listen.

Pending official approval for the funds and the establishment of the surveillance regime, Blazer was told to cancel the meeting he'd planned with Sood for the following day. The FBI agents said the bureau would finance the full $60,000 deal with Chuck Person but that the funds would come in increments.

"What did you think?" Jackson asked Blazer as they exited the building.

"Not too bad at all," Blazer lied. "It doesn't seem like it's going to be much different than before. We should have taken this approach much earlier if it meant we'd have the cash."

But to Blazer, it was clear that his freelance investigation was going to be carefully controlled, transforming his improvised efforts into an elaborate scripted drama produced by the FBI.

"When I got to the parking lot, I sat in my car by myself, holding the steering wheel tightly with both hands, and I threw my head back and let out a breath that I had been holding in for two years," Blazer said. "I wasn't crossing the finish line, and there was no question working with the FBI was going to be hard, but the day was a big win. The drive back to Pittsburgh seemed much shorter than the one I'd made that morning to Manhattan. I kept thinking that I wasn't dead in the water—not yet. I wouldn't be bullshitting Munish and Christian and Lamont and Rashan about the money I was dangling in front of them. I was certain that if the FBI actually provided the cash, there would be a feeding frenzy of corruption, and the exposure would be unparalleled. I watched the election results come in when I got home, sitting in my living room with a scotch, and it felt as if the whole world had been turned upside down. Little did I know what was about to unfold."

~

To give a realistic look to the deal with Person, Blazer drew up a draft of a standard promissory note and emailed it to the FBI agents, who agreed with the structure: a no-interest loan of $60,000 payable in four tranches of $15,000, spread out over the coming basketball season. By giving Person the full amount he wanted—instead of the $50,000 that Blazer had countered—the deal had the additional benefit of requiring the coach to list the players he'd target. For every player Person delivered as a client for Blazer, the agreement said, 20 percent of the loan would be forgiven. To Blazer's surprise, Rashan Michel happily agreed to all the terms.

After weeks of haggling with Person, Blazer set a date of November 29, 2016, to meet the coach in Auburn, Alabama. The FBI asked Blazer to send them a button-down dress shirt so they could rig it with a camera and microphone. This time when he traveled to Atlanta to rendezvous with the agents, the government paid for his airfare. As he was fitted with his wired shirt in an empty parking lot near the airport in Atlanta, Carpenter gave Blazer another key card–shaped recording device to carry as a backup. Carpenter turned the device on and hooked up the camera on Blazer's shirt, reciting into the microphone a timestamp preamble that would soon become familiar, with the date and place duly stated, along with all those present and the cooperator's avowed consent.

"This was my first operation with the FBI, so I had no idea what to expect," Blazer said. "The best way to describe it was that I felt tethered. Every move I made, every word I said—all of it was being monitored, and I felt I had no room for error or any freedom of movement . . . It was a very unnatural feeling when you know other people are watching you, listening to you, judging you. It was eerie, like I was on camera and performing."

Blazer met Michel at his clothing store in Atlanta, and the pair then drove ninety minutes southwest toward Auburn. Michel talked non-stop, either to Blazer or on his phone, invariably hollering and cursing and demanding money that was supposedly owed to him. Michel told Blazer he would do most of the talking with Person, asking how Blazer planned to deflect accusations if the coach had googled his name out of rudimentary diligence. Michel immediately corrected himself and said that Person wouldn't know—or if he did, he wouldn't care—the freeform flow of words all duly recorded by the camera and key card.

The purpose of the trip was to personally deliver $5,000 in cash to Person as a down payment and to execute the promissory note. They arrived early, so Blazer and Michel went to a mall to kill time. As Michel ate a Chick-fil-A sandwich in the food court, Blazer headed to the bathroom, encountering SAs Carpenter and Wake walking down the corridor, both investigators blanching at the sight of their cooperator heading in their direction, as if a mall full of strangers would some-how magically divine their connection. Apparently fearful that Blazer would be stupid enough to say something, the pair ducked into the bathroom he'd been intending to use. Shrugging, Blazer returned to sit with Michel, still needing to take a leak, excusing himself a cou-ple of minutes later, which elicited a curious look. Once again, Blazer encountered Carpenter and Wake walking in his direction in the mall, the pair of Keystone Kops blatantly avoiding contact by darting quickly into a music store.

"They were total fools," Blazer recalled. "It was a funny exchange on my first undercover encounter with the FBI."

They met with Person at a nearby Applebee's in the quiet lull between lunch and dinner, the coach's great height forcing him to duck slightly to enter the restaurant. A celebrity in Auburn, Person stopped to take a picture with a fan and then joined Blazer and Michel at a remote booth in the back of the establishment. Blazer's outstretched hand was engulfed in the six-foot-eight basketball player's giant palm.

The encounter was brief and perfunctory. Person spoke softly, almost in a whisper, with a deep voice and none of the wariness Blazer had anticipated. Sitting in the booth, Blazer presented the promissory note for $60,000. Person evidently knew nothing about his interlocutor's checkered history—or he did but didn't care—and he seemed to barely listen to the financial adviser's full name; Person was evidently not one of the more watchful types Blazer had encountered over the years. The coach barely skimmed through the loan document and asked if he could have an extra $5,000 in the next installment, all the dialogue captured by Blazer's shirt camera. Blazer agreed, amending the agreement and initialing it, then handing the pen to Person, who likewise executed the document.

"I couldn't believe it was that easy," Blazer remembered. "He didn't know me. He hadn't done any research on me, to my knowledge. Yet he was willing to sign anything to get that money in his hands, just based on Rashan's word that I was okay. Part of me felt sorry for Person and how desperate he was, wishing that he'd walked away or at least taken some time to work out the details a little more. Chuck had no idea the FBI was listening in, and he'd just signed his college basketball–coaching death sentence."

Promoting his services, Person told Blazer about the players he could get for him in the future, including Alabama standouts Herb Jones and

Austin Wiley, saying that in the eighties, he'd been at Auburn at the same time as Wiley's mother, who'd been a basketball medalist at the 1992 Olympics, so he had a preexisting relationship with the family he could exploit.[5] Person also singled out two potential NBA players. Blazer noted that Person was more than happy to push them into the embrace of a perfect stranger; the coach didn't ask for references or details about the services Blazer provided. Even after experiencing reckless behavior during his years in college football, Blazer was astounded that basketball seemed to be even worse; with much smaller rosters and vast NBA contracts on the line for far fewer players, the stakes on landing a prospect were higher. After slipping the envelope with $5,000 in cash under the table to Michel, Blazer watched as the two departed, certain they would divide the spoils in the parking lot while he picked up the tab.

Meeting up at the car for the drive back to Atlanta, Blazer jokingly asked Michel if he'd given Person the money. The joke didn't elicit a laugh or smile. In the car, Michel couldn't stop talking excitedly about how smoothly the meeting had gone, clearly thrilled that he'd discovered a new way to make money. Blazer pleaded with Michel to keep the relationship confidential—certain that he wouldn't—while Michel worked his phone to make arrangements to have sushi with Lawson in Atlanta that night. At the sushi joint, the tables turned as Lawson used Blazer as a phony potential investor in a sports bar. Lawson had convinced the sports bar's owner to let him have a free party for his son in return for bringing in potential investors.

"The owner left and we all had a laugh," Blazer said. "Law apologized and said it was never a bad idea to bring a white guy to a meeting to add credibility."

---

5   Jones was picked in the second round by the New Orleans Pelicans in 2021 as a senior, and he signed a three-year deal for $5.4 million, excelling as a rookie. Wiley wasn't drafted and now plays professionally in Germany.

Convening with his FBI handlers afterward, all were excited by what had just transpired. Person was evidently happy too, calling Blazer first thing the next morning. When Blazer saw Person's number, he feared the coach might have had second thoughts, but Person was only calling to ask for yet another $5,000 at their next meeting, bringing the total to $15,000.

As if the illicit nature of the arrangement weren't explicit enough, Blazer recalled that Person noted they both would lose their jobs if anyone found out about their dealings. *No,* Blazer thought, you *would lose your job.* He shook his head in disbelief as the former NBA star bragged about becoming a head coach and all the players he'd be able to provide as clients—in return for cash under the table.

"It was almost impossible to surprise me at that point in my life," Blazer recalled. "But Chuck's behavior shocked me. I couldn't figure out what was going on with him. He kept sending me texts all day, asking about wires and money. The evidence was overwhelming. I figured he'd come up through college basketball in the '80s, and the system was probably corrupt then too. He didn't seem like the kind to take drugs or gamble, so I could only speculate as to why he needed the money, but at the end of the day, that wasn't my problem.

"The big thing was that I had proved to Chuck and Rashan I wasn't full of shit. I was finally coming through with real money that showed that I could actually deliver . . . Even though I'd asked Rashan to keep the deal confidential, I hoped that he would talk about me to other coaches, to see if they were interested. Chuck said he cared about getting me business, but I knew that wasn't true. He was setting himself up to make some fast cash, and I knew it was just a matter of time until he came to me directly and cut out Rashan—like it was only a matter of time before word spread that there was a dude from Pittsburgh with deep pockets, willing to pay college basketball coaches."

CHAPTER SEVEN

This Is How You Do It in the NBA

The first intercollegiate competition in history occurred in 1852, a boat race between Harvard and Yale at Lake Winnipesaukee in the mountains of New Hampshire. From their inception, college sports were a commercial enterprise designed to provide entertainment for profit. This boating showdown was sponsored by a railroad executive with the hope of encouraging train travel up to the aspiring tourist destination. Participants in the race were given an all-expense-paid trip to the lake, along with costly prizes and a bottomless amount of alcohol to celebrate the event, enlivening the resort with bonhomie and an early version of college spirit, but with no pretense that there wasn't money involved.

College football became a national passion late in the nineteenth century, and games between Ivy League schools attracted huge crowds and consequently large gates. With big money at stake, the teams recruited the best players with payments, free tuition, and free travel, and colleges profited mightily. There were no academic requirements and no regulation of relations between schools, so players were free to migrate to multiple schools, sometimes within the same season, as they sought to make the most money and play in front of vast, adoring crowds of students dressed in their schools' colors.

Ironically, in the early twentieth century, Theodore Roosevelt signed the trust-busting Sherman Act to break up monopolies, even as the president called together the heads of Harvard, Yale, and Princeton to get them to form their own anticompetitive trust—the organization that eventually became the NCAA. Roosevelt's aim was to address violence in college football because players were killed on the field year after year, and he wanted to institute a league with rules and order. A side-idea came up, drawn from archaic English notions of fair play and good sportsmanship, that the players should no longer be paid for their performance, importing an irrelevant colonial ideal of gentility to the brutal reality of new-world sports and commerce.

The result has been decade after decade of corruption and bribery, followed by brief spasms of investigation and reform that only lead to more and larger corruption, cheating, and scandal. A report for the Carnegie Foundation in the 1930s, for example, found that college sports were "sodden with commercial and material and vested interests." Millions of dollars were swirling around, even in the earliest days of college sports, with so much money in football that a famous halfback at the University of Washington in the 1940s named Hugh McElhenny quipped that he'd have to take a pay cut when he turned pro.

"A wealthy guy puts big bucks under my pillow every time I score a touchdown," McElhenny said. "Hell, I can't afford to graduate."

In the 1940s, the supposed innocent age of college spirit and sportsmanship, another study found college sports beset with cheating, lying, and double-dealing in a way that shamed any and every other commercial venture apart from organized crime. The introduction of scholarships in the 1950s did nothing to stop the scheming, as report after report displayed, the rules farcically ignored or skirted in innumerable ways as the NCAA took on the de facto existence of a cartel. Television made college football a star attraction, which went into warp speed with the advent of ESPN and cable broadcasting. By the twenty-first century, more than a thousand colleges split billions in revenues, and the president of the NCAA earned nearly $4 million per year. Top coaches' salaries went as high as $11 million, not to mention all the sponsorship money from sneaker companies and local businesses. College sports departments had vast budgets, like the University of Oregon's total of $400 million per year, a multibillion-dollar industry rivaling Hollywood in size and importance—and all without having to pay the essential labor force, the players.

Marty Blazer didn't care to know this history, apart from his first-hand experience with the venality of college football. For more than two years, Blazer had been a freelancer for the Department of Justice, trying to entice bad actors in college sports to break the rules and thus trigger an investigation—but without the funds to make it happen. Now, as he was finally getting the money, he saw that it came with urgent obligations.

In December 2016, Blazer realized that his life and routine had been altered radically. A call from SA Carpenter instructed Blazer to get another personal cell phone. From that time on, all calls on his cell would be recorded by the FBI, he was told, even if he ordered pizza or spoke to a friend.

Then he had a contentious conference call with SA Carpenter and Lavale Jackson of the DOJ. *How long have you known Rashan Michel?* they asked, as if they didn't know the background perfectly well. *Where did you meet? Who introduced you? Have you had other dealings with him? Have you ever paid coaches before?* Their aggressive tone made Blazer defensive but also illustrated in no uncertain terms that in their eyes, he was little more than an investigative tool, not to be believed or relied on.

"It was very strange because I'd been cooperating for two years by then," Blazer recalled. "My answers were relaxed and truthful as I channeled what I'd said in my proffer. It felt like they were testing me to see if I was hiding anything. The call hit me on the head, reminding me that these people were not my friends. I was just an asset to get this case going and then move on to the next one. I told myself I was just like

Chuck Person to them. They don't care about me. They'd deal with me while I had something of value to provide. It was kill or be killed, and I was going to do everything necessary to protect myself and my family."

In his diary, Blazer sought some perspective.

"I feel nothing about exposing a situation where older men who are supposed to be mentors to these young men sell out their lives and push them into relationships for money."

Blazer was to be on call for the FBI twenty-four hours a day, seven days a week, with no exceptions or excuses. In the next six months, he would have more than five hundred calls with SA Carpenter alone. The calls weren't friendly. Carpenter and the others required Blazer to participate in strategic planning, detailed reporting, and logistical scheming with young, ambitious, often short-tempered FBI agents. He was at their mercy, he was reminded nearly constantly, a reality he had to accept in silence.

"Substantial assistance meant I had to be ready to drop whatever I was doing and be wherever I was needed," Blazer recalled. "When my phone rang, the FBI knew it was ringing and who was on the other end and what was being said. There were no excuses for not taking a call, unless I'd been instructed by them not to pick up. There were countless text exchanges as well. Each conversation was discussed and scrutinized to measure how useful and effective it had been. I was working with a seasoned, hard-driving FBI agent who was very detail oriented."

In the following months, Blazer learned that Carpenter's personality combined redneck passions like fishing, bourbon, and *Shark Week* with the casually cruel euphemisms of a former military sniper as he talked about "targets." To underline his lack of respect for formality, Carpenter cultivated a look that resembled an unkempt backwoods trucker who'd come to live in the big city, with his beard badly trimmed and a pronounced indifference to personal hygiene. Dressed in ratty jeans, rumpled shirts, and sockless boat shoes, Carpenter was the type to order a burger rare and wash it down with a couple of beers, then follow up with a satisfied belch.

Carpenter practiced an extreme form of compartmentalization and never talked about his personal life, but despite his redneck persona, he was actually from an upper-middle-class New Jersey family and had graduated from Wake Forest in North Carolina before joining the 82nd Airborne, deploying twice to Iraq. After he'd returned to the United States and joined the FBI, he'd taken to downing large quantities of vodka, even as he maintained a stellar career that included working the vast FIFA soccer corruption case, which had given him strong qualifications for the investigation that now lay ahead. For all his good old boy affectation and his rise in the bureau, Carpenter had also developed a lack of impulse control.

As soon as Blazer started receiving money from the FBI, he sensed his cooperation with the bureau was pulling him away from his family. When the first tranche of FBI money was finally wired to Blazer's account, he was on the way to a soccer tournament with his son. Blazer immediately pulled his car off the interstate and made a wire transfer to Person's account from his phone, texting the coach to confirm receipt of the funds. Blazer's son never questioned what he was doing; a chasm of secrecy in his family was growing larger by the day.

Blazer also continued to keep Trish almost entirely in the dark about what was going on. For her part, Trish knew he hadn't personally benefited from the movie crimes. As she set about building her burgeoning business, she reasoned that the less she knew about his cooperation with the FBI, the better for their relationship; she also suspected she wasn't legally permitted to know about her husband's actions for the government.

SA Carpenter told Blazer to meet with Chuck Person in Manhattan for a sting on Monday, December 12, 2016, at the same time Blazer was supposed to be in Tampa for his son's soccer team's national championship tournament. Blazer was in Tampa, in the stands with his son, as his phone rang continually with calls from FBI agents arranging his coming trip north—like it or not.

Worried that his thirteen-year-old son would have to spend the night alone in a hotel, in a strange city, Blazer offered a weak excuse and asked another dad on the team to keep an eye on his son for the day. He was filled with worry and guilt, praying he could get back to Florida in one day.

"The worst part was the conversation I had to have with Connor," Blazer recalled. "My heart aches every time I go back to that moment when I had to explain to him why out of nowhere I had to take a trip to New York to meet with some potential clients and that it was more important than spending time with him. We had been looking forward to that weekend for months. It was even more painful when he didn't question my ridiculous lie. He accepted the circumstances without asking for details, but I could tell from his expression he was hurt."

Blazer woke at four in the morning and flew north, leaving Florida for a slate-gray December day in New York. He arrived in Midtown Manhattan by midday, climbing into the back seat of SA Carpenter's Jeep near Madison Square Garden, where Auburn was set to play that night. There, Blazer was given a black camera-mounted business shirt and a clear plastic bag containing $15,000 in cash, bringing the total he'd given to Person to $30,000. Carpenter told Blazer to raise the matter of compensation but cut down on all the banter with Rashan Michel because the agents couldn't endure the tedium of listening to the endless meaningless ramblings. *You prick,* Blazer thought. *I've left my son alone in Florida, and I'm risking my personal safety for this, and all you care about is your convenience.*

Michel had also rushed to New York, and Blazer rendezvoused with him at a small café. Michel asked if Person was going to get money that day. Blazer confirmed it without specifying the amount, receiving a text at the same time from Person asking if Michel could see Blazer's phone. Blazer replied that he couldn't, so Person wrote that Blazer shouldn't tell the tailor how much money Blazer was paying out. Inwardly, Blazer rolled his eyes.

At the café, Michel said he wanted to be paid a retainer of $2,000 a month, passing Blazer his phone to enter his credit card information to pay Michel's return airfare that day as an expense that should be reimbursed. Blazer started to punch in his information, then thought better of it and said he'd think about the best terms for payments, but he wasn't going to cover expenses piecemeal or hand out his credit card information.

Person was staying at a Hilton near Madison Square Garden, but Michel didn't want to be seen in the lobby, telling Blazer that Auburn's head coach had already been sanctioned for recruiting infractions and Michel's mere presence would spark suspicions; in the cat and mouse game of NCAA corruption, certain boundaries and rituals had to be respected. While they were waiting for Person across the street, the coach texted and instructed Blazer to tell Michel the total to be paid that day was $3,000, not the $15,000 Blazer had in the bag. As Blazer stepped into a bathroom, his phone rang, and Person whispered instructions to keep $3,000 in his pocket and, once he was in Person's hotel room, to go into the bathroom and put $12,000 in the bag holding the blow-dryer and leave it under the sink, as if they were in a low-budget spy film.

Finally in Person's hotel, Blazer and Michel found his room door ajar. Person was sitting on the bed, and a tall, twenty-year-old Black man sat at the desk, seemingly confused about why he was meeting two strangers. Hugs were exchanged. These kinds of introductions usually occurred in the coach's hometown, off campus, in a private and confidential place, so Blazer was shocked to meet Auburn player Danjel Purifoy.

~

"Marty is going to be your financial adviser, and we will clear it with your mom and stepdad to make sure they are cool—but whatever you need, this guy will handle," Person said as he introduced Blazer to the player.

Person said that while Purifoy was in college, Blazer would provide the coach with $1,000 a month for his mother and an additional $500 for the player. Person explained to Purifoy that he had to be careful about how he spent the money, not buying anything extravagant that might attract attention.

"That's very important because this is a violation of the rules," Person told Purifoy. "But this is how NBA players get it done. They form partnerships. They form trust."

Purifoy nodded.

"Ray will do your suits," Person added, nodding at Michel. "Any questions?"

"No," Purifoy said, and after another round of hugs, he departed.

"That statement really made me see Chuck in a different light," Blazer remembered. "Over a decade in the NBA, playing with greats like Michael Jordan—there was no question he was a role model in Danjel's eyes. It was undeniable as well that Chuck held the future of the freshman in his hands. Danjel was powerless to say no or to question anything that was happening. He had no choice but to enter into an agreement with an absolute stranger like me."

With Purifoy gone, Person told Blazer he was looking to take a job as a head coach at a top school, and he could send him more players once he was in that position. In the meantime, if Blazer would "supplement" Person's income at Auburn, he could wait for the perfect opportunity for their mutual benefit—and of course, he'd continue to conspire to get his players into deals with Blazer. In due time, Blazer excused himself and went to the bathroom and quietly put $12,000 in cash in the hair-dryer bag, then stashed it under the sink as he'd been instructed.

Returning to the room, Blazer said he'd brought $3,000, pulling out thirty hundred-dollar bills from his pocket and palming them to

Person so that Michel would see the cash. After some small talk, Blazer and Michel returned to the lobby and parted ways. Almost immediately, Blazer received another text from Person, so he called to find the agitated coach demanding that he not tell Michel anything about their business going forward. It seemed that as soon as Blazer had left, Michel had demanded a share of the cash without knowing the true amount, and he and Person had quarreled. Michel had to be pushed out of their dealings entirely, Person said angrily, a development that Blazer had anticipated. Without Michel, Blazer would have a direct line to the coach, a prospect he might quickly parlay up to the highest level of college basketball coaching, providing entrée to the kind of household names that might really shake the foundations of the NCAA. Blazer readily agreed.

Blazer wanted to avoid a debriefing session with the FBI, in the hopes he could fly back to Florida immediately. But SA Carpenter insisted they travel to FBI headquarters in Lower Manhattan to discuss the day's events and plan next steps.

"After half an hour or so of debriefing at the FBI headquarters, a guy came in and said his name was Brian," Blazer recalled. "Brian was introduced by Scott and Jason as their supervisor. Brian was a short, pasty-faced redhead who had a lot of energy. I could tell Scott and Jason didn't like him but they had to put up with his antics. Brian was clearly an obnoxious ball buster, constantly reminding the other agents that he was in charge without having to say the words. He wanted me to know that he appreciated what I was doing, but he also seemed to want me to know that he understood how sports mobster corruption really worked—that he was streetwise in a way the others weren't. He seemed to be saying that he and I were in on the joke, not like the other knuckleheads.

"Brian said he'd been listening to my calls and that he was very impressed with everything I'd been doing. He said he knew my situation was tough, but there was nothing better someone in my position could do to prepare to deal with the prosecutors. He said I was unique because I was in with 'these people,' and that was very difficult to do successfully. I knew that was true—you couldn't just send an undercover to insert themselves into the college sports Mafia. You had to be an insider, with people who spoke the same language—like organized crime or a terror cell.

"I made it to the airport in the nick of time. I was able to talk to my son, Connor, before my flight took off. His team had lost that day, and he thought he didn't play very well. I felt terrible that I wasn't there for him. He said he'd wait up for me. In Tampa, I rented a car and drove for an hour in heavy fog, making it to the hotel just before one. It was like my life was constantly on the edge of a knife, with the thinnest of margins. I had survived that day, but I wasn't sure about tomorrow or the day after. My son was asleep in the room when I crept in, so I had a beer and some chips and looked out the window, thinking about how there was no room for error."

～

Cooperating with the government also left little room for Blazer to consult his conscience—but he did occasionally wonder about the collateral damage. The Sunday after the New York operation, Blazer was sitting in Chuck Person's kitchen in a sprawling house in an upscale Auburn suburb, watching Person's young children run down the stairs to hug their father. Introduced to Person's wife while wearing a camera mounted on his shirt, Blazer felt empathy knowing that her husband was about to be recorded committing yet more potential felonies—but Blazer did not stop doing what was necessary.

"I didn't want him to be doing this," Blazer recalled. "I couldn't understand why he was risking all that he had. But there was no going back now. These were his decisions, and there was no question he knew what he was doing was wrong."

Danjel Purifoy's mother, Waukesha, and her husband were in the kitchen as well, plainly as under the sway of Person as their son had been in New York. During his career, Blazer had participated in hundreds of kitchen meetings like this, sitting down with athletes and their families, knowing perfectly well what they wanted to hear. He went through the motions, pitching his financial-advice services, but he couldn't muster his normal enthusiasm for this part of the business.

Sensing Blazer's lack of conviction, Person jumped in, telling Purifoy's parents that Blazer was his personal financial adviser and that he also worked with his former Auburn teammate Charles Barkley. Person's lies and cavalier attitude revived Blazer; the coach was evidently taunting the fates with his casual deceptions, and the informant swiveled to fully capture the scene with his button camera. By then, Person was enthusing about Danjel's potential future with the Indiana Pacers, pushing the unsuspecting family toward accepting the money and thus endangering the future of a young man trapped in the NCAA's viselike grip; Auburn's basketball team made tens of millions for the school, and head coach Bruce Pearl would soon sign a new five-year $3.8 million per season contract, but Purifoy and his family weren't able to make a dime.

"Danjel's mother and stepfather were more interested in what I could do for them now in the form of payments than they were with what I could do for Danjel when he reached the NBA," Blazer said. "Chuck told them that I would coordinate $1,000 a month to them and $500 to Danjel, which would come to them through Person. He told them that I would help them with the cost of travel, like the game coming up against Vanderbilt in Nashville. Then he wrapped up the conversation by saying I had something for them. That was my cue to hand over the money. I stood up, careful that I had the camera fixed on Danjel's stepfather as I told him the $1,000 in the envelope was just to start, and we exchanged contact information and planned to speak again soon."

The deal with the Purifoys completed, Blazer and Person walked to the front door, and Blazer produced another envelope, quietly explaining that it contained the $5,000 they had discussed earlier, looking up nearly a full foot at the coach, who smiled for the button camera and said big things were going to happen—big, big things.

~

Afterward, the FBI agents were delighted with the progress Blazer was making, but he found it hard to be joyful over the Christmas holidays of 2016, weighed down by his predicament as well as the burden of dealing with law enforcement officials who didn't understand the unspoken rules and signals of college sports. He knew that as competitive as it was to sign players to an agent or financial manager, it was equally cutthroat for runners and agents to put themselves in a position to pay players, developing a level of trust and intimacy that enabled future stars to put their fate in the hands of people they didn't know. Blazer also knew word that he was paying out real money would travel in the small world of college basketball. Jealousies would be developed and hidden, along with grudges and expectations, with all concerned eager to step aboard the gravy train.

It was no surprise, then, when Lawson texted Blazer to warn him against dealing with the unreliable and unstable Rashan Michel. Even though Lawson had put Blazer in touch with Michel, the tailor had proposed Blazer do business with another football agent, in direct competition with Lawson, and he said he would be very offended if any business resulted from the new connection. Petty disputes like this were commonplace and acted to Blazer's advantage: he had no intention of taking any steps with the football agent, but allowing the conflict to fester would help Blazer keep the various gossipy pieces in his developing conspiracy from comparing notes and developing doubts about the sources of his payments.

Early in the new year, the FBI told Blazer they wanted him to splash more money around, staying in five-star hotels and renting luxury cars, in order to impress upon the targets the idea that he had access to large sums of cash. Blazer thought this was a crazy way to seduce potential coconspirators. Money managers shouldn't be living large, he knew, because it would only lead to suspicion or distrust; his interlocutors would reason he was overpaid, stealing, stupid, or all three.

"I wanted to tell them that the best way to make it look like I had money was to be understated," Blazer said. "The more you looked like you had big money, the more people would be suspicious. The best way to display wealth wasn't to shout but to whisper, just implying that there was plenty of money to be had. I tried to tell them if they wanted to blow the lid off this thing, they should let me act like I did when I was doing it for real. Let me entertain the targets. Let me take them for a steak dinner at Prime 112 in Miami and then to Tootsie's for a night out on the VIP floor. That would really motivate them. Nobody cared about my money unless it benefited them directly. Real wealth to those guys was your connections and the experiences you could offer, but the FBI agents just didn't understand."

CHAPTER EIGHT

Racketeering

In early January 2017, Auburn had a marquee home game against LSU, with Auburn hoping the showdown would be head coach Bruce Pearl's five hundredth win. Watching the game in his room at a hotel in Auburn, Blazer saw the TV announcers point out Auburn's three all-time greatest basketball players in attendance: Charles Barkley, Chuck Person, and Vickie Orr-Wiley. Blazer shook his head; later that night, he would offer bribes to two of them—on camera—for the FBI, a reality completely at odds with the adoring roar of the crowd.

After the game, the FBI agents met Blazer in a nearby parking lot, driving a supersize white SUV, looking like frat bros about to go barhopping. SA Carpenter handed Blazer an envelope with $10,000 in cash for Person and another with $2,000 for Orr-Wiley, the mother of the seven-foot Auburn sensation Austin Wiley. Blazer was told he wasn't to give the envelope to Orr-Wiley unless she directly asked for it. Protocols for the night were laid out, including the idea that Blazer offer Person a retainer of $10,000 per month. Blazer suggested $2,000 as a more realistic number, worried that even someone as venal as Person would find the sum suspicious since it was divorced from delivering specific players.

The meet with Person was set for eleven thirty that night, again at the coach's house in a quiet cul-de-sac, all the other houses silent and dark. Waiting for Person, Blazer was self-conscious about wearing the wire, wishing he could at least talk to himself to keep his thoughts in order for the operation. When Person arrived, Blazer followed him into the house to a small alcove near the front door, where he convened with eighteen-year-old Austin Wiley and his mother, Vickie, a member of the 1992 US Olympics basketball team who looked like she could still play.

"Why you only play me twenty minutes in the second half?" the young Wiley asked Person.

"Why you always sitting next to me on the bench?" Person asked.

"Why don't you talk to me when I sit next to you?" he demanded. "I want to talk to you."

"I'm coaching, Austin," came the sharp reply.

Wiley complained that all he'd ever received from Person was $250 to spend in a Walmart, and the coach argued back. Blazer was struck by the intimacy of the relationship—almost like a father and son. He saw that Person controlled when and where Wiley played, which meant he could make him a star—or he could hurt him. There was no way in the world, Blazer saw, that Wiley would defy Person, including regarding who would become his financial adviser, as had been the case with Danjel Purifoy. Blazer felt repulsed by the extent of the hold the basketball coach had over the kids.

"Chuck was trafficking the kid, and it was fundamentally vile to me," Blazer recalled. "I wasn't sure that the FBI grasped that this was the true essence of the investigation—the leverage coaches at that level had over their players and the power they had to manipulate them. There were many subtleties that seemed lost on the FBI."

Wiley and his mother soon departed without directly asking for the cash, so Blazer hung on to that money, allowing the participants to determine their fate and avoiding the appearance of entrapment. Alone together, Blazer offered the $2,000 monthly retainer to Person, but the coach seemed confused; as Blazer knew, receiving money for nothing made no sense in this transactional context. The coach also seemed to suspect that this small payment meant he wasn't going to get what he'd been expecting, sighing with relief when Blazer produced the envelope of $10,000.

~

Corruption in the NCAA has long been treated as a sports story with a moral component, a structural issue of amateurism that denied college players compensation for their labors. There were also the obvious racial aspects of the exploitation of many young Black men by mostly white, middle-aged head coaches who made millions from their unpaid athletes. Those narratives contained a certain amount of truth, and they were common tropes in the echo chamber of sports media.

But NCAA corruption can also be understood as a crime story, requiring less of a grasp on the ins and outs of March Madness or the NBA draft than knowledge of the ways organized crime operates. Like organized crime, endemic corruption was almost always protected by powerful forces, often with the authorities looking the other way so long as they were benefiting. The Mafia had operated that way for decades, with gambling and prostitution thriving on the complicity of countless dirty cops, and the same was true for Mexico's drug cartels and the country's political class. It seemed like everyone in college basketball was benefiting from this open secret—except, for the most part, the players. The kids and their parents usually thought they were smart enough to game the system—and occasionally they were successful—and it was true that the families of elite basketball players did all they could to cash in on the promise of the teenage players. But the reality, Blazer was coming to see, contained many deeper textures, with the families being new players to the game, pulling in nominal gains, while the colleges, coaches, agents, financial advisers, and sneaker companies were the permanent economy of the sport and the true predators.

In essence, the NCAA was a classic racket, as defined by the Racketeer Influenced and Corrupt Organizations Act, or RICO. The American amateur system was created by self-interested officials who imagined sports to be played for character, competition, community, and physical health. Lurking just beneath the surface, since its inception in 1906, the NCAA has been about class, race, and gender as well, imposing aristocratic notions from English universities on kids from poverty-stricken backgrounds. The age of amateurism was long gone—if it had ever really existed—with not even a vestige left in the days of giant network-TV contracts.

College basketball is a business, of course, but Marty was starting to wonder if the cheating and under-the-table payments were inherent and inevitable, the corruption the organizing principle that kept the wheel turning. What if the NCAA's athletic conferences had really been a way to whack up the United States into territories, like the Mob's five families of New York did once upon a time, forming an intricate weave of overlapping interests with the overriding imperative of maintaining the flow of money through the system. The NCAA alone was making more than a billion dollars, with TV rights bringing in nearly $900 million per season, not to mention the countless billions reaped by sneaker and apparel companies.

As his role in the investigation evolved, Blazer was revealing a real pattern of criminal conduct in the NCAA. In February 2017, he again reached out to University of Oklahoma State Assistant Coach Lamont Evans—by then, a clearly rising star. Blazer had been talking to Evans for more than a year, plying the coach with goodies like tickets to a sold-out Drake concert in Houston (Blazer knew DJ Irie, who was on tour with Drake) and expensive Frigo underwear. When Evans asked for a new pair of exclusive titanium Beats headphones, specifying the exact model in a text, the FBI delighted in fulfilling his wish. This kind of evidence of corruption would be devastating at trial.

In February, Blazer drove from Pittsburgh to West Virginia for an OSU game, hiring the costliest rental vehicle on offer—a boxy Volvo station wagon. Blazer had promised Evans $2,000 in cash, with much more to come, and the coach was in a jovial mood when they convened in the lobby of a nearby Holiday Inn, Blazer wearing a shirt the FBI had wired up with a camera at a nearby Dunkin' Donuts. A group of OSU players was gathered around Evans, enthralled by his charm and ease; he had a grace and sincerity that impressed Blazer. As with so much else on the human level, the FBI still hadn't considered how their informant might feel as he talked with Evans and beamed with pride about the prospect of his son playing college soccer; the coach's son was a high school–basketball star, and they suggested their sons could be college roommates one day, both actors firmly committed to the roles they were playing as proud fathers, not two men secretly circumventing NCAA rules and the law in plain sight.

In a hotel room, Blazer was introduced to an OSU standout, a swingman with a friendly smile. Evans told the unsuspecting kid that a financial adviser did much more than an agent. There were perks on offer, Evans said, pointing to a box of titanium Beats as an example.

"I wouldn't put you on to anybody not top quality," Evans told the recruit, despite knowing about Blazer's history. The player confirmed that he'd follow the direction he received from his trusted coach.

To Blazer's relief, the player left after twenty minutes. The conceit of the bribery was that the money was for the coach to give to the players to incentivize them to sign with Blazer, but it was understood that Evans would pocket most of the money—that was the essence of the crime. But Blazer and the FBI tried to avoid giving money directly to the kids or their families, because they didn't want to be seen as enticing poor college kids with large wads of cash. As previous NCAA scandals had illustrated, the specter of the FBI employing its limitless resources to destroy teenagers horrified the public. But there was another reason Blazer believed they should focus on the coaches: bribery was a criminal matter, not just a breach of NCAA rules.

Preparing to leave the room, Blazer pulled out the envelope of cash for Evans, the deal done in the same way it had been with Person. Pocketing the money, Evans said he wanted more than his illicit monthly retainer of $2,000, offering a high school recruit in Nashville, whom he could secure for an additional $10,000 in the coming months.

Walking triumphantly to meet with the waiting FBI agents, Blazer believed his infiltration was gaining yet more momentum, as the agents advanced him $10,000 in cash for Chuck Person's next installment. Head coaches had to know that money lubricated the extremely competitive recruiting process, just as colleges had to know, but as long as there was no direct or provable connection, they could benefit with impunity. Blazer was coming to believe the real story—the real conspiracy—was at the highest levels of NCAA sports at programs like Louisville, Arizona, and LSU; piercing the veil of secrecy protecting the dons of this Mafia would expose the true underworld.

"I told FBI agent Scott Carpenter how the various parts of the basketball-recruiting conspiracy worked together," Blazer said. "Coaches were connected to agents, who were connected to big athletic brands. Agents used runners like Christian Dawkins to pay coaches like Lamont Evans, who helped them with their recruiting. The big sneaker companies would sponsor AAU teams, filled with high school kids who were being recruited for the top college programs. The coaches of those grassroots teams had relationships with college coaches and runners and agents, who relied on them to steer players to them—in return for extra recruiting money. It all moved in a circle, with one hand washing the other. Then, when the player was ready for the NBA, a coach like Lamont Evans made sure the player signed with the agent who gave the coach money. I told Scott that Lamont needed the money to keep the kids coming to his program. I said that it was a form of human trafficking, with the kids as the commodities being bought and sold.

"Scott was starting to understand the investigation wasn't just revealing isolated cases of bribery. The big picture included the whole framework of college basketball. I told him that it could be bigger than all the doping scandals. Word that I was handing out money would spread like wildfire. It was only a question of how far down the rabbit hole the FBI was willing to go—and how much risk they were willing to take. No one knew where the money was really coming from, and it seemed like it was time to answer that question."

CHAPTER NINE

Single Malt

As March Madness started in 2017, Blazer watched the NCAA tournament through an entirely new lens, unsurprised to learn that two assistant coaches at Arizona had expressed interest to Sood in referring players in return for cash. Lamont Evans had bragged to Blazer that he'd helped construct the South Carolina squad that made it to the Final Four to play against Gonzaga, with his recruit PJ Dozier a linchpin. As Oregon lost to North Carolina and South Carolina lost narrowly to Gonzaga, and with the perennial contender Tar Heels winning the championship, Blazer could see the wheels-within-wheels connections he was developing with the coaches in action on the television screen.

After the tournament, the corruption continued apace, a year-round business cycle of recruiting, declaring for the NBA draft, and summer grassroots tournaments with hot dog money needed in all seasons. Because Evans preferred his monthly $2,000 to be paid in person, Blazer was forced to make a day trip to Manhattan in April to meet the coach at an Under Armour event at Basketball City. Blazer was joined by SA Carpenter, the mercurial ex-military FBI agent running the investigation, who was enraged when Evans initially misdirected them to Brooklyn and they had to race through the streets of New York to connect for the rendezvous.

In an open-plan seven-court facility overlooking the Brooklyn Bridge, Blazer was shown into the red-velvet VIP mezzanine section of the Under Armour event to meet with Evans. While waiting, he surveyed the scene from a balcony, marveling at how out of place the flotilla of white FBI agents looked as they wandered through the sea of young basketball players and coaches. Evans told Blazer about the array of high school kids he was going to recruit—and then pass along to the adviser. The high school players on the courts represented the future of their relationship: Jahvon Quinerly, Devon Dotson, Silvio De Sousa, and Nazreon "Naz" Reid would play for leading programs like Kansas, Alabama, and LSU. PJ Dozier had opted for a different agent, shunning Dawkins, but Evans assured Blazer he'd still sign on with the financial adviser. When Blazer tapped his pocket to indicate he had the cash, the coach eagerly followed him to a back entrance, where the pair sat on a bench while Blazer slid an envelope across the seat for Evans to casually tuck under his leg. It was an abiding mystery of the entire investigation—to outsiders, at least—that relatively small sums of money would entice coaches to risk their careers, but it was undeniable that the lure of easy money and the thrill of circumventing a corrupt system were irresistible; the coaches were well paid, but the demands of being expected to take care of the needs of players, no matter what, provided motivation for the coaches to game the rules—and the law.

A key concept was a form of trust, albeit a perverse one. Evans had met Blazer through Christian Dawkins, which provided him with bona fides inside the basketball world. Evans wouldn't take money from just anyone, and with a code of silence that all understood, no one was going to squeal, even if the deals didn't work out. Like wise guys in organized crime, they all had skin in the game, and no one was going to tell the NCAA. That just wasn't how it worked.

Evans said he was working on a home run for Blazer, including a future top-three pick whom agent and former Chicago Bull B.J. Armstrong was now representing.

"Singles and doubles are good for me too," Blazer said. "But home runs are always good."

Blazer noticed another pattern emerging: it seemed like no coaches in college basketball—absolutely no one—could resist the temptations Blazer placed before them. The premise that literally everyone was willing to take money was further reinforced when Blazer received a text from Rashan Michel on April 24, 2017.

We got a new one, Michel wrote, seemingly referring to a coach. Call me today, he added a few minutes later. What's up? was the third text in a row. Michel was palpably anxious about not getting what he considered to be his rightful retainer.

Used to Michel's hyperbole, Blazer didn't reply immediately, forwarding the text to SA Carpenter as usual. A week later, Michel sent a flurry of texts explaining that he had been to Tuscaloosa, Alabama, to measure his "brother" for custom suits. Blazer assumed he was referring to Alabama's head coach Avery Johnson, a former NBA star whom Blazer knew Michel had previously referred to as his "brother." It made little sense that a head coach on a rich contract would risk transacting with a tailor like Michel. A few days later, Michel called, explaining in his breathless and often confusing way that the brother he'd been referring to was actually Alabama's associate athletics director, Kobie Baker.

Michel was aware that Blazer had the leverage to demand connections with coaches, but this new initiative was taking a step further up the hierarchy. Blazer was intrigued. Michel explained that as the second-in-command of Alabama's entire athletic program, Baker had access to both basketball and football players, offering double value—an attractive proposition with so many future professional athletes churning through the school. SA Carpenter was listening to the call in real time, sharing a laugh with Blazer afterward about Michel's lack of specifics regarding what Baker wanted.

Traveling to Birmingham, Blazer and Michel went to Café Dupont, one of the finest restaurants in the city, and Michel ordered expensive appetizers to accompany his midday vodka and cranberry juice. When Kobie Baker called Michel from the street, Blazer figured it had to be because he was nervous about the meeting. When Baker came in, hesitantly, he and Blazer quickly hit it off, discussing Bama football players they knew in common. Baker was Black, casually dressed, and had a kind smile and friendly manner. Starting to relax, Baker said he'd formerly been assistant director of enforcement for basketball for the NCAA, a job tasked with mitigating violations.

The fact that someone who'd once been employed by the NCAA to crack down on the exact kind of conduct they were about to conspire over shocked the jaded Blazer. But it also made perfect sense: Baker had firsthand insider knowledge of just how broken the amateur system was. Baker's job at Alabama included—at least in part—protecting the school's many elite athletes from exploitative and predatory agents and business advisers, a mind-bending irony in the circumstances, even in a world replete with ironies.

When the waitress arrived with their orders, Baker said that just the week before he'd sent a strongly worded letter to another financial adviser, warning him to stop contacting a star player. He'd threatened to report the adviser to the NCAA. Blazer admired the way Baker was simultaneously professing innocence, even as he was implicitly making clear the value he could bring for Blazer as a gatekeeper and recruiter. If Blazer paid him, Baker could erect a wall around Alabama's various future professional athletes, a giddying prospect for Blazer if it had been for real, but also an exciting development in his campaign to avoid prison.

Baker told Blazer that it was part of his duty, in conjunction with a program run by the NBA Players Association, to educate the teenagers who came to Alabama on how to avoid acquiring the sketchy business entanglements draft picks too often brought with them when they turned pro—exactly the enterprise Blazer was proposing. Baker acted as if he hadn't done any real due diligence on Blazer, but it was hard to believe he didn't know about the SEC's allegations.

Blazer delicately inquired about Baker's relationships with the players. Was Baker willing to make business referrals, Blazer asked, tiptoeing up to the question of money. Baker said he was in a position of enormous influence with the players, as he explained his take on the subtleties of guiding future NBA and NFL players in their decisions about representation: the process should occur organically, he said, instead of hitting them over the head with the suggestion, so that they would believe hiring Blazer had been their idea in the first place. Baker said he could talk Blazer up while keeping other financial advisers away or reporting the competition to the NCAA, as a trusted and objective confidant with nothing but the players' best interests at heart—for a price. The ingenious kernel of an idea in Baker's proposal was more sophisticated than the blunt force of Chuck Person and Lamont Evans; the kids and their families wouldn't even know they were being groomed and guided by the athletic director.

Blazer glanced at Michel and looked Baker directly in the eye. The time to take the plunge had arrived.

"I don't know how much he's talked to you about money structure, but I'm all in," Blazer said to Baker.

Baker seemed taken aback—or pretended to be—as he feigned ignorance. But that lasted for only a few seconds before Baker said his understanding was that he would receive four equal payments totaling $60,000 in return for referring players. This was roughly the same structure Michel had brokered for Chuck Person, and Blazer nodded in agreement, saying he was comfortable with that proposal. Then Blazer said he had $5,000 in cash in his leather backpack as a symbol of his seriousness. Baker stiffened.

"Boy, you guys aren't fooling around," he said.

Before excusing himself to go to the bathroom, Baker said he was keen to begin their relationship. When he left, Blazer took the envelope stuffed with cash from his bag and placed it under the two cell phones Baker had left on the table. Michel smiled in appreciation at the way Blazer made the transaction work without having to openly discuss what they were doing. Blazer also handed an envelope with $2,000 to Michel, which provoked momentary complaints about wanting more, followed by grudging acceptance.

When Baker returned to the table, they discussed meeting once a month in the future, without stating that it would be to make the payments in person and thus avoid a paper trail. Baker was evidently smart, and Blazer believed he was certainly fully aware of what he was doing. Standing to leave, Baker scooped up his phones, along with the thick envelope, like a card shark expertly palming an ace, the button camera in Blazer's shirt recording the sleight of hand.

~

By February 2017, in light of all the momentum, Carpenter said he wanted to escalate the investigation.

"Let's revisit the idea of introducing a partner or backer to the situation," Carpenter said to Blazer. "What do you think?"

Blazer thought it was a capital idea. To his delight, Carpenter also told him that the FBI had assigned an undercover agent to the case, a sign of the bureau's deepening commitment. Blazer soon traveled to New York City to meet the new undercover, checking into the $1,000-a-night suite the FBI insisted he stay in, for reasons that escaped him but that he didn't complain about.

"Jeff DeAngelo" confidently sauntered into the suite and sat on the couch next to Blazer, and instantly, Blazer knew the ploy could work. DeAngelo was in his early thirties, olive skinned, six foot, clean-cut, athletic, and chisel-jawed handsome—a confident man of Italian-American heritage. He was from Long Island and effortlessly gave off a whiff of fast money and lax morals. The TAG Heuer watch, the tattoos on his ankle and taut biceps, the sense of entitlement. Jeff DeAngelo wasn't his real name but an undercover designation assigned by the FBI, Blazer understood. Still, the look and persona were very convincing.

"Jeff and I hit it off right away," Blazer remembered. "He was very smooth, with swagger that spoke of generational wealth—but from a dubious background. He could have been a character on *The Sopranos*. No one was going to question if he was up for doing some shady shit for business. Sometimes I wondered if he was in the same boat as me—someone facing criminal charges trying to avoid prison by being a cooperator—but I doubted the bureau would allow that. He was really likable and laid back, and treated me like we were on equal footing. He was much less guarded about his personal life than the other FBI agents. We bonded over soccer, and he talked a lot about his background in the military. He wasn't the power in the investigation—more like a hired gun."

For months, Blazer had been playing a part, feeling more like an actor with each passing encounter with his targets, and now DeAngelo also seemed like a performer sent by Central Casting, an actor with movie-star good looks stepping before the camera to play the idealized version of a criminal.

To Blazer's surprise, DeAngelo didn't arrive with a backstory, so Carpenter, DeAngelo, and Blazer set about imagining his past as they sat in the luxurious suite with towering views of Manhattan in the background. They quickly agreed that his character should be a wealthy New York real estate investor with a hint of shadowy connections to organized crime. With the wealthy Pittsburgh scions who had provided Blazer with hot dog money for college football players, he'd learned of an advantage to having a partner finance illicit payments: it allowed Blazer to tell Dawkins and the various coaches that he'd have to ask for approval on money questions, a way of intensifying the attraction and mystery. He also knew that it was crucial the partner remain a specter, an infrequent presence to add to the allure; it mattered that the partner wasn't in the sports business and didn't ask uncomfortable questions. The less the partner said, the better. The moneyman should be low maintenance and free spending, a fan who was just happy to be involved in the exclusive world of sports.

After Blazer introduced Jeff DeAngelo to Rashan Michel, the fast-talking tailor told him he was concerned. Michel was convinced DeAngelo had Mob connections and that if things didn't work out, someone might get killed, a reaction that delighted the FBI agents when Blazer relayed it to them. Blazer discovered that DeAngelo knew precious little about real estate and even less about investments or basketball. But Blazer believed the FBI had chosen well, and large sums of cash went nicely with dubious characters haunting tempting nightclubs and casinos. For all his inability to grasp the many subtleties of college sports corruption, DeAngelo would prove adept at playing a particular type of character: the amoral sucker.

On the morning of May 5, while Blazer and Carpenter were waiting for the right moment to activate DeAngelo, Safarrah Lawson texted Blazer a link to an article with the headline **Sports Agent Fired After Running Up $42,000 in Uber Charges on an NBA Player's Credit Card.** Blazer clicked on the link and read about Christian Dawkins using Orlando Magic guard Elfrid Payton's credit card for more than 1,800 Uber rides in less than a year, without the player's approval. The total length of the trips driven equaled three round trips from New York to India.

Since Blazer's undoing by the SEC had been publicly announced, Dawkins—who had set up the relationship with Lamont Evans—had distanced himself from Blazer, conducting his dealings with Munish Sood, a strategy Blazer now viewed as rank hypocrisy. The notion that Dawkins was too righteous to deal with Blazer had been offensive then, and now it was shown to be ridiculous. The article threw Dawkins's trustworthiness into question and likely resulted in the agent he worked for firing the runner. Blazer understood all too well the assumptions Dawkins had probably made about the athlete not reviewing his credit card statements, and he certainly didn't believe that level of abuse could have occurred by accident. Blazer could relate to the sense of hopelessness Dawkins must have been feeling, but instead of evoking pity, the news incited Blazer's predatory instinct. After all his years in the sports business, knowing the intricacies of its byzantine ways, Blazer could see what it meant immediately: a big opportunity to reactivate the Dawkins aspect of the case. Bad news traveled at the speed of light in the sports business, with rivals ready to pounce on impressionable kids and pull them away.

"I could hardly conceal my excitement," Blazer told me. "I knew better than anyone that that kind of news could be a death sentence in the business for Christian, with nowhere left to turn. I also knew something special had happened for me. I sent the story to Scott, then called him to impress on him the opportunity we had. Before this, Christian wasn't really on our radar anymore with the other leads we were following, but now he was vulnerable. I told Scott that the best way to get to Christian was through Munish. I'd calculated that Munish had invested more than $100,000 in Dawkins, and he'd know that there was now no way to get any return on that investment after word of Dawkins's plight spread, let alone get the principal back. Munish wouldn't need much convincing that the money I had behind me with Jeff as my new partner was the best way to salvage his investment in Christian. Scott said maybe this was the perfect moment to introduce my backer, and I totally agreed."

When Blazer called Sood to discuss the report about Dawkins, he said everyone was talking about it, to ramp up his former partner's fear of losing his money. Blazer said Andy Miller and ASM had stepped away from Dawkins, deliberately scaring the hedge fund manager as much as possible because it was so obviously true that Dawkins was ruined, at least for the time being, and Sood's considerable investment of time and money was eddying down the drain.

Without naming him, Blazer said he had a new partner looking to invest in the basketball space, enticing Sood to consider finding someone else to take up the business he had funded for Dawkins. Blazer's new partner could potentially take over the ongoing payments Sood was making to fund Dawkins's dealings. Relying on his uncanny ability to manipulate, Blazer appealed to Sood's fear, greed, and credulity when he suggested that this was a good time to reconnect with Dawkins and discuss options. Blazer turned up the pressure, saying he sympathized with the young runner's plight and that he had his back over the Uber nonsense, much the same way he'd viewed his movie debacle—it was a temporary setback and nothing more, Blazer claimed.

Blazer suggested that the next time Sood spoke to Dawkins, he should tell him Blazer's new financial partner might be interested in connecting. Blazer didn't overhype the money DeAngelo would bring to the table; if Blazer said his new backer was looking to invest, Sood could be confident he would have serious money, or at least easy money. As Blazer had predicted, Sood was intrigued, and they agreed to convene in their old haunt, Miami Beach.

The FBI booked the presidential suite at the Epic Hotel in Miami, with water views and a well-stocked bar—the beginning of a troubling trend of the agents playing fast and loose with the government's money. DeAngelo not only looked the part of a South Beach regular but also personified the tanned, casual sense of ease and entitlement behind his reflecting aviator sunglasses. Blazer could see the details of his wardrobe, like his untucked blue cotton shirt, had been carefully chosen to make his character believable.

Over lunch with Carpenter and DeAngelo, Blazer told the FBI undercover to stay in the background and let him do most of the talking. DeAngelo simply had to signal his agreement with Blazer's strategy of paying coaches to get players referred to his company. Don't talk about the details, Blazer said to DeAngelo, just address the big picture. Blazer had long known that the world of financial advisers for pro athletes could be an excellent way to launder illicit money, because it was done in cash without a paper trail—just like drug deals—in the form of loans that would eventually be repaid in legitimate contract money, a suggestion Carpenter wanted the undercover agent to hint at. Blazer hadn't laundered money; he had been a legitimate cheater as a financial adviser until the movie fraud, but it was what had undone the disgraced agent William "Tank" Black all those years ago, when Blazer was first getting into the business.

In Miami, Sood wanted to convene at the third-floor lounge of the Melia Hotel, a place he had frequented with Blazer. Carefully staging their arrival in case the cagey Sood was observing them, Blazer and DeAngelo approached from opposite directions and greeted each other at the entrance to the hotel, then went upstairs to find Sood waiting at the bar. DeAngelo insisted on paying for drinks, so Blazer and Sood each ordered expensive pours of single malt scotch—Macallan's eighteen-year sherry oak would become a favorite during the investigation—while DeAngelo had a vodka and soda.

Turning to basketball, Blazer talked about using Christian Dawkins to be the conduit in a new stand-alone business to recruit college coaches to take payments in return for steering their players to the money-management company they'd establish. Blazer told Sood he'd sold DeAngelo on the deal with Lamont Evans and the benefits of owning a coach. DeAngelo was an able supporting actor. Blazer could see that he and DeAngelo were both facile fibsters, able to manipulate people with ease. Everything had to be transparent, DeAngelo said, when of course the inverse was true. Sood agreed, claiming—improbably—that that was the only way he knew how to do business, while his most marked trait, in Blazer's experience, was duplicity. Blazer made it abundantly clear that he was going to be calling the shots as they developed a budget proposal.

After DeAngelo paid the tab, peeling bills from a wad of hundreds, they retired to the rooftop bar for more cocktails. The atmosphere was intoxicating, with an infinity pool and a deck teeming with beautiful young women in bikinis. Drinking in the bright sunshine, Blazer started to feel tipsy, and he wondered if the FBI agent was as well. It was a seductive environment, Blazer well knew, and he wondered what impact it might be having on DeAngelo, as the undercover plainly relished playing a wealthy and vaguely sinister investor.

"Jeff was starting to believe his own bullshit," Blazer recalled. "He was going off script. He was getting caught up in the story. It was like he enjoyed being this rich dude who had a taste for the finer things in life and had the money to start a sports business. I could see him morphing into the role, because I had done it myself. He was letting his guard down and saying things that he shouldn't, like making future plans to have a big yacht party on the Fourth of July. Jeff was excited when I pointed out two condos owned by Drake and said we were drinking in the spot where a famous rap video had been shot. It was like he knew he was entering a different world. All on the FBI's dime."

Blazer and DeAngelo were stumbling drunk by the time they made it to the debriefing with SAs Carpenter and Wake. Blazer watched with amusement as the boozy and euphoric DeAngelo offered his opinion on tactics, to the annoyance of a sober Carpenter. After a couple of rounds of drinks in the FBI's suite, Carpenter instructed Blazer to drive to Fort Lauderdale without making any stops, to avoid any possible further contact with Sood. After the still-buzzed Blazer pulled onto the main drag in Miami Beach, he collided with a car filled with pretty young models, who insisted on waiting for the police even though the damage was negligible. After the cops failed to arrive, all agreed to settle the incident later, thus avoiding a possible drunk-driving charge—which might have complicated any prosecution when it emerged that the Southern

District's star witness in subsequent trials had been driving under the influence at the express direction of the FBI after drinking too much government-purchased liquor.

Good to catch up yesterday, Sood texted first thing the following morning. This could be big.

We are committed to making this big, Blazer replied.

CHAPTER TEN

The Yacht

By the spring of 2017, Blazer was especially dreading calls from his criminal attorney, certain he would only be the bearer of bad news. So much could go wrong: Blazer's cooperation could end, the prosecution could commence, or he would be told he wasn't going to receive significant consideration for his efforts to assist the Southern District of New York. Nearly three years had passed since he'd started to cooperate, and he'd miraculously managed to keep the federal government interested enough in the investigation that he'd avoided indictment, let alone the seemingly inevitable guilty plea and prison sentence.

The only other reason Blazer's lawyer called was to collect money his client didn't have. Trish was working hard, building her agency, but they couldn't live indefinitely without his income. Blazer was effectively working full-time for the government, unable to take any other job, and his savings and patience were running out. But Blazer was intensely aware that he had to keep projecting the air of a successful and prosperous financial adviser, knowing that if his clients and the targets or the government detected the slightest whiff of desperation or poverty, they might immediately shun him—an outcome that would land him in prison.

The thing that most tormented Blazer's thoughts, as he lay awake late into the night, was the threat that the investigation—which the FBI had named Operation Ballerz—would end prematurely. The contradiction was becoming unbearable: he wanted the investigation to stop, and he was terrified the investigation *would* stop. Blazer didn't share these thoughts with SA Carpenter and the other FBI agents, fearing what they would say or do. It seemed impossible for Blazer to even hint that he needed some kind of stipend for his efforts, because the agents clearly considered his cooperation a form of compensation in that it kept him out of prison.

"By the grace of God, my maneuvers had attracted the interest of the FBI," Blazer said. "In five months with the bureau, I had made multiple undercover trips, but no one had told me how I was doing, and I wasn't sure that what I was doing was being memorialized by anyone further up in the hierarchy. No one was going to tell me how much assistance I had to give, but I knew that the crimes I had committed would have to be reckoned with and that judgment day was coming."

All these thoughts were swirling through his brain when his lawyer told him he had to report to New York for a meeting with AUSA Boone on Friday, May 19. The FBI had already lined up a full week of duties for Blazer, including a trip to provide Kobie Baker of Alabama with $10,000, but what concerned Blazer the most was that Carpenter hadn't warned him about Boone's order. Blazer wondered if the FBI and the Southern District prosecutors were talking to each other at all. Did Boone even know about all the work Blazer was doing for the FBI?

On Sunday morning, Blazer received an email from Munish Sood with an attachment from Christian Dawkins laying out a "partnership proposal." Sood said it was shared confidentially and they should discuss as soon as possible, as he and Dawkins were anxious to have a face-to-face meeting. Blazer could see that the Miami trip had worked, whetting the appetite of all concerned, as he read the attachment and saw that Dawkins's "big ask" was $250,000.

Blazer called Carpenter and said that they now had the upper hand with Dawkins, and it was a good time to make him sweat. Sood then called Blazer and said Dawkins was going to be in New York the next day, and he could meet at two o'clock, the short notice confirming Dawkins's desperation. Volleying calls back and forth nonstop, Blazer reached out to Carpenter and said they shouldn't take the meeting, adding that he wouldn't be able to make it to New York on Tuesday, a defiance he hadn't dared in the past.

"Why not?" Carpenter hissed, suddenly furious at this resistance.

Blazer said AUSA Boone needed him to come to Manhattan on Friday for a debriefing, and Blazer had to consult with his lawyer before the encounter, so he wouldn't be able to come for a sit-down with Dawkins on Tuesday. Blazer reminded Carpenter they were also supposed to meet with Kobie Baker in Atlanta on Wednesday, making the logistics of the week impossible—not to mention that he couldn't afford to book any of the flights without financial help from the bureau.

"We're going to fly you in," Carpenter said on Monday in regard to the sit-down with Dawkins the next day.

Blazer tried to explain that his criminal attorney was holding a gun to his head, demanding a retainer of $15,000, including $5,000 up front—money Blazer didn't have. Then Blazer told SA Carpenter that AUSA Boone was still insisting on the Friday meeting, and he couldn't be in two places at the same time. Blazer said that the Southern District clearly wasn't coordinating with the FBI, and he begged him to appreciate how he was being pulled in different directions. Carpenter insisted that the FBI was in charge of his case, not the lawyers in the Southern District—whom he appeared to regard as rivals.

"I'm not worried about attorneys," Carpenter said when Blazer told him about the meeting with Boone. "Fuck the lawyers."

No one had explained how the system worked, but Blazer reasoned that it was AUSA Boone who would eventually write a letter to the sentencing judge about the nature of his cooperation, not Carpenter, and that meant the attorneys were absolutely vital to his interests, whatever the FBI agent said. When Blazer objected to Carpenter's dismissal of Boone, he was reminded of the fury often lurking just below the surface, the agent barking that Blazer would do as he was told—or else.

"Don't make me go down this road," Carpenter said. "Fuck the lawyer bullshit. This is what's keeping you from going to prison, and what you're doing will most likely keep you from going to jail at all."

"I'm not a prick," Blazer replied, immediately backing away, fearing reprisals. "But you're used to this shit, and not only am I not—I never dreamed I would have to be."

Carpenter calmed down in a later call, allowing that Blazer could skip the Dawkins meeting. A sit-down had been set for that week in New York, with FBI undercover Jeff DeAngelo going alone to meet Dawkins and Sood. Missing the encounter concerned Blazer because he worried about DeAngelo's ability to improvise, but there was no other choice.

The meeting without Blazer took place at the Redeye Grill, a restaurant in Midtown Manhattan that billed itself as the "Home of the Dancing Shrimp." The purpose was to discuss the partnership proposal Sood had sent to Blazer and to introduce Dawkins to Jeff DeAngelo, with Munish Sood acting as the middleman. In this encounter, Dawkins explained his business model to DeAngelo, saying he wanted to land around a dozen NBA players as clients; Dawkins would be the manager, acting as the quarterback controlling the agents and financial advisers who also worked for the stars. Inhabiting his role, DeAngelo asked how Dawkins could "control" the players, and Dawkins told him that the key was to earn the trust of the potential clients while they were still in high school. The proposition was that Dawkins would deliver kids for DeAngelo to represent and thus profit.

Dawkins wanted to gauge DeAngelo's willingness to put real money into the effort to sign "assets." The answer was that DeAngelo was eager to invest. He said he just had a few questions about college coaches and how they figured into the business plan. Characteristically, Dawkins confidently said he had great relationships with many coaches, including head coaches like Rick Pitino at Louisville and Sean Miller at Arizona. That very day, Dawkins said, he'd spoken to ten different coaches about various players, including one five-star prospect he was aiming to "give" to Pitino.

To Dawkins, the appearance of DeAngelo was like a godsend—if it proved to be real. But in a follow-up call with Sood recorded by the FBI, Dawkins wondered aloud about DeAngelo and how he seemed ready to facilitate the investment of $250,000. DeAngelo's initial investment would guarantee Dawkins a 50 percent equity stake in the enterprise, with the hustler overvaluing his connections and experiences at a very flattering quarter of a million dollars. Observed objectively, DeAngelo's proposal was extremely beneficial to Dawkins, and it appeared he was harboring doubts or perhaps even suspicions about his legitimacy or business sense.

Privately, Dawkins told Sood it all seemed too good to be true, but this skepticism ultimately didn't stop him from seeking to cash in on his new connection; in truth, he had no alternative. Blazer told Carpenter that the logical next move was to ask Dawkins to prove that his connections still trusted him after the Uber revelations. Blazer said they should insist that Dawkins arrange for a meeting with one of the coaches he'd mentioned being connected to, like an assistant coach at Arizona named Emanuel "Book" Richardson. Carpenter eagerly agreed.

Meanwhile, Blazer had another difficult meeting with his attorney, in which he learned it was likely he would still go to prison despite his cooperation. The attorney had worked primarily on drug and gang cases, and he said that in the end, no matter how useful the cooperation was, the accused invariably received prison time when they pleaded guilty. Once again pressing Blazer for a large advance that he could not afford, the lawyer started to make off-color and unfunny jokes about his client not bending over when he dropped the soap in the prison shower.

Stressed out, Blazer explicitly told the lawyer to stop communication with the Southern District until he had figured out his legal representation moving forward.

Going against Blazer's orders, the lawyer then emailed AUSA Boone to say that "everybody needed to get their shit together" regarding communication if the basketball investigation was going to continue. This was a direct threat to the Southern District and thus to his client. Blazer was dumbfounded at his lawyer's reckless behavior. To put it mildly, Blazer needed the Southern District more than they needed him. He later discovered that Boone had replied that if the cooperation ceased, he would have US marshals immediately arrest and indict Blazer. As soon as he learned about the letter, Blazer called Boone to apologize and withdraw the demand for clarity on the benefit he would receive. It was evident that Blazer's best course of action was to shut up, keep his head down, and help the government as much as he could.

In need of an experienced lawyer with a more even temperament and experience with white-collar crime, Blazer called one of the best criminal attorneys in Pittsburgh, the former partner of a personal friend. After anxiously describing the increasingly complex situation and his lack of funds, the attorney agreed to represent him on a reduced "friend" rate. After the near debacle of threatening the Southern District, Blazer was anxious to move the investigation forward in order to have a real chance to get a reduced sentence.

On May 24, Blazer and DeAngelo arrived at Sood's low-rise glass office building in Princeton, New Jersey, driving a brand-new Maserati Levante and parking it conspicuously in the front lot. DeAngelo was wearing reflective aviator shades, as if to emphasize a hint of menacing inscrutability, and the FBI had installed an app on DeAngelo's phone that let Carpenter and other agents listen to the conversation in real time.

Sood arrived a couple of minutes late, and they all quickly agreed that DeAngelo was going to invest the reduced amount of $200,000 in a basketball-player management company in return for 50 percent share in the equity. Dawkins would have the other 50 percent of the equity, and in time, Sood would invest a small amount of capital to reduce DeAngelo's percentage of the shares. This meant DeAngelo was going to put all the money into the company, and ultimately, he wouldn't have the controlling interest—a structure so favorable to Sood and Dawkins that it passed without comment. It was a deal that was indeed too good to be true.

"I could see the wheels turning in Munish's head," Blazer recalled. "He was always trying to get something for nothing. His intention was to reap the benefits while investing as little as possible, so I knew for sure he'd be on board."

Throughout the meeting, DeAngelo kept returning to the subject of recruiting coaches to assist in signing players. Blazer was concerned that the emphasis was too strong and might prove suspicious, as DeAngelo suggested paying Dawkins a bonus for each coach he introduced to the new business. The focus on coaches made Blazer uneasy; it might appear odd to emphasize this particular strategy, so he ran interference, explaining that he'd convinced DeAngelo of the importance of coaches.

"When I talked about the $4,000 a month we were going to pay Lamont Evans, Munish pushed back, saying he had to be careful getting involved in disbursing that money because he was regulated," Blazer recalled. "Munish was full of shit. The whole business model was against all kinds of financial and tax regulations, not to mention the NCAA's rules and possible criminal liability. Munish was willing to take those risks. He just wanted something for nothing, as usual. I remembered all the deals where I'd introduced Munish to people and he'd done business with them behind my back. I wasn't going to lose any sleep over what happened to Munish. He knew my situation was bad after the SEC news, and he wasn't sure what—if anything—I was getting out of this deal, but he never asked how I was doing or if I needed any help. I kept telling myself that Munish was going to get a wake-up call soon enough."

At lunchtime, DeAngelo insisted all three of them drive together in the Maserati to a nearby tavern, a way to visually display his wealth. En route, Sood called Dawkins to discuss the proposed structure, putting him on speakerphone. Blazer talked about the attraction of an all-cash investment to DeAngelo—more than a hint that they were involved in money laundering. They all agreed they were nearing the terms for a deal.

Over lunch, an East Indian medical doctor interested in pitching real estate investments to DeAngelo joined them. The man was a friend of Sood's, and Blazer could see Sood was already trying to leverage his connection to DeAngelo into other deals. As Sood and his friend threw out far-flung ideas like buying gold in Bolivia, Sood's predatory behavior appalled but didn't surprise Blazer. It turned out that DeAngelo was inept when it came to talking about real estate—or investments in general—but Blazer kept dropping heavy hints that all-cash deals were preferred, a not very subtle way to underscore DeAngelo's shady background.

After listening live, Carpenter requested a private word with Blazer when the operation was over. With no recording devices on, just the agent and Blazer sitting in an idling car, Carpenter said he understood why Blazer had been freaking out about his lawyer's letter to the Southern District. In what felt like a warning, Carpenter said he was concerned that Blazer's legal representative didn't appear to really understand how the prosecutors worked. Carpenter went on to say that, given how Blazer's cooperation was proceeding successfully, a New York City public defender would be perfectly capable of handling the case without driving him into the ground financially. SA Wake joined Carpenter in the car and concurred that a public defender would be a good direction for Blazer, as the court-appointed attorneys really knew what the Southern District expected and what was possible.

"It's not like *My Cousin Vinny*," Carpenter said.

Blazer found himself getting emotional, asking if AUSA Boone was being kept in the loop about his activities, adding that he had no intention of stopping cooperating. Blazer was willing to cooperate for another two years, he said, if only he could get paid for his work to support his family. Blazer talked about the time that had passed since his first proffer and said he could have been finishing his sentence in a federal prison camp and preparing to rebuild his life instead of being entirely consumed by the investigation.

"You don't want any part of that path," Carpenter said. "I've been in federal prisons. And believe me, even the best of them, you wouldn't want to spend two hours in them, let alone two years."

SA Wake said he would be more considerate with the scheduling between then and September, catching himself as he spoke. Carpenter flashed Wake an angry look, as Blazer's eyes grew wide with surprise. What was going to happen in September? Blazer wondered. Was that some kind of deadline?

Blazer's mind raced as he drove away. He couldn't bring himself to tell Trish the real truth of his exposure to criminal punishment. It would only terrify her. He had no one to confide in, only increasing the pressure and contradictions.

"I wanted this all to end so badly," Blazer said. "But I was scared to death about what came next for me and my family when the music stopped. I knew it would be hard on them. Driving home, I choked up at the realization that it was only a matter of time until everyone who knew me would stand in judgment."

On the upside, the prospects to bribe coaches now appeared to be growing, with Chuck Person and Safarrah Lawson name-dropping other coaches from top programs around the country. These elite programs had just taken a star turn at March Madness. The coaches had NBA-level players on their teams and more in the pipeline. Kobie Baker at Alabama said he needed money for Collin Sexton, a future first rounder and Cleveland Cavalier, and Baker had invited Blazer to appear on a recruiting advisory panel he was putting together on the campus for student-athletes—a ludicrous notion, given the athletic director's likely knowledge of Blazer's history of fraud.

Then came the yacht.

June 6 was an unseasonably cold, gray afternoon when Blazer landed in New York City for a meeting with Dawkins and Sood to finalize the terms of the new deal and provide the first infusion of capital from DeAngelo. Sood and Dawkins hadn't been told that Blazer would be at the meeting, adding an element of surprise. Prior to the meeting, Dawkins had provided DeAngelo with a long list of coaches he proposed pitching—or bribing, to put it more bluntly—and the plan was to review the roster and prioritize targets. Blazer met with Carpenter in a mall near One World Trade Center in Lower Manhattan. DeAngelo soon joined them, toting a bag of goodies from a shopping spree—bottles of single malt whiskey and a designer pen to ink the agreement. Both FBI agents appeared excited about what was about to happen, like kids with a load of firecrackers, a box of matches, and a plan to wreak havoc.

On the rooftop of the Meliá hotel in Miami, DeAngelo had boozily talked about a friend in Manhattan with a yacht they could use to entertain players and conduct business. Blazer had assumed it was idle chatter, but DeAngelo and Carpenter led Blazer down the west side of Manhattan to a marina and stepped aboard a three-story yacht that looked slightly worse for wear. DeAngelo instructed Blazer and Carpenter to take off their shoes, despite the rainy weather and slick deck. DeAngelo had adjusted his wardrobe, with a sweater tied around his neck and Sperry yachting shoes, which he removed.

The yacht's stateroom was a hive of activity. Four FBI operatives were wiring the space with microphones and cameras. The FBI had brought in SA Jill Bailey, the pretty, athletic, and flirtatious undercover who had sometimes helped plan meetings but was now playing the role of a vague, unexplained fellow financier. In her midthirties, with blue eyes, blonde hair, and a winning smile, she looked the part of a real estate investor and interior decorator. It seemed to Blazer her main role was to provide a softer touch and some sex appeal, giving Sood in particular a woman to try to impress and further lower his defenses. She began by asking Blazer questions about Sood to prepare, and Blazer answered but couldn't help reassuring her that their plan was bound to work.

"Don't worry, Munish will love you," he said. She laughed.

The bar was stocked with the high-end liquor brands Blazer had suggested to the agents, including two bottles of Macallan eighteen-year-old whiskey intended as gifts to Dawkins and Sood. The skipper introduced himself as Vinny, a stocky, hirsute Italian-American in a polo shirt and khaki shorts who fancied himself a comedian, telling Blazer he spent so much time at sea he swayed when he peed. Wearing Crocs and chomping on an unlit cigar, Vinny didn't seem like an FBI agent at all, but Blazer doubted that a civilian would be permitted to participate in an official operation. As the FBI prepared, the skipper continued with a series of one-liners about his marriage working well because he spent so many nights sleeping on the yacht while DeAngelo stationed himself in a corner to count out $25,000 in cash. Blazer offered to make a bet, doubting that Sood would be so brazen as to accept cash.

"The setup looked over the top," Blazer recalled. "I felt like I was on a movie set. Jeff had bought an expensive Montblanc pen to sign the agreement as part of the act. Anyone in their right mind would have been suspicious. Even with the possible connection to the New York Mafia, no one would go to this much trouble for a down-on-his-luck runner like Christian Dawkins. Giving gifts on top of funding someone like Christian—who hadn't proven himself—just didn't add up. The booze, the pen, the yacht—all of it was nuts. As street smart as

Christian was, I was concerned he was going to sniff out Jeff as either really stupid or too eager and trying too hard."

As surveillance was set up, a senior FBI supervisor loudly arrived aboard, sending a ripple of masculine energy through the yacht. Blazer knew the man only as Brian; apart from SA Carpenter and Wake, all the other law enforcement officials didn't use their real names or any name at all. Brian best resembled the actor Damian Lewis, British star of *Homeland* and *Billions*: redheaded, commanding, smart, quick witted, and oozing machismo. Blazer could see why he'd risen high in the bureau. Brian was noticeably shorter than the other agents, which was the source, Blazer believed, of his aggressively domineering manner.

From the start, Brian had treated Blazer differently than the other agents, winking knowingly and sharing facial reactions as if they were both smarter and more streetwise than the others. SA Wake started to flick through channels on the yacht's giant flat-screen TV, stopping on Fox News for a minute before changing to another station.

"I better change the channel," Wake said. "Dawkins wouldn't appreciate that. I'm sure he's a Democrat."

"Your internal monologue is unbelievable, Jason," Brian said.

"Yeah," Blazer said jokingly. "That's kind of racist."

The other agents snickered as an awkward silence descended. Wake looked around in bewilderment, wondering what he'd said wrong. Brian instructed Wake to keep his thoughts to himself, and the junior agent hung his head without apologizing.

Word came in from the "eyes" tailing Dawkins and Sood that they were approaching for the sit-down. Strong pours of Macallan were handed out by Vinny as they watched the arrival of the two putative business partners, along with Sood's pretty young assistant, present for reasons that were never explained. Blazer thought the trio looked like a small flock of lost sheep as they wandered around the docks, searching for the yacht.

"The fools were shocked to see me welcoming them aboard as I stepped off the yacht to greet them," Blazer said. "No one, including me, had mentioned to Munish that I was making the trip, and he'd been communicating directly with Jeff. I thought it was a nice 'fuck you' surprise, and I was dying to hear his bullshit explanation for why he was laying the groundwork for the business with the investor I'd brought to the table without including me. It was like running into your girlfriend in a bar when you're in the middle of picking up another woman. Munish nervously embraced me and acted like my presence was expected. I returned the hug, and I was tempted to give him a kiss on the lips—like the traitor Fredo got from his brother Michael in *The Godfather*."

Likewise, Dawkins appeared crestfallen to find Blazer on the yacht. With Blazer there, Dawkins wasn't free to hustle DeAngelo with empty promises and wild exaggerations of future success because he'd risk Blazer calling him out. Blazer had thrown Dawkins a lifeline in the form of investor Jeff DeAngelo, but there was no recognition of this fact, just sullen acceptance of his presence.

Blazer had them remove their shoes and ushered them to the bar, asserting his territorial authority. The gift bottles of Macallan had been carefully placed on the coffee table to indicate where they should sit. Blazer ushered Sood to the seat opposite Jill Bailey, certain he wouldn't be able to resist her charms as she tucked one of her legs underneath herself.

Vinny entered and offered a round of drinks. Dawkins didn't drink, but Sood accepted a cocktail, as did Blazer, who was beginning to enjoy himself. Sood quizzed Vinny about the yacht, and DeAngelo interrupted to say they'd all have a tour of the boat after the meeting, adding that they could use the ship to impress athletes.

"I could tell Christian and Munish didn't understand the way Jeff was spending money," Blazer recalled. "It was an unnecessary waste to impress a kid like Christian, who wasn't mature enough to grasp the magnitude of the gestures. A four-hundred-dollar bottle of scotch didn't appeal to a kid from Saginaw, Michigan—but he was happy to accept the gift despite being a teetotaler. The FBI agents had no clue what would be attractive to someone like Christian. I did, from all my years of dealing with young Black athletes, but no one ever bothered to ask. Instead of buying objects of his desires, the agents obtained things that matched their own wishes.

"The same was true with Munish. The shabby yacht was child's play compared to his experiences playing in my sandbox in the past. He'd been around the block with me, bypassing rope lines at clubs like Story and LIV in Miami. He'd had the VIP treatment at strip clubs and been comped Las Vegas hotel suites and had free rides on private jets and partied on a secluded private island. But Christian and Munish would act as dazzled as they needed to be to get Jeff to sign the agreement to fund the company."

Dawkins had come up with a name for their shared enterprise: LOYD, Inc., the acronym for Live Out Your Dreams, his personal credo. All agreed it was a great name, as Sood explained that he had attended to the formal requirements like minute-taking, establishing a board of directors, and filing the appropriate corporate titles. Reading through the list of college coaches Dawkins had emailed earlier with the subject line "These Are My Main Guys," DeAngelo again emphasized the need to pay coaches, a monomaniacal vision that the runner seemed to find suspicious. The list was extremely impressive, Blazer could see, a veritable who's who of college coaches: Rick Pitino of Louisville, Sean Miller of Arizona State, Will Wade of LSU, Tom Izzo of Michigan State—not to mention the array of assistant coaches who were charged with the nitty-gritty of recruitment.

Dawkins was making unbelievable promises, and the up-front investment he requested was so outlandish—and without foundation—that Blazer would have killed the initiative out of hand if he'd really been investing. He was surprised that Sood didn't wonder why he wasn't expressing more skepticism. Without addressing the question of how deliverable the outsize promises really were, Dawkins talked about the expenses involved in paying players, making it clear that every single player he would recruit would receive some amount of money.

The concept underlying Dawkins's approach was to make early payments to players' families while they were still playing grassroots basketball. Dawkins also gave college coaches money as a way to "assist" in recruitment. His idea was to give these coaches money when it was required to land a recruit or to satisfy the needs of a current player. The coaches would then be indebted to him for the assistance, which would create an obligation for them to push other grassroots stars to Dawkins. But DeAngelo didn't appear to understand the basic premise of LOYD, so he kept robotically asking to pay coaches. This seemed to finally arouse wariness in Dawkins, as DeAngelo couldn't explain why he wanted to focus on paying coaches.

"What are you trying to accomplish with coaches?" Dawkins asked. "What's your goal, your end game, what you envision with coaches? What are you paying them for?"

DeAngelo started to talk in circles, reciting key words: *coaches, grassroots, schools, business model.* Blazer listened, puffed his cheeks impatiently, and took a tug of scotch, waiting for a break in the conversation. After crossing his arms and wincing, Blazer finally sat forward and asked Dawkins where things stood with Lamont Evans. Blazer knew he had to intervene, to explain DeAngelo's fixation with coaches as the key to recruiting players in a way Dawkins could understand.

"Initially, coaches were how I pitched my shit to Jeff . . ." Blazer explained to Dawkins. "What made sense to me, the guys that never wavered, the guys that stepped up to the plate were with Lamont. Whatever the structure of the business was, Lamont had no choice but to help out."

Blazer reminded Dawkins of his own words when he'd said not paying coaches was "skipping a step" and how coaches were the glue that kept the relationship together. Coaches used the funds to recruit and support players, preventing the assistant coaches from having to spend their own money, Blazer said, knowing that was precisely the model used by agents to deploy runners like Dawkins. Players might stiff an agent or a financial adviser, Blazer said, but they wouldn't betray their coach.

"We don't mind putting money toward making sure that the kid sticks with us," Blazer explained. "The kid might fuck me or you over, but when push comes to shove, they're not going to screw their coach. And once a coach takes money, we own him."

Dawkins seemed to appreciate the argument for blackmail and that DeAngelo's fixation on coaches came from Blazer proposing that approach.

Blazer said that they were looking to replicate the relationship with Lamont Evans by paying sums to other coaches who were "Lamont-esque." This piqued Dawkins's curiosity.

"How much are you paying Lamont Evans?" Dawkins wanted to know.

Blazer hesitated, fearing he'd raise a red flag. The answer was $4,000 a month, an absurd amount in a real-world relationship, given that a player like PJ Dozier was a capable guard but hardly the elite prospect of his draft year and the standout player from OSU they'd met wouldn't be drafted at all. Still, Blazer felt he needed to answer honestly.

Dawkins laughed. "You can do what you want with your money, but you're out of your fucking mind paying him that much. I'd pay Lamont as needed and that's it."

Dawkins said that Evans didn't have the resources at Oklahoma State to compete with programs like Arizona and Louisville. Now engaged in the process, Dawkins proceeded to explain to DeAngelo how the NCAA actually functioned, in his experience. To pay a monthly retainer to a coach, Dawkins said, it had to be for a superstar assistant like Book Richardson of Arizona. As an assistant at a truly elite program, Richardson worked with multiple first-round players every year. The head coach of Arizona, Sean Miller, listened to Dawkins, he said, claiming he could contact Miller anytime and figure out what he wanted or needed.

"I can call Sean and have a conversation with him and tell him what's going on," Dawkins said. "And Sean will get in line."

Dawkins compared Miller to Rick Pitino, the head coach of Louisville, whom he was also close to, he said, illustrating the power runners like him possessed with extremely rich coaches, who were dependent on the steady flow of the best high school players coming to their programs.

Pitino was a control freak, Dawkins said, and so was Miller, but the difference was that Pitino was perhaps the only big-time head coach who didn't want to know what was going on in his recruiting program. Even if Pitino did know everything that was happening, from paying players to providing prostitutes and strippers in order to lure teenage boys to play for Louisville, as had been recently revealed in yet another NCAA scandal, he was very careful with what he talked about on the phone so he could pretend ignorance, while Miller was far more reckless—or heedless.

"He's crazy," Dawkins said of Miller, shaking his head in wonder. "He talks on the phone about things he fucking shouldn't talk about."

Blazer could see DeAngelo's and Jill Bailey's eyes widen. Dawkins referenced a "highly inappropriate" conversation he'd had with Miller only days earlier, when Miller had allegedly told him he was paying for "everything" for Deandre Ayton, a Bahamian recruit who would become the first overall pick and a star in the NBA; the sum the coach was paying was up to $10,000 a month for the incoming freshman, a significant amount but a pittance compared to Miller's salary and payments from Adidas, which came to nearly $3 million a year. Dawkins noted that Ayton had been recruited to Arizona by Richardson, and Miller said he would deliver the budding superstar as a client to Dawkins because of his connection to the assistant coach, provided—and this was the big and omnipresent ask—Dawkins took over the payments from the coach and was present on the campus on June 10, when Ayton was scheduled to arrive in Arizona for his first and only season. Richardson could recruit lottery-pick players year after year, and even though the head coach and assistant coach didn't get along very well, they were indispensable to each other.

"Book is exactly what we want to do," Blazer said to Dawkins. "And we need more guys like him."

"If you're down with funding those kinds of guys, man—like then we'd be fucking running college basketball," Dawkins said.

Dawkins paused, looking around the stateroom. "What's the most you would want to put out?" he asked.

"Per month or per year?" DeAngelo replied.

"Forgive me," Blazer cut in. "I was thinking, strategically, for a budget, we would look at four more coaches like Lamont."

"I think you could do this smarter so that everyone can make some money," Dawkins said. "I don't know what you're giving him [Evans] four grand a month for. This is what you should do: let me speak to them when they need it. Because if you're giving a guy four grand a month, he's going to spend it—and it's going to have nothing to do with what's going on. Like with Book. If he's got two kids, he might need one or two grand a month—you give it to him at that point. All they should be using the money for is to take care of situations for ourselves."

"I don't mind doing a bit of both," DeAngelo said.

Dawkins insisted that only the coaches who attracted first-round picks every year should be paid recurring retainers. Blazer asked Dawkins about the logistics of arranging a meeting with Book Richardson in the coming days in New York City. Dawkins replied that Richardson had grown up in the Bronx, so it was likely he would use the forthcoming NBA draft as a reason to come to the city and do some recruiting on his home turf. Blazer said they should definitely make an appointment between June 22 and 24 in Manhattan.

"I looked at Jeff and then at Christian and said, 'Let's get it done,'" Blazer recalled. "Looking back at Jeff, what I wanted to say was, 'That's how you fucking get it done.' I could see Jeff and Jill were getting excited as Christian let loose . . . I was amazed by what Christian was saying about all the coaches he claimed he could land. He was a slick hustler, like all good runners, but there was no way he was capable of inventing this caliber of bullshit. There had to be some truth behind it—the question was, how *much* truth."

Blazer was certain that the FBI agents watching the live video feed were thrilled at the seemingly endless amount of corruption they were uncovering. Pitino at Louisville was one of the highest-profile college coaches in the country—and he was certainly among the best paid, by far the highest-paid official in the state of Kentucky. Blazer knew this was more—much, much more—than the FBI had dared to hope for. With Pitino and Miller implicated, potentially, why wouldn't all the other coaches working the system—and that's what it was: a system—also be vulnerable to exposure?

"Maybe my ass had a chance of being saved after all," Blazer recalled feeling. "All we had to do was get Christian to bring the horses to the water. As it turned out, it wouldn't take much to get them to drink."

As if to prove Blazer's thoughts, Dawkins started to talk about LSU's head coach, Will Wade, yet another prominent multimillionaire coach.

"I have to tell him, 'Please shut the fuck up,'" Dawkins said of Wade and how he talked on the phone.

Blazer took a pull on his scotch and wondered if DeAngelo was feeling the buzz he was starting to feel.

"There's nothing more to do," Sood said. "Let's sign and seal the deal and move on."

All except Blazer then executed the agreements with the Montblanc pen. As Sood signed, he avoided making eye contact with Blazer, fully aware that he was cutting his former partner out of the deal. Sood complimented DeAngelo on the "nice touch" of having a designer pen for the signing ceremony, picking it up and inspecting it with admiration. The props Blazer had thought were way over the top were seemingly working their magic.

"All right, gentlemen, congratulations," Sood said, shaking hands with Dawkins and Blazer and DeAngelo. "What I'm going to do . . ." Sood paused and turned to Blazer. "I don't know what you want." Then he continued. "But I'm going to set up emails for everybody using the company name."

"Yeah, that would be good," Blazer agreed, the question of his participation left dangling.

DeAngelo reached for the envelope he'd prepared with $25,000 in cash, presenting it to Sood and Dawkins. The scene reminded Blazer of his days studying to be a stockbroker, when he had been forced to watch videos about cash and money laundering as part of his continuing education on the finance industry; the FBI video recording the encounter amounted to an instructional tape in what not to do with large amounts of high-denomination cash. Sood was unfazed, despite not being asked for revenue projections or the timing or extent of the potential return on investment—questions any serious investor would ask. Oddly, Blazer felt a slight pang on behalf of his former partner for his lack of shame.

"This is money," DeAngelo said, dropping the thick white envelope on the coffee table next to the canapés and cocktails.

"Perfect," Sood said as DeAngelo took the cash out of the envelope and fanned it for all to be impressed by.

"You don't mess around," Dawkins blurted out.

"Make sure someone doesn't beat you up on the way to the bank," Blazer said to Sood. "I hope you don't get mugged."

The scene astounded Blazer. He'd expected Sood to refuse to take the cash, as he'd been the chairman of the board of a bank and well knew the laws about money laundering. DeAngelo was emitting the signals that he was Mob connected, but Sood didn't flinch at the money on the table. DeAngelo assured them that it would be followed by another fifty thousand that would soon be flowing into LOYD's brand-new Bank of America account. The FBI's videotape captured one of the odder moments in an investigation replete with strange and surprising developments: as DeAngelo and Sood joked back and forth about taking care of the money and the larger amounts to come, Dawkins made a comment that perfectly expressed the subtext of the yacht meeting.

"At least he's not a gangster," Dawkins said of DeAngelo, with an uneasy grin, apparently kidding but also seemingly unable to stop from vocally reassuring himself that the transaction was somehow legitimate, and all present laughed nervously at the suggestion.

"This is the way to do business, right, Christian?" Sood said, picking up the cash.

"I like it," Dawkins said.

"Very direct, getting shit done," Sood said.

"No jerking around," Blazer said, gesturing toward DeAngelo to imply how he did business. "You believe in the model and it's real."

"It's a good model," Sood said, to general agreement. "It will be fun doing it."

As Sood passed the cash to his assistant, and she joked about getting mugged, it was evident from the dynamic that the hedge fund manager was going to control the cash flow.

"You want a tour of the boat?" DeAngelo asked.

Business done, they made their way from the stateroom to the deck with Vinny. Blazer lingered behind with Sood to have a "private" word.

"Man, I really thought we were going somewhere else altogether, but you actually came through," Sood said to Blazer, putting his arm on his shoulder, the insult at the heart of the backhanded compliment evident.

"We *are* going to go somewhere else," Blazer muttered as Sood walked away. "But you're not going to like where very much."

Before Dawkins departed, he turned to Blazer, saying the meeting reminded him of the yacht scene in *The Wolf of Wall Street*, when Leonardo DiCaprio's character attempted to seduce and corrupt two FBI officers— the movie had been filmed at the same marina, according to Vinny, the confluence of Hollywood and crime now an open joke among the investigators, complete with speculation about who would play who in the movie.

"Whatever Christian's opinion of me was, he knew I had a substantial amount of experience dealing with similar hustlers," Blazer recalled. "He knew he had to go through me to get to Jeff. He knew that if he wanted the money, he was going to have to provide Jeff with what he wanted, or I would pull the plug and move on to someone else. We said our goodbyes, and the three fools left."

The celebratory squad of FBI agents descended on the lavish spread of meats, cheeses, and premium alcohol like jackals while Blazer haggled with SA Wake to have his expenses paid. He felt like he was part of a winning team, but he knew he didn't really belong.

"As they all had a drink, the supervisor, Brian, made a joke about how Christian's eyes had followed the envelope of cash all the way into the bag," Blazer recalled. "Brian said Christian had looked like he was going to cry and added that Christian was certain to get some of that cash before he left town. I admitted that I'd given Munish too much credit, doubting that he would take the cash. I told the FBI agents that I thought Christian had been serious about the coaches he could deliver and I bet it was just the tip of the iceberg.

"While they counted out cash to reimburse me for travel, I was dying to grab one of the bottles of scotch to take back to my room to quietly celebrate on my own. I felt like I was an integral part of the team, guiding the conversation to where it needed to go. I admit that playing the game was exhilarating, like signing a new player. A new chapter in the investigation had just started."

CHAPTER ELEVEN

I'm Surprised There Aren't More Murders in This Space

In the summer of 2017, the steady thrum of corruption in the basketball investigation took on the cadence of a machine gun pumping out rounds of venality and duplicity. By this time, Blazer was itching for an even more aggressive strategy, arguing to the FBI that enough time had passed since his SEC screwup for his past transgressions to be forgotten. Since the denizens of college sports often had checkered pasts, they shrugged off the legal woes of others—especially when there was real money on the line. SA Carpenter said he wanted Blazer to be innovative, but Blazer worried that he might cross a line with AUSA Boone if he got too adventurous and endanger the consideration he'd get; it was better to follow instructions and be innovative in driving conversations discreetly and subtly.

"Marty," Carpenter said, "wherever you were before, you're with us now, so it's different. We have your back one hundred percent. That's part of what this organization is known for—how we take care of the people who cooperate."

Momma Spriggs in Carlisle, Pennsylvania, was a restaurant halfway between Pittsburgh and Manhattan, where Blazer and FBI agents discussed the investigation's various machinations and the operation for the forthcoming NBA draft, particularly the planned meetings with Book Richardson of Arizona and a new lead in the form of an Adidas executive named Merl Code. Blazer had just attended the high school graduation of his eldest child, Madison, and celebrating the momentous occasion had stirred up existential dread about prison. During the ceremony, Blazer had locked eyes with Trish and contemplated the odds that he might be behind bars for the graduations of his two other children. Trish didn't know what her husband was up to or the extent of his jeopardy, but she was concerned that he didn't have a real agreement about the benefit he would receive.

There was no question Dawkins and Sood believed the new enterprise was real, but Blazer told the agents that if he could reclaim some of the swagger and arrogance of his past persona, the dragnet could grow exponentially. Ironically, the street smarts that had gotten him in trouble would be his most effective tool in assisting the FBI. SA Carpenter readily agreed. Blazer told the agents that they needed to have cash payments handy for the meetings taking place during the draft, as Book Richardson and Merl Code would be expecting immediate gratification.

Blazer traveled to Manhattan on June 19 for the NBA draft. June 19 was always a difficult day for Blazer, because his mother had suddenly died of an aneurysm on that very day more than two decades earlier. This time, the self-reproach was deeply personal. He had been raised in a loving middle-class family in the suburbs of Pittsburgh, and his mother had doted on him, as he was her only son and golden child. His father had run a demolition business, usually dealing in cash with shady figures, and his mother had raised the family of four kids. But Blazer's father had been a great father but not the best husband, leading to the end of his parents' marriage. Blazer had come to understand his father and maintained good relations with him until he died, in 2014. But he had been relieved his father wasn't alive to see his son's descent into the world of criminal justice. Like many men, in his father, Blazer had found an example of how not to act.

"I believed I was better than him," Blazer remembered. "I had vowed I wouldn't be like him, but as you get older, I don't think you can avoid carrying some of your father's traits. I loved being a braggart and a big shot. I always wanted something more, and I didn't have a lot of patience when it came to getting what I wanted. Ever.

"If my mother had been alive, I would have been much more careful and conscientious about the decisions I made personally and professionally. I wouldn't want to add hurt and embarrassment and disappointment into her life, like my father did. I wouldn't have taken out-of-control risks. Twenty-four years after her sudden death, all I could think about was what a mess I had made of my life. When she died, I had been devastated, and I knew I had lost my moral compass. I wondered if I would have been in this predicament if she hadn't passed all those years ago."

While Blazer brooded on his plight, the FBI ushered Christian Dawkins, Munish Sood, and Arizona assistant coach Book Richardson into a suite in the five-star Conrad Hotel in Manhattan. Jeff DeAngelo and Jill Bailey were there. In addition, Munish Sood and his young female assistant sat with them as Richardson explained another variation of how money circulated in and fueled college recruiting.

In preparation for the meeting, Dawkins and Richardson had agreed that the coach would pitch a player named Rawle Alkins, a standout six-five player from Brooklyn whom the pair claimed they were on the verge of signing when he entered the draft. The two had also discussed what the coach could expect from DeAngelo in terms of money—all recorded by the FBI, pursuant to a court order permitting law enforcement to record calls from Dawkins's cell phone.

"Between you and me, I think they are probably at like five for you right now, in their heads," Dawkins had told Richardson on a call, speaking of DeAngelo and Blazer as the money backers of LOYD and the $5,000-a-month retainer the coach could command. "I think you could probably get more. I hyped you to be a motherfucking Dalai Lama."

In the meeting, the Arizona assistant coach told DeAngelo and Sood how he'd recruited Alkins. To attend college, student-athletes needed a minimum number of high school credits—sixteen. But Richardson said Alkins had been one credit short.

The coach described how he'd obtained a fake transcript showing that Alkins had sufficient credits. Richardson claimed that he spent $40,000 to commit the fraud by paying a bribe to an official with access to the school records.

"So, long story short, I said okay," Richardson said. "I said, 'Fuck you, I'm not doing it.' Tried to play poker, and one week turned into a month, and I said, 'Oh shit.' I tried to get someone else to get him [Alkins] a summer school course. Couldn't do it because the school, Bishop Ford, closed down. So when the NCAA says, 'I need to see all the coursework,' the school is closed."

Richardson didn't explain how he'd funded the necessary $40,000—but that was precisely the kind of issue that LOYD could address, it was understood. A top recruiter like Richardson, consistently landing five-star players, if he wanted to become head coach, had no choice but to find ways to get over the many hurdles facing attractive recruits as they tried to satisfy bureaucrats in the NCAA's distant, air-conditioned Indiana corporate headquarters—while putting the whole program at risk if they were caught.

"Well, here's the thing," Richardson explained, regarding the possibility of getting caught, "if anything happens, it's their word against mine. And when it's cash, you know, I don't know what they're talking about."

"Right," said DeAngelo.

"But Rawle Alkins is such a great kid," Richardson continued. "I got caught up. And I felt the kid was done an injustice and a disservice because what—the high school coach [I paid], again, it was ingenious. But when you bamboozle everyone and that kid didn't get any of the forty, that's the problem I have."

Bailey nodded in agreement.

"So, again, it's something different every year," Richardson said. "It's like I said, $40,000 to do that was extreme. If I had the chance to do it again, I'd try to barter. I'd give blood. I'd give semen. Something."

"I think we're saying kinda the same thing," DeAngelo replied. "It's mainly, you know, we can provide you—I can provide you—with a pot of money each year. And then you do what you have to do."

"You know best how to take care of the situation," Bailey agreed.

~

But Richardson wanted to ratchet up the quality of service he was promising by having DeAngelo review the lists of players he was recruiting as well as examining resources like ESPN's high school–ranking system to pick out potential targets. DeAngelo said he liked the idea, adding that they wanted to personally meet the recruits through the process to establish rapport.

"As soon as they commit, it's a phone call," Richardson agreed. "All my kids call me Uncle Book. By the time this is done, they're going to call you Uncle Jeff."

Arriving at the hotel in the middle of the day for the afternoon session with Merl Code of Adidas, Blazer listened intently as Carpenter and DeAngelo proudly caught him up on the earlier Book Richardson meeting.

The FBI agents said that DeAngelo had handed Richardson $5,000 in cash in an envelope. In a call on the way to the airport—with the FBI recording calls from Dawkins's cell phone, as they had done under a court order—Richardson had joked with Dawkins about the mindlessness of DeAngelo handing out money so easily.

"But what can I do to make sure both of us are good?" Richardson had asked Dawkins, expressing the view that perhaps he should break off a piece of the money for Dawkins for facilitating the meeting.

"I'm Gucci," Dawkins had told Richardson. "And you use that money that you're getting from them to help recruit, do whatever—or go on a fucking vacation," he continued. "Who cares."

On the way back to the hotel, Dawkins called and said two of the coaches he had promised meetings with that day weren't coming to New York for the NBA draft, but he confirmed Merl Code from Adidas was on his way. Code and Dawkins had talked, with the FBI recording the conversation. The Adidas executive had seemed to act as a mentor to the runner. During the call, they had set up a strategy for Code to best hustle the seemingly gormless DeAngelo.

With the FBI listening, Dawkins and Code had joked about DeAngelo's lack of sophistication as an apparent fanboy. Dawkins had snorted and said that DeAngelo was no Sonny Vaccaro, a reference to the legendary Nike executive who'd signed Michael Jordan and for decades run ABCD Camp, the prototype for a high school grassroots development program, with alumni that included Kobe Bryant and LeBron James.

"There's nothing real complicated about the situation," Dawkins had said. "They already know who you are, obviously. Just bring up some kids' names—guys that you think you can be involved with. It's pretty simple."

"How can I do that?" Code had asked, questioning the premise of just randomly dropping the names of top prospects he didn't really know. Dawkins had encouraged him to do exactly that: just name top kids. Dawkins had said that DeAngelo and Blazer wouldn't even know who he was talking about regardless.

"I mean, but I could say Zion Williamson knowing good and damn well we ain't going to get him?" Code had asked.

"Yeah, exactly," Dawkins had joked. "That's my point. I'm going to get somebody anyway. They're not going to know how I got him. I'm just trying to get some money put in your pocket, basically."

Arriving for the sit-down, Code affected the mien of a somber businessman. During introductions, Blazer learned that the Adidas executive was a graduate of Clemson, so Blazer talked up his many football connections at the school. Code was a slightly pudgy Black man in his forties, wearing an off-the-rack suit with arms two inches too long. He didn't match Blazer's image of a slick sneaker executive running multimillion-dollar relationships with famous college coaches and players.

The seating in the suite had been carefully planned, with hidden cameras arranged to capture what was about to unfold. Jeff DeAngelo and Jill Bailey took their prearranged seats at the coffee table, joined by Blazer and Munish Sood and his assistant. Describing his background, Code explained that he'd worked for Nike for many years, running their Elite Youth Basketball League, the feeder system that nurtures and ensnares some of the best high school players before they go to college. But he'd left for Adidas after having disagreements with his boss, and because Adidas was offering more generous financial support for the grassroots and college programs he funded.

Segueing to the question of money, Code said he was involved in steering players to Adidas schools, but it wasn't necessary that a future NBA player go to a specific school associated with the company; relationships with coaches at Nike and Under Armor schools were just as important to him in the long term. The point was to get the best players to sign with Adidas when they turned pro. The stakes were extremely high, he said. NBA star James Harden had just signed a thirteen-year deal with Adidas for $200 million, with the company designing custom shoes and apparel in a transaction that could yield ten times that amount in revenue.

"Seriously, I'm surprised there aren't more murders in this space," Code said. "You're dealing with street people who are just as inclined to kill someone over their money or if they feel disrespected in any way. There's just so much money and so many people influencing decisions."

The room fell silent. Code wasn't joking, and Sood's eyes widened while his assistant, likewise, looked terrified. Blazer wasn't surprised, nor apparently was Dawkins, both fully aware that there were always dubious—even dangerous—figures lurking around star collegiate and professional athletes.

Blazer even felt a measure of professional appreciation as he listened to Code's proposed structure for their dealings. Code said the point wasn't to have a ton of players; the real money would come from having a few superstars, whom he would identify by combing through grassroots leagues for the best prospects. LOYD would then make an "investment," paying a connected assistant coach at the school to cover the cost of "taking care" of the future superstar on campus and to defray the expenses of further recruiting. From start to finish, Code said, they would control the situation, and everyone would win. The coach would then make sure the player didn't develop any other business relationships during the time they were in college, ensuring a lucrative sneaker deal and financial-management representation were settled long before the draft. All the parts fit together, like a jigsaw puzzle, with a fast and attractive return on investment. The circuit would be closed and self-sustaining, with Code and Adidas praising LOYD to the players and vice versa, all reinforced by a coach secretly on the payroll—and all without the player knowing a thing about the conspiracy to close off his options and play with his mind.

Blazer believed what Code was describing was true genius, the player trapped in a "money bubble" from the time they were in high school, with no way to know their advisers and coaches were involved in a conspiracy to control their interests—and with tens or hundreds of millions on the line.

"We're all in," DeAngelo said, "with identifying colleges, college coaches, talent at the AAU level. Do you have a number of coaches in mind? How much do you want to get paid, and how do we get it to you?"

"I haven't really thought about a number," Code said, laughing. "I'm not trying to rob you. I'm trying to save you money. It's not that I'm not interested in up-front money, but I'm more interested in the long term—in getting ten, twelve, fifteen NBA guys. Because that's where the real money is."

"I could do something now if you want," DeAngelo said.

"I'm not pressed to get into your pockets," Code said. "If that's what you want to do, great. If it's not what you want to do, I'm fine."

Blazer was beyond impressed with the performance he was witnessing. Of course Dawkins and Code had talked money before the meeting. Of course a monthly retainer had been discussed. Of course Code expected to depart with a nice chunk of tax-free money. But ice wouldn't melt in Code's mouth as he feigned indifference.

"I could see how masterful Code was in selling Adidas to kids," Blazer recalled. "He didn't need to be slick or smooth. His weapons of choice were unpretentiousness and righteousness. The best salesmen make it seem like they're not even selling. They make it seem like buying is all the customer's idea. I'd been too quick to judge him."

Code cited a top prospect going to Louisville as a potential investment opportunity for LOYD, without naming the player. Code explained that assistant coaches at the top programs were using funds from their own salaries to pay for the players' and families' requests for money; with coaches' salaries in the range of $300,000 to $400,000, the smaller sums weren't too onerous. But for a coach like Lamont Evans, with a salary in excess of half a million dollars, risking his career by taking a few thousand from Blazer and DeAngelo didn't seem to make much sense—to an outsider. But assistant coaches didn't want to spend their own money. Code said the money LOYD was spending should be used for recruiting and supporting the kids, not to line the coaches' pockets.

As Code spoke, Sood and Dawkins started a whispered sidebar conversation that Blazer joined. Blazer discovered that Sood was asking Dawkins sotto voce if Code really expected an envelope of money, intimating that it was within his power to get DeAngelo to fork over cash. Blazer interrupted and said that there was an envelope ready, stepping closer to ensure that the recording device in his pocket captured the hushed talk. Blazer wanted it to be crystal clear to a future jury that Sood understood and was on record participating in the payment that was about to happen.

Code suggested that a grassroots tournament in Las Vegas the following month might be a convenient place for DeAngelo and the others to meet the coaches he could deliver, despite the fact that Code couldn't attend in person. Dawkins waved for the undercover agent to produce the cash, and so DeAngelo did, pulling an envelope containing $2,500 from his back pocket. Code faked surprise and insisted that the money wasn't necessary, even as he slid the envelope into his breast pocket.

While Dawkins escorted Code down to the lobby, DeAngelo produced the $25,000 in cash the FBI had carefully counted beforehand, placing it on the coffee table in the middle of the room to the evident amazement of Sood and his saucer-eyed assistant, explaining that this was the second payment to LOYD and the third tranche would come in September. Whatever potential defenses or justifications Sood might have relied on were now entirely gone, the FBI's cameras capturing his grin as he accepted the cash.

Upon returning, Dawkins gleefully lit up at the sight of the cash on the coffee table. He then asked the departing Sood to "break off" $4,000 to cover his travel expenses, and he was handed the money. Then Dawkins told DeAngelo he was hungry, shunning the spread of turkey sandwiches and cut fruit the FBI had provided. The young hustler—who, in reality, was white-knuckling an attempt to start a business and would otherwise be so broke he'd have to move back into his childhood bedroom—now made this kind of demand from his new partners. They wound up going to a fancy restaurant, and it went without saying that DeAngelo would pay the tab, after Dawkins had ordered and then ostentatiously stepped outside to make a call. He barely picked at his supersize plate of chicken parmesan, washing it down with ice-cream cake with whipped cream and a cherry on top, which he popped into his mouth.

When Dawkins finally left, the FBI team convened in the suite to discuss the day's events. Blazer was excited about using Code, and for a moment, he thought of himself as part of the team, a trusted adviser and strategist. But it turned out SA Carpenter was irked, asking why Dawkins had been so demanding and difficult.

"I told Scott that Christian was so demanding because he needed to be a prima donna," Blazer recalled. "It was like the crazy backstage demands of rock stars with a contract rider requiring bowlfuls of only green Skittles to be set out for them. I'd seen it with my athletes in the past because they wanted to be pampered and catered to. In Christian's mind, he was the king, the rainmaker, the celebrity of the business. He only ate a couple of bites of his chicken because he wanted to establish that he could be rude and inconsiderate deliberately, to show he wasn't concerned with Jeff or his money . . . He was the most important figure of all of us, and he wanted that understood and acknowledged through deference. It was the cost of doing business with him, putting up with his arrogance and insolence. Christian knew exactly what he was doing. It was about power and control and showing that he was special—he was the star."

Blazer took the elevator to the lobby with Jill Bailey as he left. They exchanged congratulatory small talk, and he was shocked when Bailey leaned in for a hug as they said goodbye. Blazer didn't know what was behind the gesture, but the sign of acceptance and kindness gave him a jolt of energy—even as he contemplated having to face AUSA Robert Boone the next day.

~

While Blazer focused on his role in the investigation, the larger covert case the FBI was building continued to grow. In a recorded call after the Code meeting, Sood had laughed and told Dawkins they should "stroke [DeAngelo] off a little more," as if being around athletes aroused sexual excitement in DeAngelo. The pair agreed that paying Book Richardson $5,000 per month was a joke. DeAngelo was sleepwalking as he gave away money, Sood said derisively.

On June 26, 2017, Dawkins called DeAngelo to explain where the plan for Richardson and Code had landed. He'd consulted with the Arizona coach and the Adidas executive about the monthly payments LOYD would need to make to secure their services and access to their players. The sums Dawkins suggested were laughable amounts that no one in their right mind would ever pay. But Dawkins wasn't operating in the real world, and he intended to squeeze every dollar he could out of DeAngelo.

"So Book is saying he's going to need five a month, and Merl's saying he's going to need seventy-five hundred," Dawkins said. "How do you feel about that?"

"See, Book, to me, is in a little bit better position," DeAngelo replied. "Because he's an actual coach. He's pretty much laid it out there. He kind of sees his role is that 'Whatever kids I get, I'm going to tell them where to sign.' I mean, he said that. 'I'm going to tell them where they need to sign.'"

When Richardson traveled to meet with Sood at his New Jersey offices to receive another payment of $15,000 from DeAngelo, Sood called Dawkins afterward to share his delight—a call duly recorded by the FBI. The duo believed they had discovered a geyser of money; DeAngelo had already handed out at least $180,000 in cash.

"He left with a gift," Sood said of Richardson.

"Jeff feels good right now," Dawkins said with a chuckle.

"Dude, Jeff is, like, fucking high," Sood said.

"I figured that," Dawkins said.

"I mean, it made his whole day," Sood said. "He's so happy."

"What does DeAngelo want?" Dawkins wondered aloud, finally asking the screamingly obvious question about the investor's seemingly irrational motivation. "I mean, is he just a fan?"

The yacht, the hotel suites, the bulging envelopes stuffed with cash were more than a little suspicious. Compound those oddities with the single malt scotch and Jill Bailey's little or no recognizable purpose for the business. Or paying Book Richardson thousands of dollars with no connection to a specific player, or not questioning how Blazer had come to meet DeAngelo. None of it added up when considered rationally.

Sood sighed. "I don't know," he said, pushing aside any of the many concerns about DeAngelo that might have troubled him. "I think he's hoping that Book Richardson will send us some kids and this business will grow."

"Guys like Book are going to send me kids anyway," Dawkins replied, noting the pointlessness of the bribes. "Does he understand that?"

"No," Sood said of DeAngelo. "But it's like he's fucking dying. He's dying. Don't wake him up."

CHAPTER TWELVE

Fuck the Lawyers

At eleven a.m. sharp on June 20, 2017, Blazer and his new criminal attorney arrived at 1 Saint Andrew's Place in Manhattan—the forbidding offices of the Southern District of New York—for his debriefing with AUSA Robert Boone. The lawyer had taken a $1,000 flight to New York from Pittsburgh at Blazer's expense, money the cooperator couldn't afford. The new attorney had white-collar experience and had dealt with federal prosecutors, so Blazer was in better hands. Still, Blazer hadn't wanted him to come, considering all the maneuvering he had done on his own and the urgent need to save money, but Boone had insisted the attorney be in attendance—a foreboding signal Blazer didn't pick up on.

It was the day after Blazer's meeting with Merl Code, and his feelings of elation were undercut by worry. Blazer wasn't sure what to expect from Boone. While he was aware of the serious nature of his crimes, successful operations like the yacht meeting and the encounters with Merl Code and Kobie Baker had caused his mind to race all the way to not being indicted, and perhaps even being exonerated.

SAs Carpenter and DeAngelo were waiting for Blazer in front of the squat brutalist federal building, and together they entered through the metal detectors and made their way to a windowless prison-interrogation-like conference room. Waiting for the always-tardy Boone with the door open, Blazer was surprised by the string of law enforcement officials stopping by to say hello and shake his hand. Special agents and prosecutors told Blazer that they'd heard what a great job he was doing, patting him on the back, recognition that made him feel like a kind of celebrity.

To underscore the nonchalant, even celebratory, atmosphere Blazer had been anticipating, SA Carpenter splayed his arms and legs in his chair like a petulant teenager letting his parents know he has precisely no interest in what they said or did. DeAngelo likewise, was light-hearted and casual in manner. The FBI agents were both implicitly communicating that the meeting with Boone was a colossal waste of time and energy, an unwelcome distraction from the only thing that truly mattered: the brilliant investigation they were conducting with their innovative and valuable cooperating witness. Imagining the meeting, Blazer had wondered what would happen when the powerful egos of Boone and Carpenter encountered each other at close quarters, a clash he expected to be entertaining—if not explosive—as the investigator and prosecutor fought over their place in the hierarchy of law enforcement and a major case likely to command national headlines.

When AUSA Boone finally entered the room, he seemed hurried, his manner implying he had just left a vital meeting somewhere else and that he was in a rush to move on to something even more important. Boone didn't even glance at Carpenter, and Carpenter likewise avoided eye contact. The power dynamic was obvious to Blazer: AUSA Boone was in charge.

"Fuck the lawyers." Yeah, right, thought Blazer.

As the AUSA on the case, Boone had the myriad powers of the federal government at his fingertips, from obtaining subpoenas to ordering wiretaps and providing sentencing recommendations for cooperators that would almost certainly be followed by the judge assigned to Blazer's case. It is a little-known fact in American society, but the way the legal system has evolved over time has meant that federal prosecutors—most especially in the Southern District of New York, which views itself as an elite institution best resembling Harvard Law School—possess the closest thing the country has to absolute control over the fates of others.

Boone was accompanied by another AUSA and an intern. Blazer had hoped for the meeting to start with recognition of how far the investigation had advanced thanks to his fine work for the FBI. Something about the Merl Code meeting the day before, for example, and how ingenious it had been to rope Adidas into a case that was only just starting to come into focus in terms of scope and potential reach. Instead, what followed stunned Blazer: for hours, AUSA Boone systematically reviewed Blazer's history, from his involvement with the movies to the intricacies of misappropriating his clients' funds. Blazer's anticipation of sparks flying between Carpenter and Boone was replaced by the sinking realization that the only thing Boone wanted to talk about was Blazer's past. As Blazer responded to the questions, the prosecutor furiously took notes in his yellow legal pad, constantly searching for contradictions or evasions and lies.

Blazer hadn't talked about his crimes in detail in a long time, not since he'd confessed to the federal government, and he was worried that he would forget facts or accidentally omit fraudulent acts that would make it look like he was minimizing his conduct or trying to avoid responsibility. Blazer didn't know what further evidence the government might have amassed, but the peril was suddenly clear and present. Boone didn't accept *yes* or *no* replies, asking follow-up questions and demanding greater detail in the manner of an interrogation.

Special Agent Carpenter and the undercover DeAngelo knew few of the details about Blazer's crimes, but now both leaned forward, chins on their hands, listening with intent interest as Blazer went through his litany of criminality in humiliating detail, ashamed anew of the terrible decisions he'd made for years. The movie *Mafia*, Russell Okung, the forged signatures—it was all too much. For a moment, as Boone pressed for more detail, Blazer choked up, tears welling in his eyes, partly in regret, partly in embarrassment, but mostly because of the mortification of recalling the reckless way he'd endangered the well-being of his wife and kids. Blazer had forged a successful career as a financial adviser, living in a manner few suburban dads could imagine, but he'd let hubris, greed, and his curious mix of cynicism and naivete put him at the federal government's mercy.

Blazer didn't realize it at the time, but one of the concerns Boone needed to address was how Blazer might perform under the withering attack of defense attorneys during cross-examination in a trial. Was Blazer a habitual liar and blame shifter who'd happened to get caught, or was he a man who'd made a series of awful choices and regretted all he'd done? Did he talk back and get belligerent when pressured? Was he willing to own the entirety of his criminal conduct without offering excuses or justifications? A defense lawyer wouldn't accept yes or no answers, demanding Blazer recite all the gory minutiae. Defense attorneys also had an array of tactics to unnerve witnesses like Blazer, the cooperators who were often at the center of the most important federal cases as witnesses against their former partners in crime.

It was a truism of organized crime cases over the ages that in order to understand how conspiracies really worked, prosecutors had to have gangsters like Sammy "the Bull" Gravano explain the inner truth of the Mafia to juries at the trials of gangsters like John Gotti. College basketball was much the same. To get to the truth, the government needed to put informants on the stand—and that, apparently, now applied to Blazer. A panel of twelve peers in a jury didn't have to like Blazer, but they had to believe him, along with the overwhelming corroborating evidence of the wiretaps and recorded conversations law enforcement possessed.

As he tried to engage with Boone, Blazer leaned heavily into the truth, the whole truth, and nothing but the truth, no matter how dire. He felt like he was floating outside his body as he described awful acts committed by the man he'd been only a few years earlier, physically the same but now so different in so many ways, he believed. The arrogance and egotism were nearly gone. His crimes looked particularly awful if judged as a whole, but broken down step-by-step, Blazer knew it all made a certain kind of stupid sense, as his FBI collaborators were discovering, the justifications and half-baked excuses he'd told himself becoming more and more ridiculous as he recited the stark reality of millions of dollars disappearing into the maw of his foolish movie investments.

Staring at Boone, Blazer was also starting to understand the performative aspects of official contrition. The self-flagellation that he was being forced to rehearse had a ritualistic nature, requiring him to shed any part of the real interior monologue he had to rationalize, contextualize, or even explain away his bad acts. In a sophisticated but unspoken way, Boone was preparing Blazer for trial and illustrating how he would have to act on the stand. As a denizen of the underworld of college sports, with all its unspoken signals and wordless contracts, Blazer was a past master at picking up on the coded language the prosecutor was speaking.

As Boone relentlessly revisited the past, Blazer caught a glimpse of the blank faces of Carpenter and DeAngelo as they listened, and he couldn't help worrying that he was totally fucked. Neither of the FBI agents had said a word about the value of Blazer's cooperation. They hadn't mentioned the ideas and contributions he'd come up with or the strategies he'd suggested to the agents. Carpenter had said the FBI would have Blazer's back, and in Blazer's mind, this was the time—above all others so far—that he desperately needed support. The FBI agents weren't going to say a word, Blazer realized. He was truly on his own.

Casting back in time, Boone turned to Blazer's experience twenty-five years earlier in the boiler room, where he'd first learned to sell penny stocks to small-time investors. It appeared that Boone had scoured Blazer's entire legal record, leaving nothing out, no matter how inane or inconsequential. When asked if he had ever brandished a gun, Blazer volunteered that he had been apprehended at an airport in 2016, when he'd gone through a metal detector forgetting he was carrying his .380 revolver, but no charges had been filed. The gun had been confiscated at the airport, but when Blazer started to work with the FBI, SA Carpenter had arranged for the weapon to be returned by the FBI office in Pittsburgh—facts that Blazer relayed to Boone.

Did Blazer ever take illegal drugs? Boone demanded. No. Prostitutes? No. Domestic violence—have you ever beaten your wife? Fistfights, theft, pistol-whipping, injuring someone else? Again and again, the answer was negative. Then Boone turned to pornography, asking Blazer if he watched illegal child porn. The room filled with laughter as Blazer replied that, no, he only watched straight, red-blooded American *adult* porn.

The exhausting daylong session ended with Boone saying that the next time they met, they'd revisit Blazer's involvement in corruption with football players at the University of North Carolina nearly ten years earlier. By this time, Blazer's criminal attorney was rapidly writing in his legal pad, tallying the number of federal crimes Blazer was going to have to plead guilty to and how much time he was likely to serve. The idea of avoiding prison now seemed far-fetched. Boone hadn't asked even a single positive question about Blazer's cooperation and the state of the NCAA investigation. With his attorney totaling up the crimes, citing the sections of the laws Blazer had broken, along with minimal downward departures a judge might grant, the math said that he'd have to serve between six and seven years. The charges included wire fraud, theft, and lying to the federal government—a string of felonies that Blazer could minimize in his own mind but that a court might impose heavy sanctions for. That was more than the time it would take for his son to graduate from high school, and Blazer couldn't help pondering the premonition he'd had at his older daughter's graduation ceremony only a few weeks earlier. He'd already spent three years working for the government, and it seemed he wasn't going to get much credit for his efforts.

Mind reeling as he left the building, Blazer knew that no matter what happened, he was nowhere near a finish line. He'd hoped to be done when the arrests were made, but now he could see that he would have to do anything that was asked of him or risk his own immediate arrest, with no promise of any benefit. Blazer had no bank of goodwill to draw on, he believed, with no apparent support from the FBI, and it seemed to him that he'd gained little or nothing from his years of covert toil on behalf of the federal government. The light at the end of the tunnel he'd glimpsed now appeared to be a runaway locomotive driven by AUSA Robert Boone.

The exhilaration of the day before had evaporated, now replaced by despair. Walking silently out of the building, Blazer turned to SA Carpenter with a searching look in his eyes, as if to say, *What am I putting myself through this investigation for if this is how it's going to play out?* The only answer, Blazer knew, was that he had no choice in the matter; the government owned him lock, stock, and barrel.

CHAPTER THIRTEEN

Groundhog Day

The morning after that painful meeting with AUSA Boone, Blazer felt like things couldn't get any worse. So when SA Carpenter called to check in, Blazer commiserated about being forced to relive the lowest moments of his life in gory detail. To his surprise, Carpenter said that he'd heard a thousand times worse.

"So you ripped off some football players," Carpenter said, a position that Blazer wished the agent had expressed the previous day. "I really can't see what's the big deal."

Carpenter's opinion didn't matter compared to Boone's, Blazer understood, nor did he buy the idea that the FBI or Southern District as institutions would be fine with overlooking the misappropriation of more than $2 million. Attempting to get Blazer focused on the next stage of the investigation, Carpenter wanted to know how realistic the scenario they had created would be in the real world. Did it make sense to someone from the inside for corrupt financial advisers to pay coaches thousands of dollars to seduce players on their behalf? Was there any question that coaches were the best way to reach players? Where could the investigation focus to make the model more convincing and realistic? In shock, Blazer realized that the premise of the investigation suddenly seemed to be in doubt.

It had been shown to be extremely realistic, Blazer said confidently. But there were some things that might feel over the top, like the high-roller liquor served in the FBI's expensive suites, the lack of real deliverables in terms of specific players as a return on investment, or the yacht meeting. But it had worked, and there was no arguing with success. The essential ideas behind the investigation were solid, and he wished he'd thought of them himself when he was really working with football players. Paying coaches to recruit players was a great structure. But the real gangster move was snaring the coaches with corrupt payments, providing leverage over their livelihoods. Like a mobster being initiated into the crime family by being forced to kill someone—thus passing the point of no return—the coaches were crossing the threshold of knowingly cheating and thus were at the mercy of Blazer, DeAngelo, and LOYD, with the implicit threat of revelation and ruination always looming. In time, with sufficient funding and persistence and patience, Blazer maintained that they would be really running college basketball, as Christian Dawkins had said.

Carpenter then asked if Blazer thought there were other "Jeff DeAngelos" in the real world. Blazer reminded Carpenter that one of the first opportunities the investigation had hoped to pursue involved a player at Texas A&M whose father was allegedly accepting payments from a booster. Dawkins had asked Blazer if he would be interested in taking over those payments to secure the player's future business, which would essentially mean taking over from the booster, who was definitely another "Jeff DeAngelo," Blazer said. Blazer added that he didn't know what the booster's hustle was—how specifically he was monetizing the connection—but he was certain to be seeking a benefit for the payments; in college sports, nothing was free, despite the pretense to the contrary.

Blazer didn't know it, but he had unearthed a central truth of American college sports in the twenty-first century. Athletic coaches have enormous power over players, from admission to the school to playing time and chances to star. This was true in most popular sports like basketball and football, where professional careers were on the line, but it was equally true of minor sports like rowing, fencing, and soccer, with coaches dangling guaranteed admission to selective colleges in front of applicants and their families. In the FBI sting known as Operation Varsity Blues, which unfolded just after Blazer's operation broke into the news, law enforcement caught wealthy parents—including some celebrities—bribing coaches to get their privileged children into elite colleges by way of fake sporting credentials. While the kids were the commodity in what might be called "Operation Marty Blazer," in Operation Varsity Blues, parents paid a fixer to grease the palms of college coaches to create a "side door" with fraudulent sports résumés to get kids into schools like University of Southern California and Yale. Coaches, whose careers were inextricably linked to the talent they were able to recruit, also made money by exploiting their many powers in the upside-down and amoral world of college amateur sports.

Blazer sensed Carpenter methodically directing the investigation toward a conclusion and felt torn: Blazer wanted the ordeal to be over and done with, but rushing to end the case prematurely seemed insane. They were really just getting started, he said to Carpenter, with limitless potential ahead and the biggest names in the sport on the line. With the FBI's involvement and cash, they'd penetrated college hoops to an incredible extent in a matter of a few months—a considerable feat.

"I couldn't grasp why they might not dedicate the time to see the case through to its conclusion," Blazer told me. "What could possibly cause them to cut it short when we had so much momentum? With my paranoia, I began to worry that the timeline had to do with my prosecution. I was trying to figure out Scott's frame of mind as we spoke. The case kept growing and growing, and it was becoming so enormous I thought it might be overwhelming the FBI. Scott seemed introspective, like he knew we couldn't follow the case to its logical end point—like he wasn't sure what to do next.

"I was trying to provide him with the right ammunition to fight with the powers that be to keep the investigation going. I said that every time we meet with someone, another door opened, again and again and again, revealing even more layers to the story. I could tell he was trying to wrap his mind around how big the opportunity was. I was mostly worried that cutting it short would negatively impact the value of my cooperation, but I also have to admit that going after these targets was gratifying. There were so many moving parts it was intellectually interesting and exciting to have so many high-level coaches involved. It seemed like the Merl Code conversation had finally made Scott connect the dots and see the impact a financial figure like Jeff DeAngelo could have on the landscape of college sports. It might have been delusional, but I felt like we were all working for a common goal and doing some good.

"But it also seemed like the FBI was trying to use me less, with Jeff DeAngelo more often talking to Dawkins and others like the suit-maker Rashan Michel directly, which worried me because they had no fucking clue how to handle those guys. I was constantly reminded that I was absolutely necessary to the success of the investigation, and I was all the way in."

Blazer had landed on the crux of a paradox: On one hand, the case was getting better all the time, as Merl Code and Kobie Baker had offered new avenues to pursue. But on the other, Jeff DeAngelo's mono-maniacal fixation on coaches was stirring misgivings—if not outright contempt—from the main targets, a fact that had evidently caught the attention of AUSA Boone, and possibly DOJ officials further up the line. Another complicating factor remained the legal theory of the case. What was happening surely seemed illegal, if only because of the subterfuge and large amounts of cash. But was it indictable? Who were the victims of the bribery scheme? What was the crime? Blazer had no one to talk to about such matters, so he had to operate on the faith that the FBI and Southern District knew what they were doing.

There weren't that many examples to point to where corruption in college sports had made it to criminal prosecution. The case of Norby Walters in the 1980s had resulted in repeated appeals and an eventual conviction, but that had revolved around it being premeditated (the accused had sought legal advice before giving money to college players), a fact that didn't apply to the current investigation.

Unbeknownst to Blazer, the Southern District was relying on the federal law that made it illegal to offer a bribe to an employee of a federally funded organization. While this law was often used with government contractors, the coaches also worked for colleges that received federal funding, even if the basketball programs were wildly profitable enterprises in no need of government help. Under this theory, the victims were the colleges, who were denied the honest services of players they "paid" by way of scholarships and other incidental support. So all that mattered was that Dawkins, the coaches, and Code from Adidas had facilitated illegal payments with the intent to influence or reward the recipients. In this novel and untested interpretation of federal law, the Southern District had come up with innovative ways to apply the criminal law to college sports.

In the days leading up to the Las Vegas meetings, Blazer's misgivings about DeAngelo proved prescient, as Dawkins and Code again tried to dissuade the FBI undercover from pursuing coaches as his central strategy. Blazer believed DeAngelo should at least pretend to weigh the merits of different approaches instead of blithely insisting on coaches, coaches, coaches. Dawkins and Code appeared to think they were saving DeAngelo from folly.

"The fact of the matter is this, Jeff," Dawkins told DeAngelo on a call. "The coaches have a level of influence, but it isn't the end all, be all. Fuck, I'm more powerful than any coach you're gonna meet. No one knows you, or who you are, or your background, or what you may be. These guys have worked their whole lives to get to this point, and if one thing goes wrong, especially—not to make this a race thing or whatever the case may be—if it's a Black coach . . . If you've got one fucking thing happen to you, you'll never coach again. That's just the bottom line."

"I'm with you," DeAngelo replied disingenuously. "I would definitely like to get to where we have maybe around ten or so quality coaches that everyone's comfortable with. I believe in the model."

Two days later, on another call, DeAngelo explained to Dawkins that he was hoping that Merl Code would use the influence he had developed with various coaches during his years with Nike and Adidas to enable the investor to develop relationships with coaches, an eye-rolling level of fixation—but that didn't stop Dawkins from scheming to get his hands on the potential pile of money.

"If you want to be Santa Claus and just give people money, well, fuck, let's just take that money and go out to a strip club and buy hookers," Dawkins said to DeAngelo.

Dawkins was only joking, as he tried to convince DeAngelo that he was squandering his money.

"It's only a handful of schools that produce NBA players, bro," Dawkins told DeAngelo on yet another call.

"I'm with you," DeAngelo said, then insisted that Dawkins do as he was told and bring coaches to the table. "Here's the model. I'm funding your side of the business, and I'm staying out of your way, and you're going to do that."

All the while, on recorded calls, Dawkins continued to try to explain to the seemingly dense DeAngelo why it was bad business practice to spend more money than the company had or would bring in. There were also limits to how much money could be expended recruiting coaches, with the proposed budget of $50,000 per month simply being impossible to blow through. But DeAngelo insisted, and

Dawkins clearly felt disrespected because his advice wasn't being heeded and funds were being diverted from him.

"I respect that, if you're telling me honestly that you don't think that's the best approach," DeAngelo said before asserting his upper hand. "But that's what I'm doing. That's just the way it's going to be."

The directive was clear. Dawkins had no choice, so he called Merl Code and gave him what he thought was a clear-minded assessment: Jeff DeAngelo was a fucking idiot. Paying some coaches made sense as a way to gain access to potential stars, according to Dawkins's own reasoning, with top-echelon schools like Arizona and Louisville playing multiple NBA prospects. But throwing money at relatively low-level coaches like Lamont Evans at Oklahoma State was pointless, given the rarity of professional basketball talent at the school. The model was ingenious, as Blazer had understood, but only if was pursued with discretion and specific players in mind.

There was nothing they could do to save DeAngelo from himself, Dawkins concluded. Code believed that denizens of the basketball world were going to eat DeAngelo alive and spit him out, after separating him from as much money as possible.

In multiple calls, Code said he had tried to convince DeAngelo that throwing money at coaches wouldn't lead to results, exclaiming in exasperation that DeAngelo was "just fucking raining money."

"I talked to Jeff earlier," Dawkins told Code on a call they thought was private but that the FBI was recording. Contradicting his prior strategy of paying coaches, Dawkins lamented the emphasis on that idea. "So this is how I'm going to do this, ni**a. I'm not going to introduce him to no coaches. To me, I think the whole model doesn't make sense."

"So we just going to take these fools' money?" Code asked.

"Exactly," Dawkins replied. "Exactly."

Dawkins complained to Code that he had tried to invest DeAngelo's money the "right way": old-fashioned rule breaking by paying NCAA players directly. Buying plane tickets for their parents and girlfriends to go to games, sliding them cash to buy a car in the weeks before the draft, taking them to nightclubs and strip joints. Dawkins wanted to break the rules with the method that all concerned understood and respected, not a cockamamie coach-focused approach that had been his idea in the first place but now seemed destined to fail.

Dawkins complained to Code. "If they not going to listen, then fuck it, take they money."

"I'm with you," Code replied.

"Fuck it," Dawkins said. "It is what it is."

~

During the early summer, Blazer continued his routine work for the FBI, taking repeated calls from Auburn coach Chuck Person, who was pleading for $40,000 to pay for Austin Wiley's mother to move to Auburn to be close to her son. This was a situation Blazer had often encountered during his football years, which received surprisingly scant attention. Lamont Evans touted a one-and-done prospect he was recruiting and proposed a structure using Nike's Elite Youth Basketball League to fund a deal guaranteeing the kid would attend Oklahoma State and sign with Blazer, a similar idea to that proposed by Code at Adidas. Blazer also chased a lead to try to get a meeting with an assistant at a Nike-sponsored blue-blood school, who could grant access to players consistently picked high in the NBA draft.

"Just letting you know you can't expect to pay Honda prices if you want to drive a Bentley," a coach contact told Blazer of the coach from the Nike school.

Blazer agreed that the coach was, indeed, a metaphorical Bentley, and he was happy to pay handsomely for such a relationship. As a former NCAA-enforcement official, Kobie Baker represented a particularly attractive target, in Blazer's mind, in much the same way catching a corrupt cop was more of a challenge. Baker knew the system in all its dimensions, and he required a subtle and patient approach, while the FBI was used to employing the sledgehammer of easy cash.

But SA Carpenter no longer seemed motivated about opportunities that Blazer thought would be gold mines, like Person touting his friend, the coach from Missouri, and the connection to future Denver Nugget superstar Michael Porter, texting Blazer a screenshot of the coach's contact information in early July.[6] Blazer was left to only guess that Carpenter was struggling to settle on a new strategy, given the unspoken deadline that was looming.

Early one morning after the Fourth of July weekend, Blazer was flying down to Orlando for a follow-up meeting with Kobie Baker that Rashan Michel had set up, hoping to get back on track with Baker's bribe-installment plan. Carpenter texted to say his flight was delayed and Blazer should contact SA Jason Wake to pick him up at the airport. It was a scorching-hot day in Orlando, and Blazer decided to see if he could get the sometimes-reckless junior agent to spill the beans on the state of the investigation as they drove.

"I really need to take a piss," Wake said. "I'm going to run into Dunkin' Donuts quick. I'll keep the engine running so you have AC. But if you leave me here, I'll fucking kill you."

"Don't worry," Blazer replied, laughing.

Slamming the door, Wake left Blazer contemplating the implied insult: After seven months of reliable teamwork with the FBI, did Wake really believe Blazer would jeopardize his freedom by stealing the vehicle and driving off into thin air? Abandon his family? Outrun the law? Blazer wasn't a fugitive, and he didn't appreciate being talked to like a common criminal, particularly by someone he held in low regard.

---

6   Porter suffered a back injury in college and dropped to the fourteenth selection in the 2018 draft, but he proved to be an outstanding player for the Nuggets, signing a maximum contract extension in 2021 that will potentially earn him more than $200 million.

"As soon as Jason got back in the SUV, I started to probe him for information," Blazer remembered. "I casually asked how long he thought the case would keep going, especially after the NBA draft meeting. I told him that Scott said the lawyers could wrap the case up at any moment and he'd have to comply, no matter how promising the future prospects looked."

"It's not up to them," Wake barked. "They don't arrest anyone—we do. If the leads continue, the case continues."

Unconvinced, Blazer kept going, asking about the elements of the crimes being committed. What were the specific crimes to be charged? Who were the victims? Wake replied that the coaches seemed to think they were breaking only NCAA rules, not criminal laws. He told Blazer that AUSA Boone wanted recordings of in-person meetings with coaches and players accepting large sums of cash in front of surveillance cameras, as they'd done with Person and Evans.

"I then asked him what he thought the lasting results of the case would be once the story broke," Blazer recalled. "He guessed that convicting a handful of coaches might get rid of corruption for ten years, but then it would come back. I said that unless people went to prison, nothing would change. We both agreed that the NCAA was useless. Jason said that maybe I could get a gig as a consultant to the NCAA after the investigation was over. All I could think was that Scott would have killed Jason if he knew he'd shared his thoughts about the case with me."

Carpenter finally arrived, climbing into the SUV, and they went to rendezvous with DeAngelo, who was driving a brand-new forest-green Range Rover—another pointless extravagance, considering the meeting was set for a hotel restaurant. The sit-down with Kobie Baker and Rashan Michel at the airport Marriott didn't go as planned. Blazer cut through the small talk and brought up Alabama's Collin Sexton, a future Cleveland Cavalier. Baker said Sexton was definitely a one-and-done prospect, who would be with Bama for his freshman season, then go high in the draft. Baker said the school had helped Sexton obtain a $10 million insurance policy in case his career was ended due to injury while playing college basketball and that he was very close with the father, Darnell, but that Baker had "played it cool" with the prospect and he wasn't being paid to play.

Michel chimed in that Kentucky paid top prospects half a million to commit, but Baker seemed to want DeAngelo to think he didn't get involved in that kind of dealing. Then Baker once again turned to the panel he was putting together to give Alabama's star players advice on obtaining management, inviting Blazer, while allowing that the actual event was pointless but that it provided a chance to personally meet players and underscore which financial advisers were in the circle of trust at Alabama. Collin Sexton's rookie contract would potentially be worth more than $20 million, making him an extremely attractive prospect to a financial adviser, and Baker let it be known he was prepared to guide the way for that to happen "organically," as he put it, which was another of saying without the player's knowledge.[7]

"Kobie was ready to connect us to Collin Sexton at a minimum," Blazer recalled. "All we had to do was stop fucking around with Kobie and confirm the details. I couldn't stress enough to the FBI the power someone in Kobie Baker's position wielded. If only they had been in my shoes when I was trying to sign football players. I had seen it with Coach Johnson at Penn State. More important than giving me access to the kids, Coach Johnson could knock out the competition. The kids trusted him blindly. He held their future in the palm of his hand. Kobie didn't have to get into specifics about a rival financial adviser. All he had to do was raise an eyebrow and say he'd heard the person had a bad reputation. I had seen how easily influenced the players were. They wouldn't ask for proof. They would simply go dark on the financial adviser, even if they were getting money from him.

---

7   Sexton's four-year contract with the Cleveland Cavaliers was indeed worth more than $20 million.

"Kobie wasn't just a coach. He was an athletic director at Alabama. When a player was told that an agent or an adviser was crooked, they assumed it came from the highest levels of the school and had been fully researched. The mere act of sending a letter telling an adviser to back off implied that the adviser had acted in an unscrupulous manner. Credibility and legitimacy meant everything.

"In Orlando, Kobie said that he'd sent exactly that kind of cease and desist letter to a financial adviser trying to get close to Collin Sexton. Kobie could make or break a relationship with one word. He'd weaponized his position very well. Another part of his pitch was that he still had influential friends at NCAA enforcement from his time working there. A call from Kobie and the NCAA would look the other way, was the implication. Kobie wasn't like the other coaches. He was the most sophisticated participant we'd encountered. I just hoped the FBI understood what an attractive opportunity we had with Kobie in our pocket."

Toward the end of the meeting, DeAngelo still hadn't taken the initiative to talk about the financial structure Blazer had discussed with Baker weeks earlier in Birmingham. Blazer couldn't understand what DeAngelo was doing by refusing to talk about the cash that everyone knew Baker was awaiting. What was DeAngelo thinking? Blazer wondered as the waitress took away their dishes and they discussed meeting again in New York in August, when Alabama traveled there en route to play a series of exhibition games in Canada. Baker wasn't going to bring up the subject of money himself, and Blazer assumed they all knew this was the deal when DeAngelo was in charge of the cash.

The meal over, the group walked to the entrance of the hotel, where uneasy silence and pointless banter ensued until DeAngelo handed Michel an envelope with $2,000. This left Baker lurking in the hallway, behind Michel, peeking over his shoulder and watching the transaction with apparent envy and consternation. Taking up the cue, Michel looked expectantly at DeAngelo, waiting for the other envelope, but it wasn't produced, to Blazer's astonishment. DeAngelo had the $5,000 in cash in his pocket, all counted and ready for delivery. Instead, Michel and Baker walked away, shoulders slumped in disappointment.

"It all happened so fast that I followed Jeff's lead and said nothing," Blazer recalled. "But I was pissed. Why wouldn't Jeff give the money to Kobie, or give it to Rashan to give to Kobie? Or give it to me to give it to them? Or just say what was necessary for Kobie to admit he was waiting for a payment? After they were gone, Jeff told me that he didn't think Kobie had done or said enough to warrant the payment. I couldn't believe it. Did he forget that I'd already paid Kobie in Birmingham? Jeff said Kobie was coming to New York soon, and we could pay him then. But the damage was done. Kobie wasn't stupid. He was never going to come out and ask Jeff or me for money, especially when he was meeting Jeff for the first time. We had an agreement, and everyone was on the same page—except Jeff. Hell, even Chuck Person wouldn't say, 'Do you have my money?' when I made a payment. Jeff made me look like a fool. But I figured that maybe there was a bigger strategy at play. I didn't want to do anything to jeopardize Kobie as part of the investigation. I didn't want the deal to die on the vine because of Jeff's stupidity."

Minutes after the meeting ended, an enraged Rashan Michel called Blazer, screaming about the athletic director not receiving the expected envelope. The cooperator tried to explain that DeAngelo wasn't a mind reader, and there had been no explicit indication about getting cash that day—an excuse that Blazer knew bordered on idiotic. Of course, the whole point of getting together in person in Florida had been to hand deliver the envelope, as all the parties understood perfectly well. Why else fly to Orlando in the first place? The illicit nature of the relationship made meeting in person imperative.

In the following days, Michel remained incensed, repeatedly texting and calling late into the night, often seemingly after consuming more than a couple of cocktails, cursing at Blazer and threatening to end the relationship entirely. Blazer reassured him that Baker would get paid. DeAngelo was just a fool, Blazer told Michel, and he didn't know how the business operated, promising that it wouldn't happen again and offering to pay his expenses for the trip up to New York in August, confident that the promise of money would lure Michel back into the fold. For months, Michel had been pushing to strengthen the relationship—"We got to go from eating pussy to straight-up fucking," was how the tailor had put it—but now the entire premise was in peril, and Blazer felt the urge to figure out a solution.

Then, on a call with DeAngelo, Michel began to angrily question where the money was "really" coming from, alleging that DeAngelo was a drug dealer laundering the cash. DeAngelo calmly replied that the money came from his real estate investments, but a panicked Michel said he didn't want anything to do with DeAngelo's illegal business, threatening to wire back all the cash he'd received—an empty threat, Blazer believed.

"I knew that my cooperation wasn't supposed to be measured by the success or failure of the final result of the investigation," Blazer recalled. "But in my heart, I'd come to really care about the outcome. I was only supposed to do what I was told—to go where I was told and say what I was told to say. But that wasn't how I'm built. I was following orders when I called Rashan to calm him down, but the words and thoughts were mine. I had to get him into a rational conversation and figure out how to make that happen. If I just let it go and that line of investigation died, it would be less work on my part, but that wasn't the end result I wanted.

"I started to question a lot of decisions that were being made in the investigation. Focusing on Christian Dawkins was the easiest path, but it wasn't the most promising or impactful lead that we had, I believed. I knew we couldn't bring the whole world of amateur sports down, but I also knew there were a lot more ways to chase leads up the NCAA hierarchy. Over time, Scott and I talked hundreds of times about strategy and tactics. I appreciated when he asked for my opinion, even if the decisions weren't mine to make. I felt like I was making a difference."

A week after the trip to Florida, on the morning on July 11, 2017, SA Carpenter called with something he wanted to discuss. Blazer's stomach sank, but it turned out there was another initiative that had been looming in the background for weeks. That July, as usual, the NBA Summer League was taking place in Las Vegas, Nevada, a tournament where the pro teams scouted unsigned prospects, rookies, and G Leaguers, making it an excellent event for a hustler like Christian Dawkins to prospect for potential clients. Carpenter told Blazer that Dawkins had attended the Summer League and met with Merl Code to talk about a one-and-done high school senior they were trying to recruit to the Adidas-sponsored Louisville Cardinals. Blazer's ear perked up; the Cardinals were coached by Rick Pitino.

Carpenter explained that the player's father was going to be paid $100,000 by Adidas when he declared for Louisville. The sneaker company sponsored the school, pouring nearly $10 million a year into the college's coffers in return for the players wearing its gear—including a cool $2 million that went to Pitino personally. But it was unclear how Code could get cash to the player's father without creating a paper trail pointing to the use of corporate Adidas funds in breach of NCAA rules. This was the kind of dilemma that abounded in the amateur system, with corrupt figures contorting themselves pretzel-like to create the appearance of legitimacy. Along the way, a string of laws was likely being broken, including tax and corporate regulations. Not coincidentally, it was the kind of dilemma that LOYD was tailor made to quietly resolve to the satisfaction of all concerned—or at least, those in the know.

In Vegas, Carpenter said Code had asked Dawkins if LOYD would be willing to pay the first installment of $25,000 to the player, supposedly as a thirty-day loan, to provide Adidas with enough time to set up a front company that would produce fraudulent invoices for the sneaker company. Carpenter said that Adidas would repay the loan once the deal was funded, apparently giving LOYD the rights to represent the player in return for a short-term liquidity facility. The reality was that Dawkins didn't have the authority to make that kind of payment, so Code was really asking him to ask DeAngelo for LOYD to fund the deal.

Carpenter asked Blazer for his opinion on this development. Blazer explained that, in his opinion, the so-called "loan" to the player would never be repaid; the money was as good as gone once the FBI paid out. Blazer told Carpenter the money would be considered an investment by all, with no recourse if the player eventually decided to hire a different financial adviser; this was a cost of doing business. Blazer added that there was no chance Merl Code would take the risk of carrying cash back to DeAngelo to repay the sham loan.

This development was very exciting for Blazer. He told Carpenter he'd known that all kinds of machinations took place between the colleges and sneaker companies like Nike and Adidas, but he never thought he'd have the chance to see firsthand how it actually worked. The FBI's money had placed the investigation at the white-hot center of college sports, in the corridors of power, where five-star recruits were brokered by hustlers who conspired with sneaker-company executives to rig the sport.

When Christian Dawkins had bragged about his connections with Pitino, including meeting with him personally, it had seemed like puffery, but Blazer began to wonder if it contained some truth. Surveying the leverage that the FBI would have in the wake of the $25,000 payment, Blazer wondered aloud how high up the Adidas corporate ladder the conspiracy went. Clearly Code wasn't acting on his own volition, and he would need the connivance of a variety of executives, likely including his boss. Blazer asked if they could demand a meeting with higher Adidas officials. It seemed like a reasonable request, and the FBI recording that encounter would be devastating.

In addition to the $25,000, Carpenter then told Blazer that Code had decided his monthly retainer should be $9,500 for his "consulting services," up from the $8,000 he had demanded before. Blazer burst out laughing. The amount was beyond excessive.

"Is the consulting fee for deals he brings to us in addition to the monthly amount?" Blazer asked, amazed. "I'd prefer for us to assist with this transaction, then be a resource for similar deals. Stepping in for him on this deal would be worth its weight in gold to him. But no fucking way on the monthly ask. If we agree to that, they'll know one hundred percent that we aren't for real."

Two days later, Jeff DeAngelo traveled to Munish Sood's office in Princeton, New Jersey, delivering $25,000 in cash. In accordance with a request from Dawkins, $5,600 was set aside to cover his expenses incurred in recruiting the player, and arrangements were made for a clandestine rendezvous between Sood and the father of the athlete near LaGuardia Airport in New York City. The once supposedly legitimate Sood, the former chairman of the board of a regional bank, was now acting like a drug mule in an illegal transaction, engaging in secret trysts to hand over bags of illicit money to the father of a high school basketball player.

Drawn like a moth to a flame by the prospect of money and professional sports, Sood was smart enough to know that he had entered an entirely new area of risk. Handing over large sums of cash to the parents of basketball players wasn't a sustainable plan, Sood had to know.

"I did it," Sood told Dawkins. "It's done. But I'm not doing it again."

In the interim, the identity of the player involved had emerged: Brian "Tugs" Bowen II, from Saginaw, Michigan, the hometown of Christian Dawkins. As the details came out, events from the past started to make sense to Blazer. Merl Code had talked about a player during their first encounter, likely when the plan was germinating. Blazer learned that in the days before the yacht meeting in June, Bowen had committed to Louisville, a last-minute recruiting coup for Pitino that had appeared suspect—because it had been. Bowen had never identified Louisville as a school he was considering, but Dawkins had boasted about knowing Pitino at the yacht meeting. Blazer reasoned that Dawkins and Code had been on the hook for money for Bowen, because the decision to go to Louisville had been based on the money promised, and if they hadn't delivered, the family might have retaliated, offering an explanation for the urgency about securing funding.

"We got lucky on this one," Pitino had said to the press at the time of Bowen signing with Louisville. "In my forty years of coaching, this is the luckiest I've been."

Blazer told Carpenter they should get Adidas and the Louisville coaches to do the same thing again, with different players. Blazer also wanted to try the same structure with the other Adidas schools Code had mentioned at their last meeting: Indiana, Arizona State, Kansas, to name just a few. Lamont Evans had mentioned a connection at Nike interested in a similar deal, exposing Oklahoma State, Alabama, Arkansas, Georgia, Kentucky, Tennessee, and LSU, among others. Now that the FBI understood how to approach sneaker companies, the entire facade of NCAA sports could be revealed for what it was: a lie.

"I was able to give Scott advice, and I was kept in the loop," Blazer recalled. "But I wasn't asked to engage with Dawkins or even Sood on behalf of Jeff. The FBI had a direct line by then because of LOYD, but Jeff didn't know how to guide the situation effectively. It seemed to me that the FBI didn't recognize the leverage they had, or they simply wanted to take the easiest and shortest route to get a token result. They didn't see what was right in front of their eyes. To my knowledge, no one ever tried to figure out what Louisville coach or coaches were involved with the Bowen deal and at what level. It was completely out of character and downright suspicious for Jeff DeAngelo not to follow up with coaching introductions at Louisville. Why wasn't Jeff instructed to ask about the coach connection when he was talking to Dawkins? We were well within our rights to ask for a sit-down with Rick Pitino, after paying out twenty-five grand for a five-star Louisville recruit. And what about Merl Code and Adidas, and asking about the role of his boss, the head of marketing, Jim Gatto? Why weren't we making an effort to see if we could offer help to Adidas for other players? Adidas had opened a line of credit with us, which gave us the ability to peek behind the curtain and see how brands influenced the scheme.

"The criminal hierarchy was still developing, and there were lots of new leads. It seemed like there were avenues that would lead to the head coaches at the biggest programs. The so-called 'blue blood' schools were definitely active in this area. But the FBI and the Southern District weren't allowing the investigation to mature enough to understand who the actual perpetrators were or the nature of their motivations and the scope of the wrongdoing across all of college sports."

~

Escape from the investigation was a rare treat for Blazer, as the case devoured his waking hours for months, and he relished watching his son at a soccer camp outside Philadelphia the following weekend, trying not to think too much about his forthcoming encounter with AUSA Boone. Days later, driving to watch his son play a sunny Saturday-afternoon game back home, he looked forward to the camaraderie with the other soccer dads, normalcy that provided solace and sanity. As Blazer stopped at a light, his phone rang. He checked the unfamiliar number: the area code was New York City, likely a Brooklyn line. Blazer figured it could be one of the FBI agents calling from their home phone, and he nearly took the call, but he hesitated and let the call go to voicemail.

"I'm looking for Mr. Blazer, Marty Blazer," the woman on the message said when Blazer played it moments later.

In disbelief, Blazer listened as the caller identified herself as Rebecca O'Brien from the *Wall Street Journal*. She said she was reporting on a story about the FBI's investigation of corruption in college basketball and the involvement of Division I coaches, and she wanted to talk to him—on or off the record. Blazer had never heard of O'Brien, but he was astounded to hear her lay out a scenario that closely matched the nature of the investigation; she clearly wasn't fully informed, but she was close enough to the truth to terrify him. There was a leak in the Department of Justice, Blazer believed, and if he were suspected of talking to the press, he would be in extreme peril—and so would the case.

Blazer's first priority was to make sure the FBI and AUSA Boone knew beyond a doubt that he hadn't talked to the press or instigated any communication with anyone else. Only Blazer's wife and attorney knew what he was up to, and even that was only in vague and general terms; not even his children knew about their father's activities with law enforcement. He frantically dialed and redialed SA Carpenter's cell phone, failing to reach him. Blazer recounted how all the agents greeting him at the Southern District's Manhattan offices had seemed like a compliment, at the time, but it had also made it evident that there was widespread awareness of his activities throughout federal law enforcement in Manhattan. Were other reporters briefed? Was the story going to run even if Blazer didn't talk? What was going to be the impact on an investigation that already seemed to be on a tight and arbitrary deadline?

"The case was about to be spiked because of a fucking leak somewhere at their end," Blazer remembered. "I wasn't taking blame for their stupidity."

SA Carpenter was out on a boat, fishing, but when he and Blazer finally spoke that afternoon, he told Blazer not to worry. Leaks like the one to the *Wall Street Journal* were "not uncommon," he said, an assertion Blazer found plausible if not very reassuring. The following day, AUSA Boone reached out to Blazer's attorney and told him to tell his client not to speak to the press. Blazer hardly needed the guidance; there was no way on earth he was going to talk to any reporter. Never, ever, not until the case was over—whatever that now meant.

"If Rebecca O'Brien had published at the time, it would've been like a meteor crashing into my world," Blazer said. "In the end, she called me one more time, then she went quiet. She was the first to break the story when the investigation finally went public, so I figured maybe that's how she was silenced. All I knew was that no story ran, but another ticking time bomb had been lit under the investigation."

That week, Blazer had the next interview with AUSA Boone, and it wasn't as awful as the earlier encounters. Blazer repeated the obvious truths about his years working as a financial adviser for NFL players: every single recruit he had signed had been paid hot dog money, in one amount or another.

Once again, Boone didn't bring up Blazer's role in the ongoing investigation or the opportunity to go up the chains of power at Adidas and Louisville. The FBI agents in attendance sat mutely listening to Blazer describe his illicit payments to UNC football players in 2010. Blazer felt a cloud of despair descend as he recited all the lunacy of the years he'd run wild, deeds that seemed so far away from his current reality. Over the three years he'd cooperated with the government, Blazer had developed his superpower, wishing away the consequences of his misappropriating more than $2 million from players, hoping—somehow, someway—the government would let him walk free.

As AUSA Boone rose from the table to depart, he said, "The next step is, we're going to work up the plea." A reality that had been obvious to the prosecutor even while Blazer was still in denial.

Blazer realized he would forever be a federal felon, and it hit him like a slap in the face. Retiring with SAs Carpenter, DeAngelo, and Wake to a nearby tavern—the same one he'd gone to with his lawyers after his first proffer years earlier—talking about the investigation helped him to avoid obsessing about having to appear in court and say the word *guilty* to the judge, his family, the world.

The update from Carpenter was that the investigation was stalled. They had sent Jeff DeAngelo into the field on his own to communicate with Dawkins and Sood, but there was no further progress. Book Richardson of Arizona had been in touch with them, taking another $15,000 the week before and promising to deliver players when DeAngelo came to Tucson, but otherwise, Dawkins wasn't delivering on the coaches and relationships he'd promised.

"You guys just don't know what the fuck you're doing," Blazer wanted to say. "You don't know how to ask."

Blazer explained that if he wasn't at the meetings pressing Dawkins to deliver coaches, Dawkins would take the FBI's money and do whatever he wanted with it. Dawkins wasn't buying into the model, Blazer said, confirming that the FBI had recorded, in a call with Code, where Dawkins said he wasn't going to provide introductions to any coaches.

DeAngelo listened in silence. His years in the military and FBI had shaped his mind to institutions and rules and discipline. In college sports, everyone knew the rules were made to be broken, and deception and backstabbing were standard operating procedures. Blazer told the FBI agents that Dawkins believed giving coaches money wasn't necessary unless it was for a specific recruit or player. To Dawkins's way of thinking, the more money he gave to coaches, the less there was for him to keep. Blazer said the key to getting Dawkins to take action on coaches was to motivate Munish Sood. Blazer explained that they needed Sood to tell Dawkins to get the coaches he'd promised at the yacht meeting, or the gravy train would come to a screeching halt. Forever. Period. And the way to pressure Sood, Blazer explained, was to rely on none other than Marty Blazer.

"Munish hasn't got his money back yet," Blazer said. "He needs to get his money back. If Jeff pulls out, Dawkins becomes Munish's problem, and he can't have that. You need to give me the power to scare the shit [out] of Munish."

Permission was granted.

Blazer texted Sood on July 21, at 9:27 a.m.: Yo brother hit me up when u can just got off the phone w Lamont about a player.

Sood replied immediately, biting at the carrot that Blazer had offered, oblivious to the existence of a stick. When Blazer spoke with Sood, he told him that he'd had a call with Lamont Evans, the OSU coach who had said he had a connection to Nike. Blazer had been told by Lamont Evans that there was bad blood between the coach and Christian Dawkins, and while the details weren't clear, it seemed that other coaches were getting recruits from Dawkins that Evans wanted for OSU.

"Christian's upset because he's trying to get in touch with Lamont [Evans] to get the player to sign with LOYD," Sood said.

"I told you Christian needed to treat Lamont better, didn't I?" Blazer replied. "Christian is fucking around and won't even try to help Lamont while he's sending recruits to other schools. Now he expects Lamont to roll over and just give him the player for nothing? . . . Christian should know better. I warned him about this a month ago. He's got Jeff ready to pull the plug on funding LOYD, he's so pissed off. All the work you and I put in, he's about to fuck up this whole deal. Christian needs to stop playing fucking games."

Sood laughed nervously. Blazer had hit a pressure point. Sood had invested significant sums in Dawkins—money he had yet to receive any returns on—and the idea that Dawkins could sabotage the LOYD deal simply by angering Jeff DeAngelo was justifiably scary. Blazer poured it on, adding that DeAngelo was getting sick of the way Dawkins conducted himself. Blazer understood from his own experience that, above all else, upsetting the man with the money was a disaster.

"Christian's ego gets in the way," Sood said. "That's the problem with him and Lamont. Christian needs to pick up the phone and kiss

Lamont's ass a little more . . . Should I call Lamont? What did Christian do to make Jeff so upset?"

Blazer said he believed he could handle the situation with Lamont Evans, but DeAngelo's active disappointment and disaffection was much more consequential. Dawkins would only do more damage if he reached out to DeAngelo, Blazer said, forcing an in-person meeting between Evans and Dawkins as part of a larger strategy of getting coaches to meet with the FBI undercover.

"You know Jeff is fixated on building the business through relationships with coaches," Blazer told Sood. "Honestly, Munish, I know I created this monster, but the fact of the matter is that I've brought more coaches to Jeff than Christian. Jeff didn't have to drop twenty-five grand in my lap for me to do it either. Jeff put twenty grand in Book's hands without one player meeting set up. You know Book bragged that he could do it on the spot, but nothing is happening. Where is Deandre Ayton? Jeff told me he's starting to feel like he's being played."

Blazer paused, letting the stark implications settle in.

"We both know the game," he said. "Just don't let Christian ruin this for us, man. Even if it ain't what he thinks we need to do, Christian better get some fucking coaches on board, whatever it takes."

Sood sighed. "I'm going to kill this kid. I'll get it handled, chief. Do you know how many coaches it will take to make Jeff happy?"

"In reality, he's expecting everyone on Christian's list," Blazer said. "At least a few of them by now, right? Anything is better than what's been happening."

Sood agreed to redouble his efforts, knowing that Dawkins would be resistant and contemptuous of DeAngelo and Blazer.

"We don't need a hundred coaches," Blazer told Sood. "We just need a handful to make Jeff happy. Tell Christian he has to give Jeff what he wants, even if he doesn't think it's what he needs."

Blazer said he could handle DeAngelo for a while, but action needed to be taken immediately. The pair then discussed the forthcoming grassroots event in Las Vegas and how it would be a convenient place to set up the encounters, with coaches from the major college programs in Vegas to scout the nation's top high school talent. Blazer said he'd also work on convincing Evans to sit down with Dawkins in Las Vegas so they could settle their differences and focus on the core business for LOYD.

The fear of losing DeAngelo's mother lode of money and all that it promised was enough to prompt Sood into action. The pieces all relied on each other, like dominoes set in a row, and if constructed in the correct manner, the way they triggered the next response was predictable, even kind of beautiful. The way to ask for coaches wasn't to repeatedly ask Dawkins robotically like DeAngelo had been doing; they needed to threaten Sood, in clear and direct terms, and thus put pressure on Dawkins and then, in turn, the highly connected Merl Code.

In the upside-down world of college sports, Sood couldn't directly demand action from Dawkins. First, he had to commiserate with the young businessman, agreeing with his complaints that DeAngelo's approach didn't conform with best or even normal practices. Sood set out to guide Dawkins to the right conclusion.

"Jeff is going to fuck this whole deal up, Munish," Dawkins told Sood when he called.

"Why? What happened?"

"He keeps talking about how he wants to meet kids," Dawkins said. "He wants to meet parents. It's like, 'What are you going to talk to them about, Jeff?'"

"All right, I'll have to intervene," Sood said.

"Honestly, I'm starting to think that maybe I'll just get somebody to fucking give him his money back," Dawkins said. "Because he doesn't understand it."

"Yeah," Sood agreed.

"He doesn't understand that, like, you're not in the circle, bro," Dawkins said. "You're at the lunch table across from the cool kids.

People are going to think that, honestly, that they're being set up. That's what I'm trying to figure out. Why the fuck does he care so much? I almost want to figure out if this motherfucker is trying to do some crazy shit."

Sood pretended to sympathize with Dawkins, but following Blazer's exhortations, he insisted that Dawkins arrange for DeAngelo to meet coaches. In despair, Dawkins called Merl Code of Adidas to commiserate. Code reluctantly agreed that he would arrange for coaches to see DeAngelo, but he was growing increasingly wary of the arrangement and what lurked beneath the surface.

Dawkins knew lots of coaches, but that didn't mean he could convince them to meet with a shadowy operator like DeAngelo, particularly since no one had heard of the mysterious investor before. Dawkins had to rely on the far more connected and respected Code to convince coaches to go along with the seemingly strange plans for LOYD. But not without a word of warning from the sneaker executive.

"You and I, to protect ourselves—and I'm saying this as a guy who's real skeptical about this shit—you and I need to get some background information on Jeff and this chick," Code said to Dawkins, both overlooking Blazer's background and the elephantine question of the nature of his relationship with Jeff DeAngelo and Jill Bailey.

"Okay," Dawkins said.

"I'm just telling you to protect your own ass," Code said. "Where does she come from? Where does her money come from? We need to do some real digging. I don't want to be in no bullshit."

"I agree with you a thousand percent," Dawkins concurred.

"You got to be extra cautious about who you're associating with," Code told Dawkins, particularly in light of his recent Uber-fraud scandal. "They ain't cutting me no check for shit. They gonna pay you, and you gonna pay me. Until I feel good about these folks, I don't know them. I'm looking up Jeff DeAngelo and can't find nothing on him, and that shit is really concerning me."

"I got to get a private investigator or some shit like that," Dawkins agreed.

Instead of hiring an actual investigator, Dawkins took a short-cut—or claimed he did. He knew an older man who'd worked for the DEA for decades, and so he asked him to run a background check on DeAngelo and Bailey. The acquaintance claimed that he'd asked a contact in the FBI to see if the names popped on the bureau's criminal computer files, and they both came back clean—because both were assumed aliases, and that reality wasn't going to turn up in a cursory check. In truth, it was unlikely that an FBI agent would leave a digital footprint on the bureau's computer system showing he'd searched for the names of DeAngelo and Bailey; the risk of discovery was too high, and the so-called friend was almost certainly mollifying Dawkins by telling him what he wanted to hear, if indeed the friend even existed.

Despite all the warning signs, Dawkins was going to move forward; the hustler was going to hustle DeAngelo—or so he thought.

～

Getting Rashan Michel back on board was proving extremely expensive after Kobie Baker had been stiffed at the meeting in Florida. Without consulting Blazer, the FBI came up with the absurd idea of paying Michel $50,000 as a kind of retainer, doled out in four installments, to provide an incentive to resuscitate the Kobie Baker lead. The amount of money was so ridiculous, Blazer's biggest fear was that Dawkins and Sood and others would hear about it and instantly know that Michel—who had a dubious reputation at best—wasn't worth a fraction of that amount, not for any rational business purpose, and it would only serve to further nurture doubts about DeAngelo's motives.

Sitting with the FBI agents in a vehicle in Midtown Manhattan on a rainy Monday in July, Blazer waited to meet with Michel. The tension between SA Carpenter and the increasingly boneheaded undercover

DeAngelo boiled over. DeAngelo was idling in the Maserati again, a prop that had no value to the operation that day—the meeting would be held in a bar on the forty-eighth floor of a hotel—but he was so enamored with his luxury rides that he wanted Carpenter and Blazer to walk through the rain to get in his car to strategize, not the other way around. The senior FBI agent wasn't amused, as DeAngelo finally deferred and trudged over to Carpenter's Jeep, to Blazer's amusement. Carpenter finally snapped, pointing out how DeAngelo's incompetence had forced them to spend the time and money on another meeting with the always-infuriating Michel.

"Bro, why are you making this so hard?" Carpenter barked, as the handsome but not very bright DeAngelo stepped into the vehicle looking sheepish. "Why are you trying to fuck up my whole week right now?"

Over a vodka and cranberry juice at the Marriott's revolving rooftop bar, Michel accepted $12,500 in cash for himself and $10,000 to pass along to Kobie Baker. As Blazer and DeAngelo sat with Michel, the conversation veered from his views on his sworn path of celibacy to his consequential compulsion to masturbate—truly too much information, all of it being recorded by grimacing FBI agents. Blazer had repeatedly been told by coaches that they didn't want to deal with Michel, given his capacity to fly off the handle, only for them to continue to do business with him. In a way, Michel was essentially responsible for the whole operation, from his introduction of Dawkins to Person and Kobie Baker.

Under Michel's guidance, Baker was back in line but at a big and risky price. Rushing through the rain to catch his flight to his son's fifteenth birthday dinner, Blazer made it to his gate with seconds to spare. Taking his place at the head of the dinner table in suburban Pittsburgh that evening, wondering where he'd be for his son's sixteenth birthday, Blazer was again filled with mixed emotions about his life as an informant. With thousands of phone calls, countless text threads, and a schedule that would shame many salesmen, the case consumed Blazer's existence—an isolating reality.

"The kids were oblivious to what I was doing," Blazer recalled. "They just thought they had a father who had to travel a lot for work. I was an expert at internalizing the struggle I was going through. Trish knew what I was up to, but none of the details. With her, I tried to over-compensate by helping out when I was home and being a super-present dad. I knew that when I ran out of savings and I couldn't pay the bills anymore, the shit was going to hit the fan with Trish.

"In every way, cooperation was a game of inches for me. I had very little power over my fate, so every tiny victory—like getting home in time to celebrate Connor's birthday—was crucial for my psyche. It was maintaining the semblance of normality. It was similar to when I was conducting the movie-shell game, all the different faces I had to keep up as I had to hide what was really going on inside. I had had a heart attack, and I knew the stress was terrible for my body. I worried I could keel over at any time. I wasn't living a double life—it was a triple life, and I really don't know how I survived with all the stress and chaos, but I was doing all I could to keep my mind strong."

~

By late July, with Merl Code's guidance, Dawkins had provided DeAngelo and Blazer with a long list of coaches scheduled to meet with the LOYD team in Las Vegas. But Code wouldn't be in Vegas, seemingly displaying the common sense to distance himself from the increasingly suspect meetings. In Code's absence, Carpenter told Blazer they would meet with another senior Adidas executive.

Sood had committed to Vegas, but there were signs he was getting more and more afraid of what was happening with Blazer and DeAngelo and the giant bricks of cash changing hands. In the lead-up to Vegas, Sood and Merl Code arranged for a call with DeAngelo to clarify that the coaches who would come to meetings in Las Vegas wouldn't accept cash because they didn't know the investor. The coaches would have a courtesy meeting with DeAngelo because Code and Dawkins had vouched for him, but they certainly wouldn't be interested in receiving monthly payments in the way the FBI undercover had proposed.

Despite Sood's growing wariness, Blazer continued to work on him, enticing him with the prospect of landing big clients and getting Lamont Evans back on the hook. Blazer assumed that Sood had been spooked by his role in the extremely sketchy operation to hand over $25,000 in cash to Brian Bowen's father weeks earlier as part of the deal to get him to sign with Louisville. It had been a patently illegal transaction that broke all kinds of banking, securities, and tax laws, at the very least. Keeping Sood committed to Vegas required cajoling and hand-holding, like Blazer texting him that he'd booked hotel suites on the Strip for himself, Sood, and Evans. The suites would be comped for the trio by DeAngelo, part of Blazer's efforts to show he had valuable connections.

U all set for fri? Blazer texted Sood on July 25, the eve of the trip to Vegas. Got u set at Palazzo w me n Lamont. All in high-end suites.

Sorry can't make it, Sood texted.

Before Blazer could reply, Sood sent another text: Signing a new client.

The sudden cold feet didn't surprise Blazer. Sood was lying, Blazer believed, but it didn't really matter: Sood was already in too deep; no matter what he did, the last-minute attempt to distance himself from what was about to unfold wouldn't work.

CHAPTER FOURTEEN

Viva Las Vegas

The Adidas Summer Championship was scheduled to take place July 26–30, a grassroots tournament featuring the best high school–age basketball players in the country. The rosters would be packed with potential NBA-level talent, including future New Orleans Pelican superstar Zion Williamson, Boston Celtic–to-be Romeo Langford, and one-day New York Knick Immanuel Quickley. The amount of potential money the long-limbed teenagers represented was incredible, with Williamson alone likely a $500 million industry.

The combination of the louche sleaze of Vegas with the oily college basketball coaches, scouts, and scammers who descended on the tournament made it an irresistible setting for the crescendo of the opera Blazer had been conducting for months.

Arriving in Las Vegas for the tournament, Blazer made his way to the Palazzo at the Venetian on the Strip to meet SA Wake and pay for the suites the FBI insisted he book for himself and Lamont Evans. Wake turned up at the VIP check-in carrying a black American Express credit card in Jeff DeAngelo's undercover name, seeming proud of the fact that the government had the power to get a card issued.

The operation would be conducted at the five-star Cosmopolitan, in yet another giant government-booked suite. Riding together in a cab to the Cosmopolitan, SA Wake instructed Blazer to walk ten paces behind him through the lobby. Blazer cooperated but ultimately ended up on the same elevator. Then the FBI agent instructed him to stay behind when they reached the sixty-second floor, where there was no one else in the hallway.

"It was like being in a spy-spoof movie with the over-the-top cloak-and-dagger," Blazer recalled. "The FBI agent would hide behind pillars and avoid making eye contact with me, even though he stood out like a sore thumb . . . in his khakis and polo shirt, with the short haircut and stiff manners."

The Chelsea Suite on the sixty-first floor of the Cosmopolitan was three thousand square feet of opulence, with a towering view of Las Vegas and a sleek dining table that could seat ten. As ever, the wet bar and Sub-Zero fridge were packed with bottles of premium alcohol. The bureau's agents set up their surveillance control room in the most distant of three large bedrooms.

A senior FBI agent had been hovering over the investigation for months. Blazer knew him by only his first name: Brian. He was the short agent who had been part of the surveillance team on the yacht, dominating proceedings by asserting his superior rank.

"Brian was bouncing off the walls like he'd just drunk a case of Red Bull," Blazer recalled. "I couldn't figure out what the hell he was doing in Vegas. He hadn't come on any of our previous trips outside of New York. It had to be the sexiness of the case—the suite was like a dreamscape for an investigation."

An FBI agent from the Vegas office had also been assigned to the operation, but his duties seemed to consist of ordering room service and watching movies on the massive flat-screen TV.

With the team in place, the first coach meeting was set for ten thirty that night. Blazer was still operating on East Coast time, so for him it felt like one thirty in the morning, and he was wiped out before the operation had even begun. Dawkins had told DeAngelo that the coach to be introduced this time would function as the mule to deliver the cash for the player's mother. In anticipation of the encounter, Blazer had told the FBI agents that Merl Code had opened the floodgates, and now that they seemed to have his trust, there was no limit to what might happen.

Putting his game face on, Blazer poured himself a glass of Macallan—neat—and took a seat at the bar while the team manned their stations. They were anticipating one of the leading assistant coaches at Louisville, so when Dawkins entered in the company of two white men who looked to be in their late twenties, the team was surprised. Jordan Fair was a lanky former college point guard turned junior assistant for Louisville, and the pudgy, tall Brad Augustine ran a grassroots program in Florida called 1 Family. Fair and Augustine took seats on couches around the extra-long coffee table.

The suite had to be making an impression on Dawkins and his companions, but they feigned indifference. Indeed, the suite *had* sent a strong and unmistakable message to Dawkins, as he would later admit, that there was something deeply wrong with what was happening in Vegas. There was simply no way LOYD could afford to pay for the suite and all the liquor and champagne; the company hadn't made a cent yet. The only explanation, as Dawkins told Sood on a call during his time in Vegas, was that DeAngelo was connected to organized crime. If DeAngelo wasn't laundering money, the scene made no sense. But still, Dawkins pressed on, eager to impress DeAngelo.

In the suite, Blazer remained seated at the bar, nursing his single malt and watching carefully as Augustine breezily described 1 Family as a major program in Orlando that routinely sent players to Division I college programs. The sneaker sponsor of 1 Family was Under Armour, he said, but Merl Code and Adidas had recently taken a keen interest in the program, offering sponsorship and more, it now appeared.

"Adidas will help Louisville out with whatever they need because of Rick," Augustine said, referring to head coach Pitino and his central role in the relationship with the sneaker company. "With Adidas, nobody swings a bigger dick than Rick Pitino."

The room erupted with knowing laughter. Then Fair took up the conversation, getting down to business. Louisville was interested in having a specific player play for 1 Family as part of his preparation for their team. The pair proposed that LOYD make a payment on behalf of Code and Adidas, and instead of the player receiving the money, it would go to his parent. The teenager in question was Balša Koprivica, the seven-foot center who was a star on the Serbian national under-eighteen team and a top-ten recruit for the coming year. Fair was traveling to Belgrade the following week to try to recruit him for Louisville. His mother, former model Tatjana Čavić, had won a green card lottery and brought her beanpole son to the United States to pursue a life in basketball. They had moved into a gated community in Orlando, Augustine explained, and she needed money to stay there. When Koprivica had played for an Orlando high school with an elite basketball program, a booster had happily supplemented his family's meager income under the table, but now 1 Family wanted LOYD to step into the breach and fund them.

DeAngelo listened impassively as Fair explained that he could "ice out" any competitors for Koprivica's business once he got to Louisville and then the NBA, the assistant coach promising to put the player "in a box" to ensure Koprivica signed on with LOYD in due course. DeAngelo and Blazer had never heard of Koprivica and yet were expected to accept the unstated premise that he possessed NBA-level talent. The number of kids who didn't make it to the NBA was very high, even among supposedly five-star talents. The least DeAngelo could do was ask a few basic questions, Blazer thought, but the undercover sat stone faced.

Impatient with DeAngelo's silence, Blazer was concerned that DeAngelo's lack of curiosity or simple common sense would arouse suspicions. Blazer started to ask questions: What about the booster? Would he want to be repaid for his expenditures? Augustine said that the booster, who was purportedly a banker and a big donor to Barack Obama's campaigns, wouldn't say anything because of the illicit nature of the payments he'd made—a reality that Blazer knew all too well from his own previous dealings.

Blazer asked how much money was required, and Augustine said the total wasn't known yet. However, before the meeting, Dawkins had told DeAngelo the amount expected that night was the strangely specific sum of $12,700. Augustine lamented having to deal with the player's mother, because the brassy Balkan blonde was not to be trifled with.

"She ain't afraid to let you know," Dawkins said with a laugh. "She wants her fucking money when she wants her fucking money—like yesterday."[8]

As DeAngelo walked over to a bookshelf, where he'd stashed a mountain of cash in a hotel safe, Dawkins said that paying Čavić for her son was a cost-effective way of doing business. With foreign players, Dawkins said, the kids and their families weren't "too Americanized" and thus it was easier to get them to accept reduced prices. American kids and their parents usually knew the going rates, while a kid from a formerly Communist country could be had for pennies on the dollar. With players like Nikola Jović and Kristaps Porziņģis starting to dominate in the NBA, it was a promising area of growth, even if the predatory logic was depressingly familiar.

"Dawkins told us that if we kept her happy now, she wouldn't ever know the real value of her son due to her humble Serbian roots," Blazer remembered. "She didn't know the true asking price because she didn't have an American mindset yet."

DeAngelo fanned through scores of hundreds and handed the envelope to Augustine, with Dawkins unable to disguise his triumphant smirk. The transaction completed, Augustine turned to future business

---

8 It would later emerge that Čavić received no money from Augustine.

opportunities, claiming, bafflingly, that running a grassroots program put him in the perfect position to continue to convince Koprivica to sign with LOYD when he was drafted by the NBA—such a far-fetched idea that it was difficult to believe it was being offered seriously. But DeAngelo was handing out money like it was candy, Blazer reasoned, so it made sense for Augustine to at least try to pitch an ongoing relationship. Why not?

Likewise, Fair was keen to insinuate himself, offering a thumbnail sketch of how Rick Pitino ran Louisville's basketball program. For years, Fair said, Louisville's director of basketball operations had brought strippers to Billy Minardi Hall, the dorm that housed the team, to dance and have sex with players and recruits. There was a book on the story, Fair said, and the NCAA had suspended Pitino as a result of its exposure, compounding the scandals surrounding the program when the former wife of the team's equipment manager accused the head coach of rape—allegations that resulted in the ex-wife's conviction on extortion charges and another book to document the dysfunctional culture at Louisville.[9]

"We can do this, no problem," Fair said of his dealings with DeAngelo and Blazer, stating that Louisville was on probation with the NCAA. "We just have to be careful because of the whole stripper situation."

Pitino's awareness of the depth and extent of Louisville's NCAA rule breaking remained uncertain, but Fair said that the head coach didn't care much about what transpired with agents and business advisers, provided no one was seen hanging around the gym or casting suspicions in his direction, so the assistant could act as an ongoing facilitator for LOYD.

By then it was one in the morning in Vegas, four in the morning Pittsburgh time, and Blazer was spent when Augustine and Fair finally

---

9   *Breaking Cardinal Rules: Basketball and the Escort Queen* by Katina Powell and Dick Cady; *Guilty Until Proven Innocent: The Karen Sypher Story* by Sypher and Giovanni Rustino.

departed. But Dawkins returned from seeing the pair out in an expansive mood, eager to tell war stories to his new partners as he made himself comfortable on the couch and held court. According to Dawkins, another assistant coach at Louisville had initiated the first deal they'd made with Bowen, and Merl Code had taken on the task of finding funds for the family, but Pitino had been the motivating force behind the recruitment, deftly landing a five-star player while maintaining a safe distance from the transaction by using Adidas—an allegation that Pitino has denied. To that mix was added the preening self-regard of the multimillionaire head coach, convinced that star players were inexorably drawn into his orbit by the force of his personality and record of success, when the reality of the attraction was far simpler: money.

Dawkins snorted in contempt. "Rick thought it was all about him."

Dawkins was evidently proud of his ability to manipulate coaches, spreading out his legs, raising his arms over his head, and twisting his torso as he stretched to relax, as if the luxury suite were his natural domain—a contortion the FBI came to call "the Dawkins Pretzel."

Although he didn't doubt the validity of the stories, Dawkins sounded to Blazer like a hustler bragging to his new partners, trying to impress them with his connections. In fact, the FBI had recently recorded and transcribed conversations of Dawkins talking with the two prominent head coaches. Speaking with Dawkins in the weeks before the meetings in Vegas, Will Wade of LSU had lamented the difficulties of unsuccessfully trying to recruit future Milwaukee Bucks point guard Javonte Smart.

"I'll be honest with you," Wade had told Dawkins on the recording. "I'm fucking tired of dealing with the thing. This should not be that fucking hard."

Dawkins had agreed, as Wade said he'd made an offer to Smart that would be richer than an entry-level contract in the NBA.

"I went to him with a fucking strong-ass offer about a month ago," Wade had told Dawkins. "Fucking strong. It was a fucking hell of an offer."

But the money wouldn't go directly to Smart, it seemed from Wade's explanation to Dawkins; instead, it would be paid to the mother of the teenage player's child.

"I know why he didn't take it now," Wade had said. "It was fucking tilted toward the family a little bit. It was tilted toward taking care of the mom, taking care of the kid. Like it was tilted toward that. Now I know for a fact that he didn't explain everything to the mom. I know now—he didn't get enough of the piece of the pie in the deal."

In the previous weeks, Arizona's head coach Sean Miller had also talked with Dawkins about a high school phenomenon from Miami named Nasir "Naz" Reid. Dawkins had said that Book Richardson had told him that Will Wade and LSU were going to pay Reid $300,000, prompting Arizona to not even try to recruit him with such a high price tag.

"In essence, let me ask you this: Do you think you'll get Naz Reid?" Dawkins had asked Miller.

"No," Miller had replied. "He's going to LSU."

"Okay, he's going to LSU, so that helps," Dawkins had said.

"We're not even bringing him on a visit," Miller had said. "He's not even visiting. That's all shit. Like, I'm looking at our recruiting board—he's not even on it. All this fucking hype, fucking on the phone—it's stupid. He just probably said, 'You know what, fuck you. I don't want seventy-five; I want a hundred and twenty. I may go to Arizona.' That's all it was."

The idea of Reid using the possibility of attending Arizona as leverage against Wade and LSU to get more money had caused Dawkins to laugh.

"I told Book, 'Will Wade is like driving up the price of pussy, 'cause he's not even doing real numbers,'" Dawkins had said.

"I tell you what," Miller had replied. "He's got a big set of balls on him."

"No, Will Wade doesn't give a shit, Sean," Dawkins had replied.

Relating the essence of these tales to DeAngelo and Blazer with relish in the Vegas suite, Dawkins grinned. The sleep deprivation that had been consuming Blazer dissipated as he egged Dawkins on, displaying for the FBI in florid detail how high the conspiracies in college basketball reached. In the bedroom at the end of the hall, FBI agents hunched over devices recording the interminable conversation. At long last, as the clock ticked 3:25 a.m., a text from SA Carpenter hit Blazer's phone with a simple, desperate instruction: Stop talking.

"As soon as Christian left, the FBI agents came out of their room, and the first thing that Brian did was throw himself on the couch and imitate how Dawkins had been sitting 'like a pretzel,'" Blazer recalled. "It was disheartening to me that they just heard a conversation about leading coaches and players, explaining rampant college corruption, and the first thing they focused on was how Christian was sitting. It didn't seem like they understood how big what was happening was—the trafficking of kids at the hands of their trusted coaches."

~

Blazer woke bleary-eyed the next morning after a few hours of fitful sleep and made his way to the hotel's gym. Exercise was a way to clear his head before the long and intense day that lay ahead. Upon entering the giant suite at the Cosmopolitan, Blazer discovered that the FBI had ordered an array of expensive room service, the agents indulging in fancy baked goods, fruit platters, and bacon and eggs. To Blazer it looked like a frat boy–bachelor hangover party was going on. As he snagged a fresh croissant and a cup of premium coffee, he learned that the first meeting had been postponed until eleven that morning.

When Blazer was sent to greet Christian Dawkins and Creighton assistant coach Preston Murphy at the fourteenth-floor spa and escort them up to the suite, he encountered a friendly, solidly built basketball lifer wearing a big smile. Dawkins had instructed DeAngelo to have $6,000 ready for Murphy, three months of his $2,000 monthly retainer paid up front because it wasn't convenient to travel to Creighton's campus in Omaha, Nebraska, to make the payments in person. This was in contradiction to what Sood and Code had forewarned about coaches not accepting cash; apparently, as with the previous coaches, cash would be king.

After introductions were made, Murphy mentioned he'd grown up in Saginaw, Michigan—Dawkins's hometown—and it occurred to Blazer that the coach was likely getting money because he was a friend.

In the suite, Dawkins talked up Murphy, saying he was destined to become a head coach at a major program and that he was one of the best recruiters in the business. There was some truth to what Dawkins said, but it was equally true that, for Creighton, simply making it to the NCAA tournament every year represented a great achievement. Historically, the team only very occasionally yielded a second-round pick in the NBA draft, and few ever played in the league.

"Preston's goal was to get Creighton basketball back to its glory days," Blazer said. "In a lot of ways, he was similar to Lamont Evans at OSU. The key ingredient he confessed was doing whatever was necessary to entice top talent. Access to outside resources was necessary. Recruiting success meant landing NBA-caliber players that he would then graciously refer to LOYD for business management. That was the premise—who was to say where he would land next if Murphy had had cash on hand so that he could recruit players good enough to make it in the NBA."

~

Discussions about specific players ensued, with Dawkins and Murphy offering names that meant nothing to Blazer or DeAngelo, the pair barely paying attention to the details. With the proposal of a monthly retainer of $2,000 to recruit players for LOYD, Murphy readily agreed to the structure and was delighted to accept the envelope stuffed with hundreds, adding that he was very open to the idea of traveling to receive future payments to make the relationship easy for DeAngelo and Blazer, a courtesy that received nodding approval.

During the conversation, Blazer noted that Dawkins was constantly checking a second cell phone. In the world of sports business, a second—or "bat"—phone was a commonplace, as a way to screen calls and provide a higher level of service to the select few in your innermost circle.

After Dawkins departed with Murphy, Blazer asked DeAngelo if the FBI had Dawkins's second cell number. The second phone would potentially contain texts and calls from Dawkins's most intimate connections, making it vital for the FBI, but DeAngelo hadn't even noticed it. When Dawkins returned to the suite, Blazer inquired about the second phone as casually as possible, wondering if was from the same area code in central Michigan, only to discover it had a different area code.

"No," said Dawkins. "It's my LA phone."

Blazer then asked for the number. It would look strange to refuse to give out his private number to the people he was conducting clandestine business with.

Reluctantly, he called out the number, and Blazer wrote it down on his notepad. Blazer had just delivered the FBI another promising line of surveillance.

CHAPTER FIFTEEN

The King of LA

The University of Southern California Athletic Department's private jet banked east through the night sky from Los Angeles on the last Friday of July. Associate Head Coach Tony Bland was the lone passenger, stretching out on the twelve-seat plane's leather interior, preparing for the business of attracting elite talent to his team at the grassroots tournament in Las Vegas. Many of the richest college teams likewise had private jets at their disposal, making Bland a pampered but not singular presence as he cut through the desert sky on the forty-five-minute flight.

When Blazer and Christian Dawkins had been in South Carolina nearly eighteen months earlier, the hustler had regaled Blazer with tales of his derring-do on the long, sleet-soaked drive back to Atlanta. That trip had provided the spark of an idea that had turned into the modus operandi for Blazer and the FBI: paying coaches was an integral part of recruiting college basketball players. Dawkins had said "you're skipping a step" if you don't have the college coach on your side when trying to sign players. Dawkins had characteristically bragged about all the coaches he was connected to. As they had driven through the bad weather that night, Dawkins had specifically talked about the near-mythical powers of an assistant coach for the University of Southern California who was far more promising than the other coaches on offer: Tony Bland, "the fucking king of LA."

"Anyone meets Tony immediately wants to walk on his side of the street," Dawkins had claimed.

Back then, Dawkins had said that Bland would be interested in working together, for the absolute elite five-star recruits destined to become major stars in the NBA. Bland had been one of the top prospects Blazer had identified at the time, but months later, the SEC press release about Blazer's fraud had scared Dawkins away before an introduction to Bland had been made. It had just taken more than a year to bring Dawkins back into the fold and thus obtain access to Tony Bland. Better late than never, Blazer mused.

After assembling a list of coaches with Merl Code, Christian Dawkins had assigned different tiers of merit, from the superstar recruiters at the leading schools to the lesser programs that occasionally attracted a kid with NBA potential. Dawkins had decided who would receive money, seemingly employing the metric of real value, blended with a mix of friendship, favors owed, and those who could be counted on to actually deliver clients to LOYD.

"It felt like Christian was introducing coaches to the new basketball Don Corleone in *The Godfather*," Blazer recalled. "They were supposed to kiss the ring of Jeff DeAngelo and pledge their fealty."

The coaches at lesser schools would have only an introductory meeting with DeAngelo, with Dawkins as master of ceremonies. There, they would avow their ardent intention to take bribe money needed to recruit an NBA-level player. On the other hand, the top-level coaches would each receive an envelope bursting with thousands of dollars. Tony Bland was high on the list of top-level coaches, and with him scheduled to arrive late at night, Blazer started to think of him as a headliner. But first, the opening acts.

Throughout the course of that long day in Vegas, so many coaches came and went from the FBI's suite that it started to feel like the room had a revolving door. Among others, they took meetings with coaches from Arizona State, Clemson, the University of Connecticut, Texas A&M—and Alabama.

While some of the coaches already had relationships with Dawkins—and the anecdotes to prove it—others seemed to be there at Merl Code's behest. No matter the coaches' connections to the people in the suite, the meetings had two common threads.

First, everyone was talking about Zion Williamson, the top recruit in the country and, without question, the future top pick in the NBA draft in two years. Multiple coaches were recruiting the young star, some claiming higher levels of access than others.

During the meeting with Clemson's Steve Smith, Dawkins asked DeAngelo if he had ever heard of Zion. DeAngelo claimed he had.

"He's on the cover of *SLAM* magazine," Dawkins said. "He's a fucking celebrity. He's seriously like the next fucking LeBron James. Fucking Drake is wearing his high school jersey around the house and in videos."

Dawkins described a recent game Williamson had played against the Chicago Bulls star Lonzo Ball's younger brother that had attracted a crowd so large the police had to be called and the gym had been shut down.

"It was like the fucking Beatles," Dawkins said. "It was crazy."

"Wow," said Blazer, pretending to be suitably impressed, though, like DeAngelo, he wasn't sure who Williamson was.

"They didn't even let LeBron get in," Smith said. "Lebron came and he couldn't get in the door."

This underlined the fact that assistant coaches with designs on rising to prestigious head coach positions had to recruit stars to make names for themselves.

Or, as Raphael Chillious of the University of Connecticut put it, "If you ain't playing this game recruiting, your ass isn't in this game for very long."

Amen to that, Blazer thought, knowing Chillious's words amounted to the gospel of college basketball.

The other thread that ran through all the meetings was a relief to Blazer: to a person, every coach either accepted an envelope of cash from DeAngelo or promised that they would in the future—sometimes even showing disappointment that there wasn't cash for them right then and there.

As the hours ticked by and Blazer sat in the meetings, he found his mind wandering to the agents crammed in a room just yards away on the other side of the suite, listening as the evidence of widespread corruption throughout the NCAA piled up. Every envelope of cash that changed hands bolstered Blazer's profile as a reliable source for the FBI.

"I was amazed at how the day was going," Blazer said. "One coach after another was signing on, all eager to do our bidding in exchange for cash. These weren't small, insignificant schools either. They were major Division I programs."

After yet another coach departed, Dawkins promptly announced that the coach didn't actually have any influence over the future Boston Celtic player he'd claimed to have locked in because the player's father couldn't stand him. Dawkins said he needed $11,000 in cash to send to the specified player that very day. In the normal course of the investigation, the FBI had tried to avoid paying players directly, for reasons never explicitly addressed but almost certainly because arresting and indicting players would not provide a sympathetic or compelling case to the public. But this time, the bureau made an exception, and DeAngelo wordlessly made his way across the room and counted out the sum from the small mountain of cash he had stashed in the suite.

Dawkins said he was going to send the money from the FedEx store in the Cosmopolitan, adding that he needed to hide the cash in another box to distract the shipping company, suggesting that he had to find an old pair of shoes to place in the package. For years, Blazer had made it a practice to enclose a gift when he sent hot dog money, to disguise the contents but also to express his gratitude and respect. The gift didn't have to be big or expensive—earbuds, an item of designer clothing, a watch, any small luxury.

"What's he going to do with an old pair of shoes?" Blazer asked Dawkins. "Why the hell not send him something he will like? Sometimes that can be as important as the money. I've done this a thousand times. Believe me, I know."

Blazer was suspicious that a significant chunk of that payment would be purloined for Dawkins's personal use in the casinos and night-clubs of Vegas. Knowing full well it would infuriate Dawkins—even doing it for that very reason, in truth—Blazer volunteered to accompany him on a shopping trip to find an appropriate gift for the teenage basketball star.

Dawkins was visibly agitated, to Blazer's delight, as they took an elevator down to the hotel's shopping level with DeAngelo. The high-end stores in the Cosmopolitan were wildly overpriced, selling glitzy designer swimsuits, vintage eyeglasses, and gaudy custom jewelry, but there was an athletic shoe store called CRSVR that advertised itself as "more than just another Las Vegas sneaker store—it's a shopping destination for the world citizen."

Browsing the selection, including limited-edition apparel and Nike and Adidas shoes, Blazer was drawn to a pair of P.F. Flyers sneakers customized with CRSVR's gauche branding. The shoes were pure flash—in a good way, for a teenager wanting to impress his friends. The player wore size fourteen, Dawkins said, so DeAngelo paid for the $200 sneakers before the trio made their way to the FedEx office in the business center, money crammed into the sneakers inside the shoebox.

In order to hide the cash, Blazer told the FedEx clerk that the shoebox needed to be taped shut before it was put in a shipping box while Dawkins filled out the delivery form. The young woman behind the counter lifted the shoebox lid and flipped it over, revealing the cash, but she knew better than to ask any questions or say anything, no doubt used to dodgy casino dealings. Delivery for the next day was marked, and Blazer double-checked the address to make sure it was indeed going to the player, not to Dawkins or some third party.

The day had yielded conspiracies involving enough basketball talent to fill out a competitive roster for an NBA team. When the final coach of the day's session and Dawkins departed, the FBI team emerged from their bedroom as soon as the coast was clear. The lead agent, Brian, was excitedly cracking jokes about Dawkins and the cavalcade of coaches they'd just recorded agreeing to knowingly circumvent the law with such alacrity. Blazer's main concern was getting his planned meeting with Lamont Evans on the schedule for the following night so he could fly home to Pittsburgh first thing Saturday morning, in time to have an evening with his wife and kids.

Brian insisted on the encounter with Evans being pushed to Saturday morning. The only explanation that Blazer could divine was that the FBI agents were having a blast in Vegas and wanted another night on the town, wining and dining courtesy of the government. This thought reminded Blazer that he had long ached to have a confidant. Trish and his attorney were the only other folks in the world who knew where he was and had a rough idea of what he was doing, but they had no clue of the crosswinds and hidden agendas that abounded. Blazer was left to muse into his diary in the evenings and on flights to and from assignments, his solitary adventure putting him at the fulcrum of corruption and law enforcement in a manner he could never have anticipated, let alone prepared for. The solitary nature of his mission, with all the subplots and intrigues, had left him alone with his story, and that had made him lonely.

"Tell Evans that Jeff is getting a cabana at the Boulevard Pool, so we'll get everything sorted out between him and Christian then," Brian said to Blazer of Evans.

Blazer dialed Evans, only to encounter an aggrieved coach who felt like the last-minute time change was disrespectful. Carpenter stood next to Blazer, furiously writing notes to prompt him on what to say to mollify the coach, but it became evident that they were confronting a real problem. Carpenter scribbled for Blazer to tell Evans that it was Vegas and he'd just have to deal with it, but Evans was angry, and when riled, he was an unpredictable—even mercurial—figure.

"What y'all have going on that's so important you can't fit me in tonight?" Evans insisted.

Backed into a corner, the FBI pulled out its one surefire tactic: money. Blazer was instructed to offer Evans a prepayment of his next month's bribe, putting another $4,000 in his pocket and thus winning his acquiescence.

To celebrate the day, the FBI agents went for a late dinner at the Blue Ribbon Brasserie, a high-end steakhouse in the Cosmopolitan that offered an expensive and expansive menu of rib eyes and oysters on the half shell, as well as caviar and famously expensive fried chicken. The four FBI agents ordered an array of Flintstone-size steaks and extravagant sides, with wineglasses and beer glasses scattered around the table, all at government expense—and, ominously, all paid for with Jeff DeAngelo's government-backed credit card.

"Treating themselves to that kind of obnoxious display was not a good sign," Blazer remembered. "As I watched the FBI agents go to town on their meals, I could see that they were being taken in by their surroundings. They were four regular guys enjoying an all-expenses-paid business trip, and in this case, the 'company' they worked for was the United States government, and they were blowing taxpayer dollars. I had a lot of experience blurring the lines between business and pleasure, and I could easily identify someone getting carried away, and these dudes were definitely getting caught up. It was what had happened to me with the movie business. All the glamour and the celebrities swept me up and then swept me away. The difference was that the FBI agents held my life in their hands, and if they were caught up in the fantasy of Vegas and fancy meals and giant suites, it could be a disaster for me."

At a booth in the far rear of the restaurant, out of sight of the bustling crowd, Blazer took a place on the exterior of the banquette seat, but SA Jason Wake admonished him, telling him he had to sit in the middle, a less comfortable spot akin to the middle seat in a coach-class flight. Lording it over Blazer was Wake's way of asserting some version of control, serving only to emphasize the cooperator's lowly status.

But this time Brian didn't let SA Wake belittle Blazer.

"Don't get in, Marty," Brian said. "Just sit on the end. Jason, *you* slide over."

SA Wake complied sullenly, avoiding eye contact and falling into silence for the rest of the meal. After they'd finished and made their way back up to the suite, they discovered that the Vegas FBI agent assigned to the case had managed to turn off the air-conditioning by leaving a balcony door ajar, making the room exceedingly hot and ripe with the odors from the agent's room service meal.

All through the Vegas operation, Brian continued to ride SA Wake. Up in the FBI's ultra-luxurious penthouse suite, Wake began the usual time-and-date stamp for the recording of the late-night session's first encounter.

"This is agent Jason Wake," he said into the microphone. "We are in Las Vegas, New York."

"It's Nevada, dumbass," Brian said. "Las Vegas, N-E-V-A-D-A."

Blazer watched as Wake dropped his head again, saying nothing. Brian wasn't finished with him, imitating Wake's voice as he pretended to speak into a microphone. "Ahh, Dear diary, ahh, it happened to me again today . . ."

All the others broke out in laughter, and Blazer felt the collective tension ease into an air of macho camaraderie.

"There was so much corruption and wrongdoing in front of us it seemed like we now had a real shot at bringing down the whole system," Blazer said. "The biggest crime would be to not pursue every single one of the connections Christian and Merl had provided to the fullest extent possible. Courtesy of Rashan Michel, we also had Chuck Person and Kobie Baker to explore. It was starting to feel like we were developing a true blueprint for how the system worked. What would happen if we really started to apply the same formula in a more strategic way to exploit all of these alliances?"

Nearing midnight, Tony Bland landed in Vegas on USC's private jet. Not long after, Bland arrived at the Cosmopolitan, and Blazer headed down to the fourteenth floor to meet Bland and Dawkins. After the endless churn of coaches, Bland was the star act.

The moment Blazer cast his eyes on Tony Bland, he knew he was in the presence of the most charismatic and confident college coach he'd yet encountered. It wasn't just that Bland inspired confidence, dressed smart-casual in a crisp white T-shirt, designer chinos, and spotless Air Force 1 sneakers; it was also his easy and effortless sense of command, aided by a jocular swagger. His intelligent eyes were obviously observant, and he was tall, fit, clean shaven, in his late thirties or early forties, with a whippet-thin build. With his blend of avuncular familiarity and trustworthy worldliness, he personified the ideal for coaches dealing with top recruits.

Riding the elevator up to the suite, Bland established an instant rapport with Blazer without mentioning the business at hand, and when he was introduced to DeAngelo, he immediately made a joke about the muscles accented by the tight-fitting T-shirts the undercover and Blazer were wearing, as if they were old acquaintances having fun teasing each other.

"Damn, Marty, you and Jeff must have been doing push-ups in here before we came," Bland said, laughing.

Making himself comfortable on the couch, remarking on the suite's beautiful view of the late-night Strip blinking below, Bland apologized for the late hour of the meeting. He'd only just arrived in town. Asked by Blazer what type of plane he'd flown in—Blazer claimed intimate knowledge of a wide array of private jets—the coach replied that he didn't know, just that he'd been "alone on a big, beautiful twelve-seater."

"I used the private-jet-travel conversation as an excuse to roll out all the connections I had in Miami with hotels and nightclubs," Blazer recalled. "Tony picked up the conversation eagerly. He was definitely the type to be willing to accept any hookups and perks I could offer in South Beach . . . I was excited about the potential of the relationship with Tony, but getting stirred up was a two-edged sword for me. I would get carried away talking about the high times I had had, and I had a bunch of crazy true stories about private islands and indulging in the best of everything, forgetting that every word I said was being recorded and would be reviewed by Robert Boone. Seeing how excited Tony was to talk about the VIP life was like a drug for me.

"But I had to be careful I didn't draw unwanted attention to my past. I dreaded the thought of getting a call from Robert Boone someday to ask about something I'd said in the heat of the battle in Vegas that could get me in trouble or put me in more jeopardy."

Bland was happy to reply in kind to Blazer's grandiosity, explaining that part of the reason he'd arrived late that evening was because he'd been visiting with a college recruit, Marvin Bagley III, a six-eleven power forward widely considered to be one of the best recruits of his year, and a future second overall pick with a $50 million contract playing for the Sacramento Kings.[10] Thus, as ever, the conversation neatly segued to the most relevant subject when star college basketball players were being discussed: money. Recruiting Bagley would be a coup that could potentially snare Bland a head coach job, so it was a critical effort. Bagley had moved from Arizona to Southern California in high school, insinuating that he'd been attracted by financial incentives provided by Nike. Bland said that Bagley was actually a junior in high school, but he was aiming to reclassify as a senior to go to college that year,

---

10   In 2023, Bagley signed a three-year $37.5 million contract with the Detroit Pistons.

hastening his arrival in the pros, and that USC was helping the player take summer courses to qualify.

"USC has got him," Bland said. "He got into USC, and he's going to USC. UCLA doesn't have a chance. No way he's picking Duke. He ain't going to leave LA to live out on the East Coast. He loves the Southern Californian sunshine too much for that shit."

Talking with extreme confidence, Bland said that USC was a Nike school, so Bagley's previous relationship with the brand would ease his recruitment, offering another possible path to lure another sneaker brand into the web the FBI was weaving. Bland was also supremely confident about his ability to deliver the player into LOYD's embrace.

"The minute the dude steps on campus, your ass needs to be there," Bland said of Bagley. "He ain't going to come cheap, but what he asks, you all need to be prepared to do on the spot, and then he's yours. I can make sure nobody else even comes close to getting access."

Blazer and DeAngelo agreed that they were willing to spend whatever was necessary to secure Bagley as a client for LOYD, as did Dawkins. Dawkins's silence in the earlier conversation about Zion Williamson was now replaced with enthusiasm bordering on ecstasy as he emphasized the importance of Bagley as a client. Bagley was elite and promised to make more than $100 million in a career, likely significantly more; clipping a few percentage points from such a large sum represented an attractive proposition. But the larger importance for LOYD of having Bagley as a client was the marketing and branding value to future players, all of whom would be aware of the player's representation.

"Marvin's the type of kid you can build your business on," Bland said. "You get him, and you'll need to hire a bunch of people just to handle the clients that come your way from signing him. Dudes will want to fuck with you just 'cause Marvin fucks with you. But you won't have time because you'll be too busy dealing with lottery picks like him. All you got to say is, 'We rep Bagley, Bagley with us.'"

The prearranged sum of $13,000 was presented, consisting of one hundred and thirty $100 bills, bulging from the envelope DeAngelo produced. There had been no conversation Blazer had been privy to about the specific uses for the money, though it was understood it was for something related to Bagley, and it was clear that it was considered only the first of many payments in the months and years to come, a relationship that the coach vowed would be mutually beneficial—if not for the players involved.

"With my kids, ain't no thinkin' 'bout it when it comes to this," Bland avowed. "If I say this is what you're gon' do, then that's what they're gon' to do 'cause nobody need to play any fucking guessing games, you know what I mean?"

Plans were made for further meetings, and Blazer suggested they rendezvous in Miami Beach to use his connections there. Bland readily agreed, as they discussed the convenience of also employing Las Vegas as a meeting place for the West Coast–based coach. On his way out, Bland invited DeAngelo and Blazer to join him at the huge, multi-level Omnia nightclub atop Caesar's Palace for a party to celebrate a friend's birthday, joking that the pair was already dressed for clubbing in their stylish, tight T-shirts. Blazer and DeAngelo politely declined, while Dawkins said he would meet him later as he prepared to escort him down to the lobby.

"What it is, I trust Christian with everything implicitly," Bland said as he departed.

Blazer was inwardly astonished that Bland would have (or profess) such faith in Dawkins. The coach was clearly a rising star, with a bright future and a career quickly moving up to the highest levels of the game, and he was trusting a hustler and a roomful of shady characters with a crucial element of his future—the risk didn't add up for Blazer.

When Dawkins returned, he was eager to receive praise for all the amazing meetings he had arranged that day, most especially Tony Bland of USC.

"If he's not a fucking major college head coach soon, then it'll only be because he'll be coaching in the fucking NBA," Dawkins said.

Dawkins added that for all the slick and sophisticated appearances, Bland actually came from South Central LA. Dawkins referenced a story about a relative of Bland's nicknamed Big Magic, who was one of the leaders of the Crips. In a video that Dawkins said was all over the internet, Big Magic had confronted the rapper Lil Wayne outside a club in LA a few years earlier, warning Lil Wayne that if he wanted to come to South Central LA in the future, he needed to "check in" to get Big Magic's personal approval—though spoken through a stream of curse words and threats.

"Tony ain't no fucking joke," Dawkins said. "Man, the dude has some serious-ass gangster roots."

Blazer hadn't fully considered the idea of retaliation until that moment, and a shiver of dread went to his gut as he wondered, once again, what he'd got himself into and what the hell he was doing.

CHAPTER SIXTEEN

The Cabana

On Saturday morning, as Blazer drank a cup of coffee and picked at the croissants and fruit the FBI had ordered for the suite at the Cosmopolitan, he watched the federal agents slather themselves in sunscreen in anticipation of a day spent poolside. It was seemingly obvious that the lone reason they'd had for moving the meeting with Lamont Evans and Christian Dawkins to the following day was to give themselves a free day in Vegas at the government's expense. The frat-boy attitude that Brian and the others were displaying struck Blazer as craven. Behind the veneer of serious law enforcement lay the urges of a bunch of knuckleheads who wanted to partake of the thrills of Sin City; for all the bravado, they were just clichéd bros looking for some bro action.

The cabana the FBI had rented at the Cosmopolitan was up a flight of stairs from the pool, offering commanding and uninterrupted views of the Vegas Strip, with thick luxury towels, expensive beach furniture, and a well-stocked bar and fridge. DeAngelo had dressed as the quintessential moneyed lounge lizard, in linen shorts and an unbuttoned linen shirt covering a white tank shirt, with his hair slicked back and eyes hidden behind gaudy Gucci aviator shades. As another elaborate platter of food arrived, Blazer's cell phone pinged with a text from Evans seeking an additional five hundred dollars, apparently a surcharge for the inconvenience of postponing the meeting, despite all his expenses for the trip to Vegas being covered by the FBI—via DeAngelo.

The agents groaned in protest, but DeAngelo walked over to the towel cabinet and counted out five hundred-dollar bills to add to the $5,000 Evans was scheduled to collect. The scene had been set to get Evans back on track with the case, effectively paying him to reconcile with Christian Dawkins after they'd fallen out over recruiting issues, and the bureau wasn't going to blow it over five hundred dollars. With Evans about to appear, Brian and the other agents went down to sit by the pool and visually monitor the coming encounter, leaving Blazer and DeAngelo alone.

"There was a cool vibe around the cabana, not a cloud in the sky," Blazer said. "There were beautiful people all jockeying for position around the pool, with misters spraying, and music was being piped through the air, and there were limitless mojitos on offer. I knew this kind of scene from my past life, and I knew how seductive it was."

Evans arrived on time, dressed in an Oklahoma State Cowboys black-and-orange polo shirt, shorts, and the latest Nike-fashion footwear. He hugged Blazer and shared a laugh that reflected their seemingly genuine affection for each other. DeAngelo hadn't met Evans, so introductions were made, but the coach largely ignored the undercover and focused his attention on Marty Blazer: the man he thought he'd known for more than eighteen months. Christian Dawkins turned up soon after, dressed in his standard designer jeans, buttoned-up polo shirt, and high-end sneakers, despite the heat.

"This guy, I don't think he even owns a pair of shorts," Evans said with a laugh. "Man, I've never seen him in anything other than these pants."

Dawkins laughed because it was true; his outfit amounted to a uniform. Dawkins and Evans started to clear the air between them, with Blazer learning that the coach was upset over the recruit Brian

Bowen, who had enrolled at Louisville. OSU had allegedly offered the Bowen family $150,000, but the school had been spurned—Evans believed, at least in part, because Dawkins hadn't been sufficiently supportive. Blazer was surprised he hadn't been kept in the loop, given all the money he and DeAngelo had paid the coach and Bowen's father. Evans said he'd been dealing with Bowen's father and that there had been genuine interest in hooking up a Nike-financed deal to rival the scheme that Adidas had, in the end, arranged at Louisville.

"Listen, Lamont," Dawkins said. "The Bowen thing, there was just nothing I could fucking do, for you or for fucking Creighton—that's just the way it was. Look, no amount of money, no way that kid or his fucking dad was going to swallow going to Stillwater, Oklahoma, or fucking Omaha, Nebraska, for that matter. Just wasn't going to happen, so whatever the dad said to you was a fucking lie."

What Dawkins said had the ring of truth, and the men quickly moved past the disagreement. The way Dawkins was trading gossip about players, withholding information, and providing hints, Blazer could tell that Evans was second tier at best in Dawkins's eyes, ranking below Book Richardson of Arizona and Tony Bland of USC.

After Dawkins departed with the pair reconciled, Evans asked Blazer to arrange for a night at the strip club Tootsie's in Miami for the next payment, and DeAngelo handed the coach the envelope of cash. Evans left happy, apparently not wondering why he'd received such large sums of cash for so little return on investment.

At the debriefing in the suite afterward, Blazer could sense the impatience of SA Carpenter and Brian, as he was reimbursed for his expenses and sent on his way with another pat on the back. Given how Brian interacted with his subordinate FBI agent, Blazer thought the trip appeared to be heading for a train wreck. Putting a lot of alcohol and the Vegas atmosphere together with large egos, macho attitudes, and piles of government cash wasn't a great idea, Blazer believed; someone had to be tracking the money, the former financial adviser was nearly certain, but as the days passed and the pile was replenished, the controls had seemed to loosen and fray.

"Brian was a narcissist, which led to a bad dynamic," Blazer said. "Brian was the type of person who would lure his colleagues into a trap by encouraging them to think that he was cool with something and then change his mind and attack them with extreme prejudice. He was the type to dish it out but never take any pushback. The worst part was that there was no reason for Brian to be in Vegas. He wasn't adding anything to the investigation, but his presence created a whole different dynamic."

Sitting in coach on the flight back to Pittsburgh, surfing through sports websites on his iPad, Blazer imagined the headlines that would follow the public disclosure of the case. He was sure they wouldn't be flattering. The FBI now had proof that corruption wasn't just rife in college basketball; it was endemic to college sports. It was as if the FBI were investigating air, so pervasive were the greed and cheating. If they'd approached one hundred coaches, Blazer felt certain that all of them would have accepted money to steer players toward LOYD, but he'd begun to fear more and more that the FBI would pull the plug on the case just as it was gaining real momentum.

"Las Vegas was just another step in an ever-evolving process. Whatever we did next was going to bring about even bigger revelations. We had coaches ready to go to work, Adidas in our pocket, and there were multiple head coaches at major programs on the horizon. Ordering the end of the investigation would be gross negligence—or at the very least, massive incompetence.

"We had the ball, in full stride, running down the field with the end zone in sight and not a soul within twenty yards of us," Blazer recalled. "The only thing in the world that could trip us up . . . was us."

CHAPTER SEVENTEEN

Keep on Playing Those Mind Games

Blazer knew from bitter experience that lies had a way of building on each other. As the deceptions grew increasingly dark and complicated, it became harder and harder to stop, let alone return to the truth.

Blazer had been told repeatedly by the FBI that if he lied to the bureau or Southern District about one thing—no matter how trivial or meaningless—he would be arrested, put on trial or pleaded guilty, and then sent directly to prison, with no consideration for all the efforts he had put into the investigation. If he lied about what he'd had for lunch, or his expenses, or his prior relationship with a target of the investigation—it didn't matter. The bond of trust had to be earned and maintained at all times.

The policy of radical and naked truth telling had created in Blazer an expectation of similar truthfulness from the government, most especially the FBI, as he put his life in their hands. Over hundreds of conversations, Blazer and Carpenter had forged an understanding that depended on mutual trust.

In the past, Carpenter had always checked in on Blazer after every operation, making sure he'd gotten home safely and wanting to discuss what came next in the investigation. When Blazer didn't receive a call or text from Carpenter by noon the day after he returned from Vegas, it was impossible for the cooperator to still his thoughts.

Despite the party vibe in Vegas, the ex-military disciplinarian Carpenter wasn't the type to sleep in or take a mental health day and let the investigation slide. Despite his misgivings, Blazer was happy to enjoy the company of his wife and three kids over a leisurely coffee on a lovely summer Sunday, without the FBI's interference.

"As the afternoon wore on and I had no word from Scott, I had to force myself to not dwell on the radio silence. Making sure I wasn't lying in a ditch somewhere was highly irregular for him. Something wasn't right," Blazer said.

At 2:54, Blazer's cell phone dinged. It was a text from SA Jason Wake, an extremely odd development. Blazer read the text silently.

Hey just checking in, Wake's text said. Scott's phone is not working. If you need to reach us, please call my number.

It was a seemingly trivial matter but clearly a lie. There was no chance SA Carpenter had broken his phone in a nightclub or a bedroom with a prostitute, or whatever it was the FBI agents had got up to on their night of letting their hair down. If Carpenter had actually damaged his phone, it certainly wouldn't stop him from communicating directly; he could borrow SA Wake's phone or shoot Blazer an email. This text from Wake was the equivalent of saying *The dog ate my homework.*

Blazer reasoned that Wake wouldn't lie without direction, and that almost certainly meant Brian had instructed him to text Blazer.

Blazer flirted with the idea of inventing a pretext to call Wake and probe him for evidence of what was going on, but he had learned since his downfall it was often judicious to remain silent and let events play out. Blazer needed time to think, plan, and brace himself for whatever came next.

OK got it thanks, Blazer replied by text. All good here though.

As Blazer parsed through the possible explanations, each less likely than the one before, he began to feel a sense of dread. He tried not to obsess about the text and what it meant for the investigation and him personally, but he knew beyond a doubt that Carpenter wouldn't have voluntarily ceded authority over his cooperating witness, and most certainly not to a dimwit like SA Wake.

～

On Monday morning, Blazer's cell phone predictably lit up with calls: Munish Sood, Lamont Evans, Chuck Person, and Rashan Michel all wanted to forge plans for the future use of DeAngelo's abundant cash. An aggrieved Person was threatening to repay the so-called loans he'd received if Blazer and DeAngelo didn't agree to fund Austin Wiley's mother's moving expenses. Sensing it was an empty threat, Blazer told Person that he and DeAngelo wanted to meet Person's coach connection in Missouri, as had been discussed. Rashan Michel then called about brokering next steps with Kobie Baker, telling Blazer that the $10,000 payment in New York City the prior week had been successfully delivered to the Alabama athletic director. After that, OSU coach Evans called to follow up on their Vegas conversation, asking how much of the money he'd received had come from Munish Sood, for reasons that weren't clear. Soon after, inevitably, Sood called to congratulate himself on all the meetings he'd forced Dawkins to set up in Vegas, as if he'd been the motivating force behind the encounters.

Blazer was used to sharing the conversations and the various implications in great detail with Carpenter. But all day Monday, there was still no word from Carpenter, so Blazer put dealings from Vegas on hold. Inwardly, he now feared that the investigation was being shut down.

Unbeknownst to Blazer, the FBI was scrambling to clean up after an epic Vegas night that was impossible to sweep under the rug. Shortly after Blazer had left Las Vegas, excited by the progress they had made in the case, the FBI agents had continued relaxing by the pool. The cabana included a minimum spend of $1,500 that had to be used on food and drink, and the agents were intent on getting the most from the full amount. Soaking up the sun, the four agents had proceeded to partake of the government's largesse, with SA Carpenter downing a six-pack of beer and chasing it with nearly an entire bottle of vodka. Then the agents had returned to the FBI's suite in the Cosmopolitan to shower and change for a night on the town. While they were getting ready, Carpenter had drunkenly opened the suite's safe and removed $10,000 in cash for gambling. The group of law enforcement officials had then taken the purloined money to a high roller room at the Bellagio, where Carpenter started to play high-stakes blackjack. The other three had sat in an adjacent bar, drinking while Carpenter lost the money he'd purloined. Carpenter had intended to replace the money when he won—truly an inebriated delusion, much like Blazer's determination to replace the movie money he'd misappropriated—but by the time Blazer's plane was landing in Pittsburgh, Carpenter was broke.

Carpenter could have stopped there, but the trouble had been compounded when he demanded that Jeff DeAngelo give him another $3,500 from the safe. DeAngelo had complied, and Carpenter lost that sum in no time, just another Vegas rube losing to the house. In all, Carpenter had lost $13,500 of the government's money that night.

~

After Vegas, Blazer had dozens more calls that week, all of them recorded, but he had no idea if anyone cared anymore. When he sat down to dinner with his wife and kids on Thursday, August 3, he deliberately left his phone in his home office so he wouldn't stare at it obsessively. After dinner, unable to resist the impulse to check his phone, he saw that SA Wake had called but not left a voicemail. When Blazer called back, Wake picked up on the first ring.

For months, Wake had treated Blazer with contempt, both as the low man on the totem pole but also because he seemed to harshly judge the cooperator's criminal history. But now there was an entirely new and jarring tone to his voice—one of supplication.

"Hi, Marty," Wake said meekly as he picked up Blazer's call. "I was calling to let you know—please don't try to contact Scott or Jeff for a while, if that's okay. Unfortunately, I'm going to be your primary contact for now."

Blazer had long wondered why both Carpenter and DeAngelo were AWOL. The word *unfortunately* felt like a tell. Wake wasn't capable of strategizing, Blazer knew. Blazer wondered if Wake meant his involvement as the primary contact was unfortunate for the cooperator, the investigation, the agent, or all three—as seemed most likely.

Something had broken inside Blazer when the FBI lied to him about Carpenter's phone, a seemingly minuscule deception that was now being implicitly acknowledged but not admitted. Blazer let the silence linger as Wake fumbled for words and tried to avoid speaking out of turn or giving away the actual truth.

"There's nothing to worry about, Marty," Wake continued. "Both Scott and Jeff are safe. It's just some background stuff, and they won't be able to continue for the time being."

Telling Blazer not to worry could evoke only one possible response: worry. Why on earth would Blazer fear for the safety of the two buff ex-military federal agents? Did Wake think Blazer was concerned that Carpenter and DeAngelo had been beaten up in a bar brawl, or had a drunken car crash, or been involved in an unreported airplane crash out of Vegas?

"Even if you try to make a call to either Scott or Jeff, they probably won't pick up," Wake continued.

"Did I have anything to do with the changes, or did I do something wrong?" Blazer asked in a plaintive voice—aware that he'd done nothing of the sort.

"No, Marty. It's not about you, and you didn't do anything that I know of that was wrong," Wake replied. "Scott and Jeff just have to step away for a while."

Blazer listened in silent amazement.

"Brian knew full well that Jason was a fucking idiot," Blazer remembered. "But who else was there left to make the call to me? At this point I was beyond exhausted by having to navigate so many obstacles. The call was surreal, coming immediately on the heels of the amazing Vegas operation. Coming from anyone but Jason, I would have thought they were messing with my head, but I knew I wasn't being punked. Jason wasn't sophisticated enough to think of such a thing."

"Was it something that happened on Saturday night in Vegas?" Blazer finally asked, turning to the obvious explanation. "What did they do?"

Wake stumbled and stuttered, telling Blazer he didn't want to discuss what had happened on the phone but that the case was still active. Jill Bailey would be stepping up her role, along with another agent Blazer would meet shortly.

"If it's possible and it doesn't inconvenience you," Wake offered tentatively, "could you make a trip to New York sometime next week to talk about the changes and what's going on moving forward?"

Blazer again let silence fill the air as Wake breathed heavily and awaited his reply. Carpenter had always been the boss, instructing Blazer on what to do, but now Wake was asking for the cooperator's permission, and Blazer wasn't going to let the moment pass. Finally, Blazer offered that he'd have to check his calendar but he might be able to find time on the following Tuesday or Thursday.

"Great, great. We can make some calls, listen to some calls, go over plans going forward, and I'll get you up to speed on what happened with Scott and Jeff then," Wake said.

"Okay, sounds good," Blazer replied, before hanging up.

Blazer sat in the quiet of his home office. It was obvious that Carpenter and DeAngelo were permanently gone. The timing for this particular FBI disaster couldn't have been worse, with the lead agent off the case and thus the ability to strategize hampered, not to mention that DeAngelo had been the main face of the operation. Losing DeAngelo, Blazer decided, could actually be a plus if Blazer was permitted to participate in forming strategies. But explaining DeAngelo's sudden absence was going to be difficult.

~

"I believed Scott was the person a judge would listen to when he recommended probation instead of prison," Blazer recalled. "He was a criminal cooperator's FBI agent. He understood the mentality of someone like me, who'd fucked up, done bad things, got caught, and wanted to figure out how to work himself out of the predicament. Scott had intimate knowledge of the full extent of my cooperation, including the more subtle elements like the tactics I had suggested. Now he was completely gone. Who would stand up for me with a true and accurate depiction of all that I had done?"

Blazer hadn't yet quite twisted the Rubik's Cube of the power dynamic to this particular configuration, but in truth, the FBI was now unable to effectively threaten or intimidate the cooperator. To the contrary, the bureau would have to make sure Blazer didn't pose a threat to the investigation or the institution by revealing the fact that something had gone seriously wrong in Las Vegas.

SA Wake called Blazer a few times in the following days without divulging more. With a call to Sood scheduled for Blazer one afternoon,

Wake begrudgingly admitted that DeAngelo had already talked to Sood about his need to go away for the time being. Blazer was appalled that the FBI hadn't bothered to tell him, as he could have easily inadvertently blown the case wide open. The excuse for DeAngelo's absence was preposterous. Wake said that DeAngelo had told Sood he had to travel to Italy on an indefinite trip to tend to a sick aunt. DeAngelo had left Blazer and Jill Bailey as the points of contact for further payments and communication, as if somehow Italy didn't have cell phones or internet.

"I was at a loss for why no one had talked to me about how to address DeAngelo's absence beforehand," Blazer recalled. "It was pure luck that Jason told me about Jeff's story before I spoke to Munish and got blindsided. Jeff was my investor. How could I not know that he'd left indefinitely for Italy to visit an aunt? Worse, I could have told the FBI that none of the targets cared where Jeff was going so long as the money kept flowing. Making up a story about Italy only risked raising eyebrows. The story wasn't believable. Just saying he was taking his girlfriend for a monthlong vacation in Europe would have been easier to swallow."

If Blazer had been on the other side of the deal, if he'd been involved with a dicey investor like DeAngelo who suddenly departed for Europe and became incommunicado, he would have assumed that DeAngelo was either on the run from people he owed money to, or from the law, or both, or that he had already been arrested. Whatever way, it spelled trouble. Blazer would have insisted on abandoning the project—or slowing down at the very least—until DeAngelo reemerged, and even then, it would take a lot of persuading to convince the former financial adviser to continue.

For months, DeAngelo had been itching to be introduced to coaches, and he'd just met with no fewer than ten coaches in Las Vegas, from some of the leading programs in the country. Now he was ghosting LOYD, after pouring hundreds of thousands of dollars into it? Without a plan to follow up on all the leads from Vegas? Without demanding some tangible return for his money? The situation was idiotic, Blazer believed, and he waited in dread for Dawkins or Sood to start asking questions—but amazingly, neither did. Still, even if Dawkins and Sood didn't seem concerned, Blazer couldn't stop wondering what had actually happened after he left Vegas.

CHAPTER EIGHTEEN

We Have Your Playbook

SA Carpenter had seemed the embodiment of a certain variety of para-military manliness, but his replacement, Special Agent John Vourderis, was the polar opposite, a diminutive and slope-shouldered five-five FBI investigator best resembling an IRS auditor or a mild-mannered metro-sexual commuter heading for the suburbs. SA Wake introduced Blazer to his new FBI handler in a Starbucks near the Southern District in Manhattan on the morning of August 10, 2017, before the cooperator's meeting with AUSA Boone that day. Vourderis's soft handshake and gentle manner were surprising. Carrying an iced latte, Vourderis held the plastic cup with a napkin beneath so his hands wouldn't get damp or chilly, an affect that Carpenter would have not only noted—as Blazer had—but mocked the moment the new agent left the room, if not to his face. Blazer had to keep from laughing as Vourderis complained about his poodle puppy keeping him up the night before.

But Blazer liked Vourderis from the start. The agent began by thanking him for making the trip to New York City, an unthinkable gesture for Carpenter. Vourderis's hairline was receding, and his guile-less, deep-set brown eyes were framed by an easy smile and an open and frank communication style, the kind of camaraderie Blazer had long craved. Vourderis was dressed informally but crisply, in a blue suit with a button-down shirt, and he was carrying a leather shoulder-strap bag, the type worn by yuppies the world over.

"You might say John didn't have a strong alpha personality," Blazer said. "He wasn't a prick. I never even knew if Scott Carpenter was married, and he only gave out the absolute minimum of humanity, allowing for no whining in his tough-guy world. Scott wouldn't be caught dead carrying a shoulder bag. But John was smart, I could see, and all we needed to do now was prioritize and execute on the leads Scott and I had created . . . He was actually nice to me and calm about taking over the case. I felt like I could confide in John."

Walking toward the Southern District with Vourderis for his meeting with AUSA Boone, Blazer was hit by a premonition. For years he'd ignored red flags, with his fraud and the subsequent cover-up, with profound consequences. But throughout the multiple clusterfucks that had constituted the past half a dozen years for Blazer, he'd weathered several moments that would prove decisive to his future—for good or ill. Blazer was no philosopher, but he had learned the hard way that he needed to pay attention to what the universe was telling him.

Lining up at the security scan in the Southern District's building, waiting to empty his pockets and walk through the X-ray machine, Blazer noticed a man in front of him looking like he'd been badly beaten, with a swollen black eye and fresh cuts all over his face, his lip bloody and split, his arm bandaged; as he shuffled forward meekly to be searched by security, he limped badly. The striking thing to Blazer was the man's size: at least six-three and 250 pounds, he had wraparound sunglasses on the top of his shaved head and a scowl on his face. He looked like he'd literally been run over by a truck, or perhaps he'd gotten on the wrong side of some bad people and received a serious beatdown, but Blazer watched in alarm as he was accompanied by a US marshal through the security check.

"A bolt of lightning couldn't have been a more obvious omen," Blazer said. "I hadn't been handcuffed or had the shit kicked out of me, so looking at that dude, I realized that my situation could be a lot worse than it was. No one was trying to kill me. I wasn't going to have to ruin the lives of my kids by going into witness protection when the case broke. In many ways, I was fortunate."

Riding up in the elevator, Blazer decided he wasn't going to sulk or try to shame or manipulate the Southern District into taking the case to the fullest-possible extent. He resolved to practice some gratitude and accept whatever direction the government wanted to take. In truth, it was a realization that was long overdue. He'd misappropriated millions of dollars, and there was a serious chance that he would never darken the door of a prison cell. The facial expressions, the self-pity, the determination to bring down college basketball and the NCAA—all his prior motivations evaporated as the sinking feeling of dread he'd been enduring was replaced by something like acceptance.

In place of AUSA Boone, an older and apparently more senior prosecutor named AUSA Russell Capone was waiting for Blazer and Vourderis. Blazer had met Capone in the past during one of his debriefs with Boone. The attorney had seemed to relish wielding his power over the lives of others. Much like the FBI supervisor Brian, the height-challenged Capone wasn't quite sadistic, but he had an evident ruthlessness, matched by a skepticism that manifested in how he constantly scanned for inconsistencies or omissions or signs that Blazer wasn't being fully forthright.

Instead of the usual dank, windowless conference room, this time Blazer was ushered into a large, well-appointed corporate-style meeting room with towering views of Lower Manhattan. As if he could sense that he needed to address the presence of an elephant in the room, Capone started by apologizing for the disappearance of Carpenter and DeAngelo, searching Blazer's face to see if he could detect a response that could signal danger.

"Sorry, but administrative issues have made us have to make a change," Capone said.

"Administrative issues." Blazer knew better than to ask any questions about what had happened in Vegas, as much as he wanted to know. Capone asked if Blazer was willing to continue with the investigation, adding that AUSA Boone would be joining them shortly. Capone said that he'd seen "some" of the video evidence from Vegas. Two weeks had passed since Vegas, and Blazer had assumed—or, more accurately, hoped—they'd been poring over the evidence, developing strategies, debating late into the night about tactics. With SA Vourderis sitting quietly in the corner, Blazer believed that the institutional memory of the case had been permanently and irretrievably lost.

Blazer offered a watered-down version of his pitch to the government, all the while resigned to the outcome, saying he'd been amazed by the harvest of new leads that arose from Vegas. The $25,000 in cash for the Adidas-Bowen-Louisville deal had cemented Blazer's motley crew's place in the society of college basketball insiders, he said, providing entrée to the most secretive transactions at the biggest schools and creating the enticing prospect of doing the same thing for Nike and other major athletic brands. Reviewing the new coaches who had been recruited in Vegas, Blazer prioritized the list for Capone, starting with Tony Bland of USC and top prospect and future NBA player Marvin Bagley. As Blazer ran down the names, pointing out how actionable the leads were, Capone seemed distracted, until the prosecutor finally skipped ahead and asked about Book Richardson of Arizona. Blazer allowed that he had been only peripherally involved in the efforts with Richardson.

Over the hours that followed, Blazer came to the realization that the Southern District wasn't going to pursue the Vegas leads, apart from Tony Bland and Book Richardson, and that the focus of the prosecution had narrowed drastically. Richardson was a priority, it seemed, but Blazer wouldn't be included in that aspect of the case. The same was true for Bland. The lone target he would now be used for was Kobie Baker, a vital initiative if Blazer was allowed time to insinuate himself into the various aspects of both the Alabama basketball and football programs.

The aperture that Blazer and the FBI had managed to open onto the business of NCAA corruption would be shrunk, not opened. Blazer was told he would continue to deal with Rashan Michel and arrange for a meeting with Baker about Alabama's star freshman basketball player Collin Sexton in August, but other than that, it appeared this chapter of his cooperation was coming to a sudden and inglorious conclusion. The main emphasis of Capone's questions seemed to be to determine what—if anything—Blazer knew about Carpenter and DeAngelo, as an exercise in damage control.

AUSA Boone arrived at long last, hurrying in as usual, always giving the impression that he'd left an important meeting and had another pending. But Boone was much friendlier than usual with Blazer, asking after his son's soccer team and calling him Marty instead of Mr. Blazer. Boone no longer looked like the junior associate he had appeared to be three years earlier; wearing a tailored suit and polished shoes, he had grown in confidence and command. As Boone and Capone disappeared with Vourderis—apparently to discuss the fate of the case and the cooperator—Blazer sat silently by himself, contemplating all that had happened and how, in the end, he really had Boone to thank for this chance. If Boone hadn't taken the risk on Blazer and possessed the vision for a potential case, Blazer's life would have gone very differently. The day was rapidly approaching when he would learn if Boone valued the quality and quantity of his cooperation when it most mattered.

In a few minutes, Boone returned with Vourderis. Once again, he started going over Blazer's past, this time concentrating on his financial encounters with University of North Carolina football players nearly a decade earlier. The investigation was looking backward, Blazer realized. Blazer hoped his wife hadn't been right when she had pushed him to insist on getting a binding assurance that he would receive consideration from the Southern District when the chips were down.

"Trish urged me to be skeptical about what I was being asked to do without assurances from the government," Blazer remembered. "I didn't fault her for not trusting the people I was dealing with. She had warned me about working with athletes and getting involved in movies, so I knew I should listen to her advice. The last thing I wanted was for Trish to be right yet again . . . But I . . . I believed in my gut Boone was a man of integrity."

~

Blazer checked his voicemails when he left the meeting with the Southern District. He'd received multiple calls from unknown numbers. His heart sank. A cub reporter from a financial publication called *Advisors Magazine* had called, asking for an interview.

"I want to discuss with you how the movies turned out, to know if they made any money," the journalist said. "Please call me back when you can."

The SEC had again issued a press release about his case, Blazer realized. He had been in ongoing discussions with the SEC, but another press release was dumbfounding. One arm of the government seemed to be actively and effectively crippling another. But worse—it was to no apparent end. Delaying a press release until the investigation was complete wouldn't change the outcome for the SEC in the slightest, but reminding the public of his history risked obvious bad consequences. All Tony Bland or Kobie Baker or Book Richardson would have to do was turn on ESPN or flick through a newspaper—both highly likely activities—to be reminded of Blazer's legal history.

The next series of calls came from Rebecca O'Brien of the *Wall Street Journal*, the same reporter who had contacted him weeks earlier. After three calls in a row in which she'd simply hung up, she finally left a voicemail explaining that she wanted to interview him about college basketball and the FBI, echoing her earlier request. Evidently, O'Brien still had a source inside the government. She claimed to be working on a story about "a federal investigation into Division I college coaches and basketball players as well as your role in the investigation." Feeling a rising dismay at the rank incompetence of the federal government, when he made it to the FBI office, Blazer informed SA Wake about the press release and the calls from reporters. Pulling up the SEC release on a computer, Blazer and Wake read the headline: "Court Orders Financial Advisor to Pay Nearly $2M in Case of Defrauding Athletes."

The press release was damning. It identified Blazer by name and continued: "The Securities and Exchange Commission announced that it has obtained a final judgment against a Pittsburgh, PA–based financial advisor accused of taking money without permission from the accounts of several professional athletes in order to invest in movie projects and make Ponzi-like payments and then lying to SEC examiners who uncovered the unauthorized withdrawals."

FBI agent Wake made excuses for the SEC, arguing that the regulator spun it like the financial adviser's case had been resolved, as if the main import were the finality of the outcome, not the underlying criminality. Wake was seemingly unable to grasp that the coaches might distance themselves from anything that had a whiff of law enforcement attached.

But again, Blazer's fears were proven wrong. Even the SEC press release didn't alert or alarm Rashan Michel or Kobie Baker. Back home in Pittsburgh, fielding calls from Chuck Person and Lamont Evans on a nearly daily basis with no guidance or encouragement from the FBI, Blazer played dumb and avoided taking any action.

"The Southern District was only interested in dealing with what was already on its plate," Blazer recalled. "They weren't even trying to tie up loose ends and put a big red ribbon on the investigation before the indictments were brought down, instead of going after the real truth about corruption in college sports."

Blazer was concerned about the use of Jill Bailey in DeAngelo's place—her vague backstory was suspect, and she hadn't added anything to the previous conversations about business. Blazer doubted her ability to provide illicit bribes on DeAngelo's behalf. Fortunately, again, Dawkins and Sood were so deeply involved that they didn't question Bailey's highly improbable involvement.

In mid-August, SA Vourderis called Blazer at home and instructed him to "go soft" on Munish Sood during their planned forthcoming call, by which he meant not to push for new initiatives. Talking carefully, the FBI agent said Sood had already spoken to Bailey and that they had agreed to travel across the country together to meet with Book Richardson in Arizona and Tony Bland of USC later in the month. Vourderis then told Blazer that he should cut Rashan Michel out of the deal with Kobie Baker and talk directly to the athletic director. Blazer thought the volatile Michel would go berserk if he learned he'd been short-circuited. Vourderis silently contemplated the implications—including potential violence or Michel going to the NCAA and anonymously snitching on the entire operation, thus blowing it up—and then consented to Blazer continuing to engage with Michel.

Later that day, Blazer's call with Michel went well, the $12,500 Michel had just received in Manhattan apparently successfully greasing the wheels of commerce. Blazer agreed to meet with Michel and Kobie Baker in Atlanta right before the long Labor Day weekend, in the lead-up to Alabama's first football game of the season. The cash he planned to bring would presumably provide funds for Collin Sexton, the Alabama freshman standout. All the money Blazer was providing for the player would have to be funneled through Baker, Michel said, a term that Blazer readily agreed to, ending their shockingly pleasant and productive phone call.

Munish Sood was a different story. Blazer's former partner was imperious and dismissive when they connected. Sood relayed how he'd already made arrangements with Jill Bailey to travel to Arizona and California. As always, Sood was blinded by greed or his considerable ego, making it impossible for him to see he was being played for a fool by the very man he held in contempt as he chewed loudly on a sandwich and talked derisively on the phone.

"Munish was happy because he had a beautiful woman as his traveling companion," Blazer recalled. "The whole deal wasn't costing him a dime. To him it was the perfect scenario, all upside and no risk. He was too blinded to notice the entire thing was too good to be true. He thought he was smarter than everyone else and that he was slowly slipping the knife into my back."

The trip to Arizona and California seemed to go off without a hitch, with the FBI recording Jill Bailey and Munish Sood bribing Book Richardson and Tony Bland, but Blazer was only vaguely aware of what had been happening, and SA Vourderis provided scant information.

In the aftermath of the Vegas cash spree, a giddy sky-is-the-limit feeling had overcome Christian Dawkins and Merl Code. As far as they knew, DeAngelo and Bailey were willing to throw hundreds of thousands of dollars into college basketball in order to build a roster of NBA clients. As crazy as the scheme had first seemed, a question began to haunt the pair as they connived together: What if DeAngelo and Blazer were right? What if players like Zion Williamson and Markelle Fultz signed with LOYD under the watchful tutelage of their college coaches? What if millions upon millions of dollars were at stake, and all Code got was a lousy monthly stipend?

"My fear is because it's not structured, and we haven't really discussed value," Code said to Dawkins on a call on August 24. "I'm a little concerned, man, that these folks we dealing with are going to try to devalue me."

"Uh-huh," Dawkins murmured.

"I'm just being honest with you," Code said. "They don't understand this is the kind of shit I bring to the table. It's a pipeline of motherfuckers. I don't want them to come back and say, 'All right, Merl, we'll give you twenty percent.' Fuck that. You put some money in, yes, but you don't get none of that shit done without me and you."

Code had provided virtually all the meaningful connections in Vegas. Dawkins had been tinkering along with lower-level coaches like Lamont Evans and Preston Murphy of Creighton, but Code's reputation and record had brought Richardson and Bland into the mix, as well as Louisville and potentially another half dozen elite programs over time. The strategy Code had disapproved of—"just fucking rain money"—had a kernel of genius inside it, he now feared; the money bubble that Blazer had recognized in their first meeting looked like it could well come to life.

"The lifeblood and lifeline of this shit is what I do, what I've done for almost twenty fucking years," Code said. "I don't want to be shortchanged."

Dawkins replied that they should "keep a salary, a set number—you know, a consulting fee, whatever you want to call it—and then have an equity piece too. That's why I'm doing it—because there ain't going to be no fucking money—"

"Not initially," Code said. "I realize that."

Dawkins didn't have the luxury of considering delayed gratification, in all likelihood, as he'd been desperate to find someone—anyone—to fund the basketball business after he'd been cut loose by Andy Miller of ASM. The FBI had created the equity structure as a Venus flytrap, the irresistible temptation to become a 50 percent owner of a company that took its name from his fondest wish—to Live Out Your Dreams. Now those dreams seemed poised to come true, and Code didn't want Dawkins and the others to benefit at his expense.

"I'm saying when paydays do come, I just don't want to be shortchanged," Code said. "That's all."

"I think the best way for you and I both is to have an equity piece and also have a salary piece," Dawkins said, telling Code what he wanted to hear, knowing he had no power to force any change in the equity structure or promise Code a salary.

~

As August continued to pass in deafening silence from the FBI, Blazer reached out to SA Jason Wake for guidance on what to do about Chuck Person. The former NBA star was ceaselessly pushing for money to pay for Austin Wiley's mother's moving expenses, a promise the coach had made but wasn't able to fulfill. Or perhaps Person just needed more money for his own use, to pay off debts or whatever it was that compelled his constant demands. When Blazer called, Wake was evasive and distant. Wake then asked Blazer for records of the various instances when wires of money had been sent during the investigation—information the FBI should have been tracking and had in their files, but apparently affairs were so strained or broken internally that they couldn't ask Scott Carpenter. In Blazer's mind, there must have been some kind of misuse of the stack of federal cash involved or an irreparable confrontation—something that disqualified Carpenter from having any ongoing role in the case.

When Marvin Bagley, one of the players Tony Bland had promised for USC in the Las Vegas meeting, opted at the last moment to play for Duke for his freshman season, Blazer saw a promising opening to put pressure on the USC coach. Bland had taken the money and failed to deliver, creating a debt in the relationship bank. Blazer reminded Wake of the leverage the FBI possessed, citing Dawkins's statement that they had the coaches by the balls once they'd taken money.

"Now, who is this again?" Wake asked, sighing heavily, apparently unable to remember the name of the player, as if keeping track of all the names were an onerous burden. "Can you spell his name for me? There are so many."

Blazer explained that Bagley was an outstanding player who would dominate college basketball the following season before declaring for the draft as a freshman and heading to a lucrative career in the NBA—a player that LOYD could have used as a springboard to recruit other elite talent. Wake seemed to be barely listening. If Wake had acted with initiative, USC could have been even more deeply implicated.

Blazer had had no income for more than three years, and he was living on fumes. As the family had to rely on Trish's earnings, Blazer had set about compensating by being the most diligent and helpful spouse and parent he could be, a form of penance that had the strange effect of actually making him a better person. He'd long been addicted to the travel and bright lights of South Beach and all the other glamorous places he'd frequented with his players, but now he took the most pleasure from hanging out with the soccer dads in the stands at games or helping his daughter prepare for her first year in college. Even simple rituals he'd let the kids acquire in the aftermath of the movie fraud, like walking the dog, provided Blazer with a new kind of suburban satisfaction. The man who had never seemed to grow up had paradoxically been saved by his own downfall, and his wife and kids could see the changes.

At this point, Blazer was in contact with only SAs Vourderis and Wake for the most part and kept in the dark about developments in the case, while he continued to deal with Rashan Michel and arrange for the meeting with Kobie Baker on August 31 in Atlanta. On a call with Michel, Blazer was told that Sexton's father, Darnell, would attend the meeting, not the player, with Baker wanting to build an "organic" connection. But then Michel suddenly said he didn't think the meeting with Baker and Sexton was going to happen.

"I'ma be real honest with you, Marty," Michel said on one of their many logistical calls. "I just don't think this is going to work."

"What isn't going to work now, Rashan?" Blazer asked, exasperated. Michel explained that the Sexton family was already doing business with other financial advisers, as well as agents, a development that Kobie Baker had allegedly shared, along with the revelation that the athletic director was no longer certain he could deliver the player—organically or otherwise. Sexton was an outstanding point guard, closely tracked by basketball insiders and destined to be picked in the first round, so it followed that other agents and financial advisers would be keen to insinuate themselves into the player's life. Blazer was aware of the way to deal with such developments: add money to the pot.

"How much money do we need to bring to the table to make Mr. Sexton have a change of heart about those other people," Blazer asked wearily.

He recounted the way the deal had developed at Baker's insistence. Blazer added that if Michel wanted to have any prospect of a long-term relationship with DeAngelo, this first deal absolutely had to happen—no excuses or hedging allowed. Baker had bragged about his ability to command loyalty, saying to Blazer and DeAngelo things like, "You are my people, so it's a done deal with the players—end of story." Michel uncharacteristically didn't offer a denial or far-fetched justification. The meeting with the Sextons had to happen, Blazer said, and Michel agreed that he'd talk to Baker and finalize the plan to meet in Atlanta with the player's father.

On the night of the Sexton dinner in Atlanta in early September, SA Vourderis picked Blazer up at the airport in a rented compact Dodge Dart. He impressed upon Blazer that it was vital Kobie Baker endorse him as a financial adviser on the wire in order to create a criminal nexus; there would be no more outlandish exotic vehicles or over-the-top luxury-hotel suites. Then Vourderis asked a question that startled Blazer with its simplicity and clarity—but also its moral implications. Driving through the dense humidity of late-summer night in Georgia, Vourderis asked if the teenage basketball player Collin Sexton would be harmed by what they were doing that evening. The query stopped Blazer short.

"The NCAA might give him a slap on the wrist if he gets caught," Blazer said. "But he's good enough that it shouldn't affect him much."

"Now, that's good. I will sleep a lot better tonight knowing that," Vourderis said, shocking Blazer. This was the first time anyone involved in the case had ever expressed any ethical or emotional doubts about the consequences of the investigation, let alone the sense of proportion and resources employed.

"I was glad to hear that John's conscience was clear," Blazer recalled, with more than a little hurt evident in his voice. "But . . . he didn't recognize the implications of what he was saying and how it reflected on my character—it didn't even seem to occur to him. What did it say about me that I could do what I was going to do and sleep like a baby that night?"

Here, at last, one of the investigation's most treacherous fault lines became visible. Blazer had walked into the Southern District three years earlier to confess his crimes and discovered he could make a bargain with the government—or devil, depending on how events were perceived. The sting operation offered only an opportunity to break the law to the targets, without harassing or urging or encouraging the conduct in order to avoid legal entrapment, but the universality of corruption in college basketball made the temptation irresistible. Blazer had repeatedly had pangs of guilt when he had seduced coaches into destroying their careers, and parents into endangering the futures of their children. But SA Carpenter had never expressed any doubt about the merits of the case or how it was a destructive force in the targets' lives.

For weeks, Blazer had been tracking all the ways that Carpenter and Vourderis were different. When Blazer had been provided with a hidden camera for surveillance, Carpenter had returned his shirt in a rumpled and scuffed mess, while Vourderis offered a selection of Blazer's shirts he'd carefully ironed himself. When Vourderis tried to install the camera, he had to ask for Blazer's assistance, apparently new to the procedure. Even the security precautions varied widely. Vourderis had booked rooms for himself and Blazer in the same modest hotel, a lack of concern about potential exposure that Carpenter would never have permitted.

Nearing the designated restaurant, Blazer got out of the car a couple of blocks away and walked to the steak house in the oppressive humidity, encountering Baker in the parking lot, talking on his cell phone. Baker finished his call and hugged Blazer before the pair joined Rashan Michel and Darnell Sexton at a table on the back deck, an area selected for the privacy and nearly pitch-dark lighting to avoid prying eyes. In addition to the $15,000 in bribe money he had in a bag, Blazer had a thousand in cash in his pocket to buy dinner, money he'd been reluctantly given by Vourderis after the agent innocently expressed wonder that four people could spend that much on one meal.

Assuming that Blazer was picking up the tab, Michel ordered a brace of appetizers, including Japanese Wagyu short ribs and lobster fritters. Baker introduced Blazer to Sexton as his "partner," while the father asked the waitress for Johnnie Walker Scotch, enabling Blazer to break the ice by talking about his taste for single malts and pull out the ultra-expensive Gurkha cigars he'd brought as gifts to smoke after dinner. They ordered dry-aged rib eye and filet mignon steaks, the priciest items on offer.

Sexton said he'd coached his son all through his grassroots years and he'd been involved in the decision to attend Alabama. The Crimson Tide basketball team had multiple future NBA players that season in addition to his son, Sexton said. In scarcely a few minutes, Sexton was offering to recruit another player for him, making it clear that the father was willing to do business with LOYD if the terms were right.

As the scotch flowed, Sexton appeared to relax, as did the others. Blazer could see that Sexton wasn't a naïf; he understood all aspects of the game and the game within the game, and there was no doubt that he and Baker had discussed the money to be expected in the hope of landing his son's business.

The meal over, the men lit their cigars and ordered another round of cocktails. Michel excused himself to go the bathroom. A minute later Blazer received two texts. **Meet me in the bathroom**, the first one said, with the second one saying that Baker wanted to talk to Sexton privately. The conversation had clearly been arranged by Michel with Baker in advance, but it presented him with a dilemma: the cash he was set to deliver was in a bag sitting on the floor. Taking the bag to the toilet would look awkward and distrustful, but leaving $15,000 in cash meant it could vanish; he didn't want to risk another fiasco by losing track of the FBI's money. Torn, Blazer decided to just let the bag remain where it was. He got up and excused himself.

Michel was waiting by the sinks in the darkly lit restroom as Blazer entered knowing he was about to disappoint and potentially enrage him with the news that he had $15,000 in total, to be divided with $10,000 going to Baker and $5,000 fulfilling a request for Person—short from the sum that Michel had requested. Baker and Michel and Sexton could chop up the fifteen grand however they liked, Blazer said, but that was all he had, and they had to be clear and precise in expressing his expectations moving forward. Conceding sullenly, Michel asked Blazer to fetch the cash. Blazer returned to the table, and Baker and Sexton ignored what was blatantly happening as he bent over and picked up the bag, wordlessly returning to the men's room. Handing the cash to Michel, Blazer said that DeAngelo only needed him to get visual affirmation that Baker had received the cash directly and immediately.

Walking back to the table, Blazer could see the three men exchange nods and silently confirm that Michel now had the cash. After they all agreed to meet in New York when Alabama was in the city for a tournament that Thanksgiving, there was a fake tussle over the check, which Blazer covered—a $650 tab. The quartet walked outside to the parking lot, and Michel and Baker and Sexton removed themselves to another vehicle as Blazer duly trained the shirt camera on the trio while an envelope was handed to the athletic director and roars of hilarity and hearty embraces followed; in the poorly lit parking lot, it was difficult for Blazer to see the transaction clearly, and the footage from the camera would prove grainy and ambiguous. Michel returned to say that Baker left happy, and he would send a text to DeAngelo confirming receipt of the money. All then went their separate ways, leaving Blazer to walk through the heat of the night to reconnect with the waiting FBI agent.

Back in Pittsburgh, on Labor Day, Blazer received a call from Vourderis. The FBI agent asked Blazer to contact Baker to confirm that he'd received the money from Michel. Blazer assumed that in telling Baker to confirm receipt of the money directly by text to DeAngelo, there would be digital evidence. Vourderis reluctantly admitted that the FBI didn't have access to DeAngelo's phone anymore. The text appeared to have vanished into the ether unread, so the FBI needed to have irrefutable proof in the form of a recorded call or a text.

Blazer knew that he couldn't directly ask Baker to text him about the payment because the athletic director would be reluctant to provide a digital record of him taking a bribe; simply making the request might elicit suspicion. Instead, Blazer decided to act indirectly, as he often did, first calling Rashan Michel to say that DeAngelo was asking for confirmation of the receipt of the money to ensure Michel hadn't pocketed a larger share of money intended for the athletic director. Michel again referred to the text that had already been sent to DeAngelo but added that if Blazer needed further confirmation, he should call Baker directly, though his mother was in the hospital, so he might be difficult to reach. Blazer waited a day. He then texted Baker, inquiring about his mother and offering his best wishes, adding he'd like to know when they could next talk. Three days went by. Blazer called at the end of the week, and Baker picked up and breezily confirmed on a recorded call that he'd received the ten grand in cash, as expected. The two were looking forward to meeting in New York at Thanksgiving, when Sexton and his father would both be in town and they could all get together and nail down the details.

"The call offered the chance to continue to pursue opportunities with Kobie Baker," Blazer remembered. "We were just getting started with him and Alabama—one of the great machines of collegiate sports turning out professional athletes every year like clockwork, with an NBA-bound basketball player or two from the Crimson Tide, but the real riches at the school were on the football side . . . Kobie was destined to become the next athletic director, with his résumé and connections. I had established a trusting relationship with him. The football program sent double-digit players to the NFL draft every year . . . I hoped that someone in authority at the Southern District would reconsider their position and decide to let the investigation continue. It would improve the impact of my cooperation and help in getting a sentence reduction, but it was also because I wanted the case to succeed the way I knew it could. But in my heart, I knew they wouldn't."

CHAPTER NINETEEN

Guilty, Your Honor

After more than three years as a CI, Blazer had become an expert at living a double and triple life. Now he was about to be transformed from a CI into a CW with the takedown that loomed in the fall of 2017; instead of being a cooperator, he would be the prosecution's star witness in the trials that would ensue from the takedown if the defendants chose to plead not guilty.

But first he had to plead guilty to his own crimes, he was informed by AUSA Boone, with a court date set for September 15, 2017, when he would rise in front of a judge in Manhattan, swear an oath, and say aloud that he was guilty of fraud and thus declare himself a federal felon for life.

The days leading up to the plea were fraught, with Blazer facing a pared-down indictment that included five different varieties of federal crime. In theory, the sentencing guidelines recommended a maximum sentence of sixty-seven years—effectively a life sentence for Marty, who was in his late forties.

Whatever sentence he received, Blazer realized he had to prepare his immediate family. The news would be splashed on the front page of newspapers all over the country. Blazer figured he should tell his eldest daughter, Madison, first. She was an intelligent college freshman, and in many ways she appeared to be just another suburban kid. But Blazer knew that beneath the exterior, she was as close to him as anyone on the planet in terms of personality and adaptability. He hoped she'd be able to see the necessity of what he'd done for the FBI—and she might even take a little pride that her dad had fought so hard for his family.

Taking Madison out onto the back deck of their house on a pleasant September afternoon, Blazer gave her a brief rundown on what had happened over the past few years. She listened quietly, eyes widening. She looked like she was scanning her father's face to see if he was pranking her. Madison had seen the athletes and rappers and country music stars coming and going from her father's life, so she understood that pretty much anything was possible where he was concerned.

"I know you can handle this," Blazer told his eldest daughter in summation. "You're strong. We're not going to tell Connor and Ari for now. We'll tell them at some point. When they find out, they are going to look to you and react based on what you do. If they see you can handle it and you're okay, then they'll be okay. I need you to be strong."

Madison didn't flinch. She didn't fully comprehend everything that her father was saying, but it was clear she wasn't scared or shaken. As Blazer had hoped, she would be able to handle whatever was coming, which provided a welcome wave of relief.

The next hurdle was forewarning Blazer's inner social circle, including Trish's younger sister. The siblings were two years apart but inseparable. They also needed to tell their close friends. They scheduled a dinner party days before Blazer had to travel to New York, and the three couples convened at the home of Trish's sister. Blazer had warned Trish that he was going to tell their friends the great secret he'd been carrying for years.

Dinner was awkward for Blazer as he downed a stiff whiskey and silently rehearsed his confession. He picked at his gourmet meal, looking around the room at the happy people he loved and respected, wondering what they were going to make of him when he dropped a bombshell into the middle of their dinner party. Blazer's stories had long been wilder than any of the other fathers', and he figured his friends could withstand the shock. They all knew the vague outlines of Blazer's difficulties with the SEC and that he'd undergone the indignity of his movie projects failing, but those issues had faded with time.

"There's something I need to tell you all," Blazer said, once the main course was concluded. "You're going to hear about this pretty soon."

He paused to clear his throat, the candlelight glowing on the faces of his attentive friends.

"You know that I got into trouble with the SEC over the movie stuff a while back," Blazer reminded them, eliciting murmurs of acknowledgment. "Well, for the last three years, I've been working undercover for the federal government."

The tinkle of wineglasses stopped, and there was a pregnant pause as nervous glances were exchanged around the table. Trish kept her eyes trained on her plate, as her husband continued his confession.

"I've been an undercover cooperator with the FBI, working on an investigation into corruption in college basketball."

Blazer glanced around the table. He was feeling the impact of the whiskey. He noticed that his brother-in-law and friend were both smirking, like they were waiting for Blazer to admit that he was joking. Blazer gave them a watered-down version of the events of the past couple of years, from the clusterfuck of *Mafia* to confessing to prosecutors in the Southern District of New York about his misappropriation of money from his players. Blazer said he had taken the government into the world of college sports to search for corruption. He told the silent, shocked, and increasingly dumbfounded folks that he'd worn wires for the FBI in a complex and top-secret operation that reached across the country and ensnared more than a dozen college coaches and sneaker executives in a scheme to covertly take bribes.

"What the fuck?" Blazer's brother-in-law blurted in amused disbelief as the details poured out.

"Are you going to be okay?" Blazer's friend asked.

"I think so, but I don't know," Blazer said.

He sighed and shrugged. Plowing ahead, he shifted gears: he had to plead guilty to multiple felony fraud counts in federal court in New York City in the coming days, allowing that he didn't know how it was going to go; he might have to go to prison, or he might be released on probation if the judge decided to give him credit for his extensive cooperation. The specter of prison seemed to capture their attention—or horror—as the group turned to Trish and searched her eyes, as if to silently ask if it was true, only to be met with a resigned look and shrug.

"We're here for you, whatever you need, if you've got to go to jail," Blazer's brother-in-law said.

The others nodded in agreement. They would stand by Blazer as he navigated the criminal justice system. Now, with the arrests looming, Blazer wanted those closest to him to know the truth—as good, bad, and crazy and improbable as it was.

With his friends and his daughter looped in, Blazer began anticipating the takedown, imagining the reaction of the targets when they were arrested, most especially the unpredictable and mercurial Rashan Michel, who would quite possibly turn up on his doorstep in Pittsburgh, menacingly demanding answers. When Blazer learned that his hearing would be held in open court in Manhattan, with any member of the press free to attend, he had his lawyer beg Boone to keep the proceeding off the docket so it wouldn't attract the attention of Rebecca O'Brien of the *Wall Street Journal* or any of the other reporters who roamed the corridors of the federal courthouse looking for sensational stories.

Blazer's son had his first high school homecoming the week following the plea, and Trish was planning to host his entire class at their home for a celebration before the dance—a mortifying prospect if his father's name was splashed all over the news. His son also had no real knowledge of what his father had been up to, and Blazer would have to pray that word didn't get out.

Blazer woke at four in the morning on the day of his plea and arrived in New York before noon to admit his guilt. When he convened with SA Vourderis, the agent was astounded to learn that Blazer had never had his door kicked in by the FBI or even so much as felt a pair of handcuffs constrict his wrists, let alone endured the miseries and indignities of the criminal bureaucracy.

DOJ investigator Lavale Jackson was back in the picture, greeting Blazer warmly at the courthouse and saying he'd accompany him as he went through the degrading process of being entered in the federal system as a convicted felon; the former financier was going to receive the criminal justice version of VIP service. AUSA Boone also arrived, telling Blazer not to be too nervous, acting in an uncharacteristically light and reassuring way as he reviewed the plea agreement and told him what the judge might ask in court.

"It felt like the culmination of all the stupid things I'd done in the athlete business," Blazer recalled. "I had always been teetering on the edge of murky affairs that I was badly equipped to handle, and it turned out I had the perfect profile for someone to get in trouble. My affinity for cutting corners, my desire to be the man at any cost, the crooked nature of dealing with athletes, years of using unethical means to justify my ends, all the gray area that I had operated in—it came together when combined with my personality. I was too weak to say no, and I was too lazy to be straight, or honest, or at least ask for help. I thought I had to get my hands dirty, so I got them dirty, and this was where it landed me, pleading guilty to five felonies in federal court. By the end, I just wanted the whole thing over and done with."

Walking through the corridors of the courthouse, Blazer scanned passersby for any signs of journalists trailing him or registering his presence, but no one seemed to clock the small flotilla making its way to the fifth floor.

The courtroom seemed huge to Blazer as he sat at the defendant's table, nervously eyeing the door, terrified that a reporter could walk in at any moment and the guilty plea would wind up in the news. The doors to the court were open, to Blazer's consternation, and he anxiously tapped his feet and swallowed hard when two casually dressed white men entered and left, followed by a young Black woman carrying a notebook, who sat in the back, convincing the defendant that she was a reporter about to score a great scoop.

AUSA Boone and the judge exchanged some banter as Blazer's criminal attorney leaned over and whispered to him that federal judges weren't known for joking around in court, taking it as a good sign. When asked by the judge if he was ready to make a statement to the court before the plea was entered, Blazer noticed with relief that the young woman was gone, and he read his prepared statement in a wavering voice, inwardly cursing at himself for being such a fool. *You chickenshit,* he thought as he read his statement, recalling how he could have just said no to the whole movie fiasco when the money first ran out.

"Guilty, Your Honor," Blazer repeated as the five charges were read out.

The judge postponed sentencing indefinitely, leaving Blazer in limbo until the targets of the Operation Ballerz case were arrested and prosecuted, and the cooperator performed the last task of testifying in court at their trials. Blazer was told that the record would be placed under seal, keeping the press from learning about the day's events and ensuring continued anonymity—at least for now.

Blazer was a convicted and self-confessed felon. Lavale Jackson took him to be processed by the US marshals in the basement who had greeted the countless notorious criminals who had graced the same hallways, the most famous displayed in a mural on the walls as totems of the illustrious past, like a hall of fame: John Gotti; Bernard Madoff; Ramzi Yousef, the World Trade bomber of 1993—they were all commemorated with collages. Blazer joked that Operation Ballerz might get to join them on the wall one day, and Jackson grunted with laughter.

Fingerprinted and photographed by a bully-boy US marshal whose military highhandedness and casual unconscious racism led him to assume that Jackson, the Black investigator, was the convict there to be registered, not the white man in a suit and tie. Blazer's DNA swabs were taken and his biometrics entered into the government's database. After being "tagged," as the process was known, Blazer was at the mercy of the marshals in the dank and carefully staged bowels of the building; the glaring fluorescent lights and the temperature kept just above freezing seemed intended to engender fear. As with Carpenter's hard-ass act, Blazer refused to take the US marshal's bait and respond to the taunting, replying to questions as politely and briefly as possible.

Escorted to the bonding office, Blazer was grateful to find himself able to pee for the drug test, in a room covered in mirrors and with someone watching him. Jackson told Blazer that if he hadn't been accompanied by a federal agent, the marshals could have kept him for hours if they'd wanted. To complete the procedure, Blazer met with Boone to sign the bond that would release him on his own recognizance, the felon telling the prosecutor that he was holding up okay—it could have been a lot worse, he said.

Turning to the pending takedown, Boone said that the arrests were going to happen in a matter of weeks, not months, so Blazer should brace for what would follow, adding that he should call SA Vourderis or Lavale Jackson if he was contacted by anyone involved in the case or if he felt afraid—alternatively, he could simply dial 911.

"Even though I'd just pleaded guilty to five felonies, I weirdly felt the need to celebrate that another phase of my journey had come to an end," Blazer said of the evening, when he'd returned home to Pittsburgh. "I was going to be a felon for the rest of my life, but one small victory was that the convictions were placed under seal by the judge, so I wouldn't be in the press just yet. My wife was happy, and my son's first homecoming party would go off without a hitch. When I got home that night, I had a couple of drinks to distract myself from thinking about the shitstorm that was on the horizon and the people who had no idea that their lives were about to be changed forever."

~

On September 25, 2017, Christian Dawkins was in New York for a meeting with Jeff DeAngelo, who had finally returned from his strange extended trip to Italy. The sit-down was meant to set strategy for LOYD for the coming basketball season. The meeting was to take place at the W Hotel in Times Square, in a suite the FBI had rented for the occasion.

"Christian, I'm an undercover FBI agent," SA Bailey said to Dawkins upon his arrival in the suite, displaying her badge. "You can save yourself."

Staring at Bailey, Dawkins started laughing maniacally, like he had just figured out that he was on *Candid Camera* or an episode of *Punk'd*.

"You got to be shitting me," Dawkins said in disbelief. "You're fucking lying."

When Bailey reiterated that she was telling the truth, Dawkins stared at her in disbelief.

"I don't even fucking believe this is real," he said.

Bailey explained that the FBI wanted Dawkins to cooperate with their ongoing investigation. Dawkins was told that if he cooperated with the bureau, he might ameliorate the dire legal consequences he faced, including federal indictments for serious felonies that could result in decades in prison. Contemplating this new reality, Dawkins started to feel like he couldn't breathe. He stood up, terror stealing over his body, fighting the urge to flee, and began to peel off his clothes.

"Okay, I'll work with y'all," Dawkins said finally, hoping to strike an agreement and make a quick exit from the suite. "Fuck it, what do you want? I'll do it."

Dawkins immediately suggested Marty Blazer as a target for the FBI, but Bailey said they weren't interested in Blazer but that Dawkins would have to start making calls to coaches immediately. Dawkins balked.

"What's going to happen?" he asked. "I'm not going to actually go to jail or anything like that?"

When Dawkins finally said he needed to speak to a lawyer, the doors of the suite burst open, and an FBI SWAT-style team stormed the room, carrying Glock pistols and submachine guns and screaming for him to put up his hands. Dawkins was then handcuffed and taken downtown to the Metropolitan Correction Center, a notoriously intimidating twelve-story building that housed up to nine hundred criminal defendants awaiting trial, including the notorious Mexican narco El Chapo.

～

On the evening of Monday, September 25, as he drove his son home from soccer training, Marty Blazer learned that the major takedown for Operation Ballerz was imminent. For weeks, Blazer had been left in limbo, keeping the various and sundry participants in different machinations at bay while he awaited the arrests. In Vegas in July, he and DeAngelo had been the eager and avid funders of multiple coaches, pushing the venture into uncharted waters by adding more and more coaches and more and more promises with a seemingly endless supply of cash. Now, in September, just a matter of weeks later, Blazer was inexplicably difficult for Dawkins and Sood and the various other characters to reach by phone and impossible to do business with, as he stalled and deflected and avoided action for reasons that defied any sensible explanation. But the agony was coming to an end—to be replaced by other agonies.

"Tomorrow is D-Day," FBI special agent John Vourderis told Blazer that evening.

Blazer had to talk in code to Vourderis to ensure that his son didn't pick up on what they were discussing, but it quickly became apparent that the government wasn't planning to unseal the details of his plea. Vourderis said the FBI was going to make a mass of arrests the following morning but that Blazer's name would be withheld from the press; in the unlikely event he was contacted by the media in the aftermath of the busts, he should be prepared. Blazer wasn't told he shouldn't talk to the press, but it was clear to him that it would be against his interests to comment on cases where he would have to testify—a prospect he hadn't fully digested until that moment. There was no way on earth he was going to speak to any reporters—not yet and perhaps not ever.

"My head started racing like crazy," Blazer recalled. "In a few hours, the whole country was going to know what I'd been doing for the past three years. A part of me felt sympathy for guys like Lamont Evans and Chuck Person, who I liked personally. I knew the indictments were going to ruin their careers and cause enormous personal pain. Part of the reason I didn't want the investigation to end was that I wanted to avoid the awful truth of that moment."

When he got home, Blazer took Trish aside and quietly told her what was about to occur. She asked if he thought they were in danger—were the targets really capable of retaliation? Blazer said no, even though he was very concerned about that possibility; admitting his fear would only upset his wife. He told her his name wasn't going to come out, and he planned to pretend he was amazed that he hadn't been arrested as well in the ensuing chaos and confusion, to at least buy himself some time.

Lying awake that night, Blazer pictured all the people who were about to have their worlds upended, including Munish Sood, who was scheduled to visit him in Pittsburgh the next morning for the first time in weeks. In recent days, Sood had reached out to say that he had been in contact with a former high-net-worth client of Blazer's about a real estate deal, yet another of Blazer's connections Sood had been willing to pilfer with no consultation or compensation, citing Blazer's SEC woes as the reason. There were many ways to work around the rules, and Sood was a master at such maneuvers, but he seemed to prefer to stiff Blazer almost as a matter of principle.

The sleep-deprived Blazer got out of bed at six a.m. on the morning of September 26. He fixed himself a cup of coffee and fired up the desktop computer in his home office. Figuring that the FBI preferred to make its raids before dawn, Blazer searched the internet for the names of Lamont Evans and Munish Sood to see if they were in the news.

At that same time, as the sun also started to rise over the suburbs of Princeton, New Jersey, Munish Sood stripped naked and stepped into his shower in preparation for his short flight to Pittsburgh and the encounter with Blazer. Sood had much to be excited about, with Blazer effectively locked out of the Vegas deals that had been developed and the incipient partnership with Dawkins and DeAngelo set to thrive. Gold from Bolivia, a real estate deal, bribing college basketball coaches, a prosperous hedge fund . . . Sood's portfolio of interests was unique and disjointed—or, more charitably, *diversified*—but promising.

As the expectant Sood felt the warm water wash over his balding pate, the FBI walked past the Maserati Levante parked in his driveway—the same vehicle undercover Jeff DeAngelo had driven to one of their meetings, which apparently had made a big impression. Soon there was a commotion in the house, as multiple agents hammered on the front door and entered as if they were on a tactical military mission or raiding the redoubt of a major drug dealer, startling his wife and sleeping kids. Sood was buck naked when FBI agents placed the dripping-wet defendant under arrest, causing an early-morning stir in his quiet residential neighborhood while his wife and children looked on in horror, wondering what on earth the mild-mannered man had done to be treated like an armed felon.

While Sood was dressed and perp-walked to the waiting FBI's vehicles under the bleary-eyed gaze of his bewildered neighbors, Blazer was at his desk, constantly refreshing his online searches. At seven thirty, his cell phone rang, and the name *Lamont Evans* appeared on the screen. Blazer didn't pick up. Six times in a row, Evans called and hung up when Blazer didn't answer, leaving no voicemail. Blazer believed that Evans was in Tampa, traveling on business, so he would likely be in a hotel, and he must have gotten wind that something was about to go terribly wrong for him.

"I was getting nervous, anxious, certain that I was going to get calls from Munish and Chuck and Christian and Rashan, so I decided to turn off the phone the FBI was monitoring," Blazer recalled. "The stress was overwhelming. I was on the edge of my seat."

At ten a.m., SA Vourderis called Blazer on his personal cell.

"Google *college basketball*," Vourderis said to Blazer. "It's all out there. It's done."

Blazer said that Evans had tried to call him. What if others were able to connect the dots? Blazer asked. The FBI agent reassured him that was unlikely to happen.

"We went to great lengths to make sure your name wasn't in any of the affidavits," Vourderis said.

Clearly excited by the day's events, Vourderis said that Dawkins had started to strip off his clothes like he was on fire when he'd been busted in Manhattan, adding with delight that Sood had been pulled naked from his shower. Blazer didn't entirely share Vourderis's schadenfreude, nor did he feel sorry for Dawkins or Sood. Vourderis said that Blazer should call him immediately if he received any threatening calls or texts.

In all, a dozen people were arrested, and the office of Andy Miller's agency ASM was raided, leading to live coverage across cable news and

sports networks, precisely the kind of media frenzy Blazer had anticipated. Following the news minute by minute, Blazer learned that the
FBI had also arrested Merl Code and an Adidas executive named Jim
Gatto, indicating that the bureau had pursued the Bowen case after
all—but frustrating Blazer because it was only the tip of the iceberg
for sneaker-company corruption. Book Richardson, Tony Bland—the
names of the coaches came rolling in, but to Blazer's mystification,
others were missing. Some were not arrested or even charged, including
Kobie Baker and two of the coaches who'd taken money in Vegas—
Preston Murphy of Creighton and Corey Barker of TCU.

ESPN said the Southern District would hold a press conference
at noon, to be broadcast live as the sensational news rippled across the
sports world. Trish and her partner came home from work to watch
with Blazer as AUSA Joon Kim took to the podium in New York,
along with Assistant FBI Director Bill Sweeney and a string of officials
standing on the dais. Large diagrams propped up on easels illustrated
the way money flowed from the FBI undercover agent to Dawkins to
coaches and players, with Adidas included in the scheme.

"Today we announce charges of fraud and corruption in college
basketball," Kim said. "Coaches at some of the nation's top programs
were soliciting and accepting cash bribes. Managers and financial advisers circled blue-chip prospects like coyotes."

Dozens of reporters sat in rapt silence as the cameras rolled.

"The madness of college basketball went well beyond the Big
Dance," Kim continued, clearly reveling in taking the credit for the
takedown and determined to exhaust every cliché he could muster.
"Month after month, the defendants exploited the hoop dreams of student-athletes around the country, allegedly treating them as little more
than opportunities to enrich themselves through bribery and fraud
schemes."

In this formulation, under this construction of the moral universe
of college sports, the schools were the victims, as they had been denied

the honest services of state employees because of the bribes paid to coaches, neatly avoiding the question at the center of the case: the rule of amateurism in a multibillion-dollar industry. As Blazer watched Kim take questions from the large press contingent crowding the room, it seemed to him that the AUSA had a poor grasp of the legal and factual landscape of the case—or the real importance of the investigation.

FBI Assistant Director Sweeney was asked a shouted question that he repeated to the assembled reporters: How did law enforcement get involved in the case in the first place? Based on the seemingly impressive and comprehensive nature of the accusations, it appeared that the FBI had been working on the investigation for years, burrowing deeper and deeper into a widespread conspiracy that stretched across the nation and involved multiple schools and myriad coaches—a case that resembled some of the biggest organized crime investigations the Southern District had long been famous for.

"So, for those who couldn't hear the question, the question was, How did we get involved, and how did we start this case?" Sweeney said, before pausing. "You should know I'm not going to answer that," he added, to universal laughter from the press.

The question was part of the government's ritualistic interaction with the media when a major case was announced. Everyone in the room understood that information would be carefully controlled, with prosecutions and guilty pleas looming in the future, so the FBI and Southern District would be stingy with parsing details, even as they strove to receive the maximum impact in the press.

Watching in his home office, Blazer turned to Trish and sighed, the pair sharing relief that his name wouldn't come out in the press conference, a story that was already burning up the airwaves and would command banner headlines and in-depth coverage for days and weeks. Sparing Blazer the agony of multitudes of reporters ripping up his front yard with their vans, at least for a time, was all that he had hoped for.

But then something strange happened. "I might answer some of it," Acting USA Kim said, stepping up to the microphone unbidden as reporters hollered questions. Kim said that in the public criminal complaint, the role of a cooperating witness had been referred to; the official designation was "CW-1," as a way to hide Blazer's identity, which was standard practice in federal cases. Kim then added that CW-1 had engaged in similar criminal conduct in the past, including bribing college players and making corrupt payments in breach of NCAA rules. For unknown reasons, Kim then added that the complaint named a certain CW-1 who had also been charged with fraud by the SEC and become a cooperating witness—providing not just a hint but an absolute direct line to Blazer. It wouldn't be a matter of weeks or days before the press figured out who Kim was referring to; it would take minutes and a Google search, at most, for reporters to uncover the identity of one Louis Martin "Marty" Blazer.

"Why the fuck would Kim do that?" Blazer recalled in amazement. "I knew I wasn't going to stay anonymous forever, but why make the task of identifying me so much easier? I could see Robert Boone was up on the podium next to Kim, and he looked as bewildered as I was. They had gone to great lengths for that not to happen, to disguise my identity until it was necessary to reveal me—if ever. There was a chance that everyone would plead guilty and there would be no trials . . . I told Trish that figuring out who I was wouldn't take long, and she started to freak out. Then the FBI assistant director stepped forward and said to everyone involved in college basketball, 'We have your playbook,' which was a ridiculous overstatement. I didn't think the top officials really understood the case or what had actually occurred. The press conference was a complete clown show."

Blazer wondered if Scott Carpenter was sitting in a bar somewhere, nursing a beer and a grudge as he watched the press conference, and how he'd feel about not getting any credit for the case, such as it was. As he feared, Blazer learned that his guilty plea hadn't been sealed after all, and the banner headlines started to appear online within hours, with the local *Pittsburgh Tribune-Review* reporting that Blazer was the secret cooperator in the NCAA case. The coverage was brutal, with the press immediately seizing on the villainous nature of Blazer's prior conduct, revealing how he'd siphoned off millions in an attempt to aggrandize himself as a movie producer.

"I'm not sure how I could have imagined anything else, but I'd hoped it would be different," Blazer remembered. "I had done wrong. But I'd tried to do some good by helping with the investigation of corruption."

After the press conference, Blazer summoned the courage to turn on the cell phone the FBI was monitoring again. The voicemail box was maxed out, with twenty messages, and there were twenty-eight texts. Almost all the messages were from the press, but one text was from Safarrah Lawson, the agent who'd given Blazer the connection to Rashan Michel, which had led to his meeting Christian Dawkins in a hotel bar in Atlanta years earlier. The memories came flooding back. Lawson was brief and more than a little menacing. Long ago, when Blazer had still been representing football players, he and Lawson had discussed the merits of various forms of life insurance policies. "Marty, still need that life insurance, buddy," Lawson taunted.

That afternoon, TV vans turned up on the lawn of the Blazer home, as he'd feared, but Blazer refused to comment. Inevitably, the indefatigable Rebecca O'Brien from the *Wall Street Journal* called Blazer's criminal attorney. After consulting with Blazer, the lawyer spoke to O'Brien, careful not to share any information that wasn't already in the public domain. O'Brien knew about the case, it turned out, but she hadn't known that Blazer was cooperating with the FBI. O'Brien told the lawyer that "a source" had alerted her to the fact that there had been a significant screwup during the investigation, asking if Blazer cared to comment on the FBI's alleged misconduct.

"She had a better chance of speaking to Jesus Christ himself than getting me to talk," Blazer recalled. "I was still subject to my cooperation agreement with the Southern District, and they could terminate that at any time and throw me in jail. Boone didn't tell me I couldn't talk, but it was clear to me that I had to keep my mouth shut when other people talked all kinds of shit about me. I just wished that someone would notice that I'd tried to expose a broken system and that I had been fighting for my family."

At least yet another phase of Blazer's cooperation had come to an end. While Trish was appalled by the media attention and the open scorn her husband was receiving, Blazer's daughter, Madison, could see the absurdities of the situation, laughing with him when someone posted on Twitter, "Good Morning to everyone EXCEPT Marty Blazer." Her high school friends saw Blazer as defying authority and being involved in the lives of the biggest stars and coaches in college basketball; whatever else might be said about Blazer, he wasn't boring or predictable like his suburban surroundings.

Blazer stayed in the house for days on end, emerging only to watch his son play soccer, and even then, he sat by himself in the stands. He was, as the inevitable Rebecca O'Brien *Wall Street Journal* report headlined, **The Man Who Exposed College Basketball.**

CHAPTER TWENTY

Catch Me If You Can

As he awaited the beginning of potential trials, expecting most—if not all—of the defendants to plead guilty in the face of overwhelming evidence, Blazer started measuring his life in a series of events: six trips to New York for twelve sessions of trial preparation with AUSA Robert Boone, totaling seventy hours of questioning. Blazer was told to treat the process like he was a prizefighter getting ready for a heavyweight bout, with his prosecutor trainers preparing him to anticipate every feint and left hook a clever defense attorney might throw his way.

Blazer wasn't required to participate in the first trial, in the fall of 2018, a case that focused on the relationship between the University of Louisville and Adidas and the payments to the father of Brian Bowen II that resulted in the conviction of two sneaker executives and Christian Dawkins, each receiving a nine-month prison sentence. Blazer wasn't surprised when Tony Bland of USC and Book Richardson of Arizona pleaded guilty, but Blazer dreaded the prospect of having to testify against the unpredictable Rashan Michel. As the weeks passed, it became evident that Dawkins and Merl Code weren't going to plead out, after all, a turn of events that only seemed to harden Boone's already very hardened resolve.

"He wants a trial, so we're going to give him one," Boone said to Blazer of the still-defiant Dawkins.

In the end, both Michel and Lamont Evans also pleaded guilty, leaving only Dawkins and Code at the defense table as Blazer took the stand armed with the training he'd received from the Southern District. He'd learned not to defend his bad prior actions or take the bait when a defense lawyer claimed the case was Blazer's attempt to stay out of prison. Blazer knew to fully admit to his previous lies and calmly state that he was trying to do better in his life going forward.

To prepare for cross-examination, no fewer than six lawyers from the Southern District had raked him over the coals, including the implication that he'd somehow entrapped the targets of the investigation, with Boone deliberately insulting and agitating Blazer. Blazer had been warned that Dawkins's attorney in particular was loud and abrasive, with the affect of a Mob lawyer. He was given to long speeches and flights of rhetoric as a way to unnerve the witness, so Blazer wasn't surprised when the attorney for the defendant came out of the gate swinging hard.

"You're a liar," he half hollered at Blazer. "You are a thief. The only reason you stopped lying and stealing is because you got caught, isn't it? You're sorry you got caught, aren't you?"

Blazer wanted to defend himself against what he considered a surprisingly effective onslaught, but he sat quietly as the lawyer held forth and offered a lengthy account of the defense's theory of the case. The jury had already been treated to two days of Blazer's heavily matter-of-fact testimony for the prosecution, guided by Boone, evidence accompanied by scores of recordings and transcripts.

"I don't care about Christian Dawkins or hurting him," Blazer replied when asked about the runner. "I don't hate Christian. I have no feelings toward him personally at all. As for jail, I'm only here today to cooperate by telling the truth—my truth—because I was there when it all happened, and that's all I'm focused on. I'm not worried about anything other than telling the truth."

The court was packed with national media for Blazer's testimony. He knew the press would be brutal to him, and it was, but he had to fulfill his obligation to the federal government. Even Geoffrey Berman, the United States Attorney for the Southern District, was present to see him withstand cross-examination for three days.

At the end of the cross-examination, AUSA Boone's redirect of Blazer was devastating to the defense, as a CBS reporter pointed out, with Boone methodically asking Blazer how he had come to be introduced to a dozen different college coaches, most of the encounters set up by Dawkins or Code and all the coaches accepting money—proof positive that the defendants and the coaches had been the authors of their own fates. One by one, Boone named the coaches, with Blazer replying to a litany that each of the coaches had been introduced by the defendants, the cadence of repetition increasingly damning.

"No further questions," Boone concluded confidently.

Blazer got home to Pittsburgh at ten thirty at night on the final day of testimony, physically drained and on the verge of an emotional breakdown. Two weeks later, the jury found Dawkins and Code guilty of bribery and conspiracy to commit bribery, returning not-guilty verdicts on other charges like wire fraud. But Blazer still wasn't done with his ordeal, as much as he wished it were over.

"I never dreamed how much the whole trial process would take out of me—so much more than anything else during the cooperation."

But after the testimony and convictions, Blazer still had to worry about his unscheduled sentencing hearing and the prospect of getting at least some prison time. There was nothing more he could do to assist his cause, it seemed, and the Southern District had fallen silent again, so he was stuck in purgatory. Until his criminal attorney called one day in the spring of 2019 to say that he had been contacted by AUSA Boone. The NCAA had reached out to Boone and asked if

Blazer would be willing to talk to the organization about corruption in college sports and his knowledge of NCAA violations. This was a surprising but interesting turn of events. SA Jason Wake had once suggested to Blazer that he could get a lucrative consulting gig with the NCAA when the case was done, educating the sports association on what went on in the industry they were supposed to regulate and police. The idea had intrigued Blazer.

"The NCAA was a joke," Blazer recalled. "I had been violating their rules for more than a decade before I was caught, and I had never had to try too hard to disguise what I was doing. Use cash, don't create a paper trail, don't talk about breaking the rules on the phone—it was simple to circumvent NCAA rules. Everyone involved in college sports knew that the NCAA regulators were incompetent fools. The main threat was someone blowing the whistle on a rival as a way to get revenge or to try to steal a player. But that almost never happened. The coaches and agents and financial advisers and runners all knew they were in on a good thing and that scandals helped no one in the long term when the status quo was so lucrative.

"In the Mafia, there were countless snitches and turncoats, but in the organized crime syndicates that operate college sports, there were no incentives to turn on rivals. You would win some deals and lose some deals, but always brush yourself off and keep moving forward. It was a cultural thing, a kind of understanding that that just wasn't done. That was part of what made my investigation so unusual. I was an insider who spoke the language, so I had been able to take FBI so far into that world."

In the most severe NCAA scandals, the punishment was generally some sort of long-delayed and largely symbolic suspension, and it was usually the players who paid the price, or maybe an assistant coach, rarely the schools or the head coaches. Or the NCAA overreacted to minor infractions in order to show that it took cheating seriously—even as serious cheating was rampant.

~

Blazer had followed the NCAA's reaction carefully since the takedown in the fall of 2017, making records of officials' quotes in his notebooks. A few weeks after the arrests and the onset of the massive scandal, Blazer had read how then NCAA President Mark Emmert had participated in a seminar at Harvard, where he had been asked if the NCAA had any teeth in punishing bad actors in college sports. Emmert had rejected any personal responsibility, claiming that the Operation Ballerz basketball scandal was the function of a group of specific relationships that had devolved over time to create an unhealthy environment—as if it were a unique and aberrant case, not symptomatic of the system. It was evident to Blazer that the relationship between federal prosecutors and the NCAA was dysfunctional, if not toxic, and no one had briefed the association on the case's wide sweep.

Now that Blazer had been asked to talk to the NCAA in the spring of 2019, he longed to tell them that he could easily have involved dozens or scores or even hundreds of coaches in the scheme to pay for players, and not only in basketball—football was even more corrupt. This was Blazer's chance to be part of the solution, he hoped; he was an insider who could tell them the truth. But he knew he had to be careful about what he said to the NCAA, lest it upset or rile the Southern District or disclose the internal workings of the FBI. He didn't want to do anything that could jeopardize his forthcoming sentencing hearing. Blazer was also aware that the prosecutors weren't fully cooperating with the NCAA, and though their reasons were unstated, he believed it was because true transparency would risk revealing whatever had happened in Vegas with SA Scott Carpenter. The NCAA hadn't sent any observers to the trials, a fact that had been noted in the press. To Blazer it looked like powerful forces were aiming to protect themselves.

"I knew that Boone wouldn't tell me how to handle the NCAA request, the same as he'd done with the press," Blazer recalled. "He wouldn't tell me to talk, but he wouldn't tell me not to talk. He was like an inscrutable God. He created moral dilemmas, and I had the freedom to make decisions. Was it a trap? Was it a good idea? Then the NCAA offered to write a letter of support to my sentencing judge, and it became a no-brainer."

The first meeting with the NCAA was set for Pittsburgh, at Blazer's insistence, in a large conference room in the airport Marriott on the morning of July 18. Ten officials from the NCAA had flown in early that morning, and they were seated at a long table. Clearly, the organization was taking the session seriously, or at least recognized the stakes and dangers. All the NCAA officials were white, apart from one Black man, the director of basketball enforcement, who expressed regret that he'd been unable to detect any of what Blazer had been up to.

"All this shit happened on my watch," he said.

Blazer laughed, thinking that the official had no idea how true that was. The session began with the NCAA officials introducing themselves and their roles, and then the lead investigator asked Blazer to provide a narrative of his personal background and dealings with the federal government, from the tactics he'd used to recruit football players over the years, to the $12,000 in a hotel hair-dryer bag for Auburn coach Chuck Person and all the many events in between. Many of the facts that Blazer was describing had never emerged, because of the indicted coaches' guilty pleas and the cooperator's silence in the press, together with the lack of cooperation with the Southern District.

Blazer concluded after an hour of nonstop talking, and the NCAA official running the meeting sighed and said, "You hit everything on my list. So I have no questions."

Blazer blinked and looked around the room at the wide-eyed NCAA investigators. No one had a single question about the crazy story he'd just told them? The regulators in charge of the NCAA had just heard about widespread corruption happening, and they were ready to move on without so much as a query or follow-up? Apparently so; no one dared to dip their toes in these waters.

The session turned to allegations involving the various specific colleges involved, with the NCAA patching in lawyers for each school when the roles of their coaches and players came up for discussion. But it quickly became evident the colleges had been instructed to keep their phones on mute and ask no questions. Blazer learned that all the questions from the schools had to have been asked in advance and would only be put to him by the relevant NCAA official, an odd procedure that seemed designed to limit if not stifle a free-flowing conversation. With the limited evidence that had emerged at trial, the colleges had no way to know in advance what to ask, a kind of bureaucratic end run that seemed more than a little dubious to Blazer.

"We had an understanding that you were not to speak to Mr. Blazer directly," a senior NCAA official in the meeting said angrily on the speakerphone to the attorneys for Auburn when they had the temerity to ask Blazer about Chuck Person's conduct—facts that were new to them because there had been no trial in the case. A contentious exchange followed, with the Auburn attorney expressing frustration, and the proceeding was halted until his phone was muted again.

"That is not what this is," the NCAA official said. "We explicitly instructed you to email your questions prior to the interview for us to consider. You did not. If that creates a problem, then we are willing to proceed without you."

Watching the process, Blazer was visited by a familiar sensation— this was yet another charade. The NCAA was attempting to save face and symbolically punish schools, Blazer believed, not actually understand the mechanics of corruption. The schools were intent on avoiding blame and claiming ignorance when it was painfully obvious from Blazer's story that the issue wasn't an occasional bad apple; it was the whole orchard. School after school cast doubt on events and questioned the facts that Blazer was sharing with them, their disbelief betraying their lack of capacity—or desire—to grasp the reality he was describing.

"I had zero tolerance for the NCAA or the schools challenging facts that I knew were indisputable," Blazer said. "A lot of what I was saying was new to the schools, and you could hear a pin drop as I talked, but the schools kept saying that what I was saying couldn't possibly be true—when of course it was. I wanted to tell them that I knew what I was talking about because I was in the fucking room when it all went down."

The session proceeded without a break for lunch, until Blazer asked for a sandwich and was permitted to order a room service club sandwich, noting that the NCAA didn't even pay for his meal. No one else ate a bite. The pretense to moral superiority, displayed in not paying for a twelve-dollar soggy sandwich of limp bacon and sagging lettuce, was comical, in a way, as Blazer chewed and asked to take a bathroom break.

In the midafternoon, an employee of the hotel entered to refresh the coffee urns and pastry platters that had been sitting untouched since eight a.m. As the employee crept toward the food, trying not to be noticed, she seemed to sense the hushed tension electrifying the room. She stopped in her tracks when she noticed the assembled officials were staring in stern and heavy silence; then she beat a hasty retreat, fleeing the room like she'd stumbled on the scene of a crime, it seemed to Blazer.

"I think I saw an ESPN patch on her shirt," Blazer joked, as if she'd been a reporter from the sports channel coming to plant a bug to record the conversation.

All laughed, apart from the director of enforcement.

"I have to say for the record, that's not funny," the NCAA director said.

But to Blazer, the entire session was a joke. For eleven hours straight, Blazer offered a portrait of the NCAA as a cesspool, the high-level lawyers and investigators charged with policing the multibillion-dollar industry glumly listening. They weren't asking who the real victims were, or what he thought should be done to change the system, or if there was an alternative business model for college sports other than human trafficking.

"I'm like the dude in *Catch Me If You Can*," Blazer told the NCAA officials. "I'm your *Catch Me If You Can*. I know how cheating works. I'm not trying to burn anyone or protect anyone in the athlete business. I have no axe to grind. I will never again work with athletes in any business capacity again, so I have no ulterior motive. I can tell the NCAA who is doing the deals—more important, the where, the when, the why, the how it's all going down. The FBI had cut the investigation short. It could have grown exponentially with the number of coaches involved and the amount of money that was being taken, if the FBI had kept going. I can show how the system works."

The offer fell on deaf ears.

As a follow-up, Blazer traveled to Indiana soon after to meet at the NCAA's sleek corporate headquarters. In the wake of the scandal caused by Blazer's case, the association had come up with the idea of instituting a policy of allowing student-athletes to benefit commercially from the use of their name, image, or likeness—or NIL, as it is known. The officials wanted to know Blazer's opinion of such an approach. It avoided paying students, thus making them employees, with all the expense and complications that came with that reality—the thing the NCAA most wanted to avoid—and hopefully it would help with the publicity nightmare of serial scandals and failed investigations.

"I told them that the NIL system had to be properly regulated," Blazer recalled. "If you left it wide open—if NIL became the Wild West—an endless parade of dudes like me would prey on the kids. It would be one hundred times worse than coach-bribery corruption. The top players would probably be okay—the kids who could command national attention from reputable companies. But the midlevel kids would be ripped off and lured into terrible contracts by advisers and agents and runners and hustlers. The kids wouldn't understand, let alone perceive all the ways a clever businessperson could take advantage and make millions off them. The NCAA absolutely had to protect the kids—but of course they didn't, and it is only a matter of time before the NIL system blows up in their face. The NCAA is throwing students to the wolves."

CHAPTER
TWENTY-ONE

The Supremes

On the morning of February 6, 2020, Marty Blazer was scheduled to appear before Federal District Court Judge Edgardo Ramos in Lower Manhattan, the jurist who had presided over both basketball trials and thus was acutely aware of the value of his cooperation and testimony. It was a cold winter day, the streets slippery with sleet as Blazer shuffled across the federal square in rush hour with his wife and attorney to meet his fate. With COVID beginning to sow its awful harvest, Blazer was in a fog as he entered the courthouse. It was his youngest daughter Arianna's birthday, a fact that haunted him, as he feared she would forever remember the date as the time when her father had been sentenced to federal prison.

"Hey, in the event Judge Ramos sentences you to prison, I'm going to ask that you be allowed to self-report and that it be to FCI Morgantown," his attorney said as they stood in the security line.

Blazer and Trish locked eyes in horror, making their way glumly to the sixth floor. The lawyer was referencing a minimum-security prison with a reputation for catering to white-collar criminals, but it was still a terrifying proposition. In anticipation of the hearing, a small mountain of documentation had been prepared. Letters from family and friends had been entered into the record, along with the all-important 5k letter from the federal government that described the nature and value of his cooperation in detail. "To say that Blazer's cooperation was helpful to the government would be an understatement," the Southern District's letter said. "His cooperation contributed significantly to the government's successful prosecution of ten defendants in three related corruption cases. And he testified in a highly publicized trial that resulted not only in three convictions of a former Adidas consultant and an aspiring manager, but also in an important ongoing public discourse about corruption in college athletics."

As with his proffer years earlier, Blazer was dressed carefully for court, not wearing cologne or loafers, and displaying an attitude of abject remorse, now actually heartfelt. Blazer's attorney began the proceedings by asking if the judge had received the expected letter from the NCAA. The judge had not, a final gesture of indifference and incompetence from the association.

Blazer winced when Ramos reviewed the offense level involved for sentencing, using terms like *concurrent* and *consecutive* and *mandatory minimum*, which had profound implications for Blazer's life. He could be facing up to seven years in prison, in addition to the six he'd already spent as a cooperator.

"And with that, Mr. Boone, do you wish to be heard prior to the imposition of sentence?" Judge Ramos asked.

"Yes, Your Honor," Boone replied. "Briefly."

This was the moment Blazer had been bracing for. Boone could use his discretion to help the cooperator or he could shrug and remain indifferent, or even indicate, by way of emphasis and implication, that the accused was less than fully repentant. Blazer didn't dare turn around and look at his wife, for fear he'd start weeping, with the members of the press crowding the gallery to bear witness.

Rising, Boone said Blazer had come to the government voluntarily, before a criminal investigation had been started by the government. Judge Ramos asked what stage the SEC had been at in their proceedings at the time, and Boone said that the government hadn't yet instigated the case, eliding the fact that Blazer had been instructed to hire a criminal attorney and an indictment was imminent.

"It is perhaps more often the case that an individual has been charged with a crime and, after charges are brought at some point later, then decides to cooperate with the government," Boone said. "Mr. Blazer stands out for that reason."

"And I am correct that at the time, the only wrongdoing of which they were aware was Mr. Blazer's misappropriation with respect to his financial-advising business?" Judge Ramos asked.

"Not only did Mr. Blazer come in on his own to confess, he also volunteered information he believed showed misconduct by him, but also volunteered his guidance in helping the government discover similar misconduct by others," Boone said. "What I'm talking about there is his NCAA-related conduct. That was not an investigation the government had going. And so you're correct in separating the fact that what he initially came to talk about and what the government knew about was really separate from what ultimately became his cooperation."

None of the money had gone into Blazer's pocket, Boone told the judge, and all the funds had been used solely for the failed entertainment endeavors. Boone pointed out that for a long time, Blazer had flown around the country using his own money to instigate the investigation and that he had never hesitated in recording conversations wearing a wire—a dangerous operation, the prosecution said.

"Your Honor obviously knows what the end result of Mr. Blazer's cooperation was," Boone said, noting the ten convictions and two separate trials. "As we've stated in our submission, it's one of the biggest prosecutions and investigations of corruption in college athletics. That case simply doesn't get made without Marty Blazer's cooperation."

Blazer resisted the urge to pump his fist, with the public vindication of his role in the case officially acknowledged. He began to tear up as Boone calmly and convincingly offered details from Blazer's cooperation—facts that the former financial adviser was sure would be forgotten. Boone added that Blazer had been nothing but courteous and uncomplaining with the federal government, praising how he'd been proactive because he had genuinely wanted to assist the investigation.

"There is no justification or excuse for my actions," Blazer said from the defense table when the judge asked what he had to say for himself. "I take one hundred percent responsibility for every terrible decision I made that brought me here today. I know an apology to the individuals I harmed will never be enough, but I am deeply sorry. These guys trusted me to protect them, and I betrayed their trust. There hasn't been a moment—and there never will be a moment—that I don't deeply regret my actions and know that this shame will forever live with me."

There was a long pause, the judge again consulting the documents, and then the decision was announced: time served. For a man who had misappropriated more than $2 million, it was nothing short of a miracle. It was the kind of consideration provided to only the most exclusive class of cooperators, particularly in the bare-knuckled Southern District. As Blazer listened to Judge Ramos refer to how the cooperator's children understood the difference between right and wrong because their father had taught them better—words that stung to the quick—he realized that the sentencing was over.

"I couldn't resist going in for a hug with Boone," Blazer recalled. "He reluctantly reciprocated . . . Personally, the path I chose was hell. My soul experienced a million little cuts, and the uncertainty of cooperating was a nonstop mindfuck. I'm not a very religious person, but I prayed for strength every day. I had a quote on my desk that I looked at all the time to keep me going, as I lived in the penitentiary of my mind. 'God wouldn't put a Goliath in your life if He didn't know there was a David in you,' the saying read."

~

During his ruling, Judge Ramos brought up the question of instituting a system to compensate college players or at least provide them some form of financial support, but he dismissed the issue as irrelevant to the case before him. Both basketball trials had been appealed, and both attempts failed on appeal.

But a separate case involving the NCAA reached the Supreme Court. The 2021 case *NCAA vs. Alston* adjudicated a claim brought by student-athletes challenging the monopoly power of the NCAA and claiming it breached antitrust laws. After an exhaustive trial, the judge decided not to overturn the NCAA's rules, but he issued an injunction stopping the organization from limiting the benefits schools could pay to athletes for education-related matters, opening the way for colleges to allow students to receive compensation in forms that didn't directly contravene the amateur regime, a decision that the Supreme Court upheld.

Signaling peril in the future, however, in a concurring opinion, Justice Brett Kavanaugh was scathing.

"The NCAA's business model would be flatly illegal in almost any other industry in America," Kavanaugh wrote. "All of the restaurants in a region cannot come together to cut cooks' wages on the theory that 'customers prefer' to eat food from low-paid cooks. Law firms can't conspire to cabin lawyers' salaries out of a 'love for the law.' Hospitals cannot agree to cap nurses' incomes in order to create a 'purer' form of helping the sick. News organizations cannot join forces to pay reporters less to preserve a 'tradition' of public-minded journalism. Movie studios cannot collude to slash benefits to camera crews to kindle a 'spirit of amateurism' in Hollywood."

Price-fixing was price-fixing was price fixing, Kavanaugh observed, noting the billions in revenue generated by student-athletes. "These enormous sums of money flow to seemingly everyone except the student-athletes," he continued. "College presidents, athletic directors, coaches, conference commissioners, and NCAA executives take in six- and seven-figure salaries. Colleges build lavish new facilities. But the student-athletes who generated the revenues, many of whom are African American and from lower-income backgrounds, end up with little or nothing."

Days later, the NCAA issued new regulations allowing student-athletes to benefit from their name, image, and likeness—the NIL policy the NCAA had discussed with Blazer two years earlier. On the tick of midnight on July 1, 2021, scores and then hundreds and thousands of students started to endorse everything from local car dealerships to sneakers and energy drinks and mobile phone carriers. The worst excesses of more than a century of hypocrisy and duplicity and corruption were coming to an end, it appeared, but the NCAA wasn't going to reform itself thoughtfully. Instead, college athletes were exposed to a new breed of scammers and connivers looking to exploit the name, image, and likeness of kids still in their teens—as Blazer had forewarned.

"The NIL makes the situation worse for college athletes," Blazer said. "I told the NCAA that ninety-nine percent of the kids would get small deals—ten or twenty thousand dollars. For agents and financial advisers, the NIL deals would be loss leaders. The real money would be made on the back end, with all the deals that could be set up for cars and jewelry and the big commissions on contracts and insurance policies, money the kids wouldn't know their representatives were making. There is no regulation, and the NCAA took no responsibility for the system they have created. The kids will still be preyed on by men like me. What the hell else is the NCAA for if not to protect the athletes, instead of the schools and system and its own financial interests?"

As former Arizona assistant coach Book Richardson rode up the winding mountain road to Otisville Federal Correctional Camp in New York's Catskills to serve his prison sentence, Arizona head coach Sean Miller continued to thrive, even though he had been caught on tape conspiring with Christian Dawkins; he was eventually fired in 2021, only to be promptly hired by Xavier. LSU's Will Wade had flat-out denied any involvement in paying players despite the blatant FBI recordings leaking, essentially telling the world they should believe him, not their lying ears. In the wake of the scandal, Rick Pitino—who insists to this day that he was falsely accused—was let go by Louisville; at the time of this writing, he was the coach of St. John's.

The consequences for players directly involved were dire. Brian Bowen II was suspended from the Louisville basketball team, for example, so he transferred to the University of South Carolina, but the NCAA ruled that he would have to sit out for two seasons. He tried to enter the draft in 2018 and 2019, but in the end, instead, he was forced to play professionally in Australia, thus denying him crucial years of development against NCAA-level talent. Bowen never recovered from the setback, as he alleged in a racketeering lawsuit he brought against Adidas, claiming that the company had preyed on people who were "unsophisticated and come from poor or modest backgrounds." In 2021, a federal judge dismissed the case, granting Adidas summary judgment, in essence finding that Bowen had no hope of prevailing at trial.

On the first of March in 2022, Christian Dawkins reported to federal prison to serve an eighteen-month sentence, and on the same day, Merl Code published a book, *Black Market: An Insider's Journey into the High-Stakes World of College Basketball*. It was a strange account, unapologetically chronicling the ways Code had broken the NCAA's sham amateurism rules in general terms—"I did my damn job, plain and simple," he concluded—even as he said that he wasn't going to name the coaches and sneaker-company executives he had conspired with in the case who remained unindicted.

Later that year, former FBI special agent Scott Carpenter rose in court in Las Vegas to plead guilty to a misdemeanor count of embezzlement of $13,500 in federal funds, the crime ironically—or perhaps, predictably—captured on the casino's security camera. The plea stated, "Even though Carpenter had been drinking on Saturday at the cabana and at the Bellagio while gambling, he knew that he was gambling with money belonging to the United States. As an FBI agent and the lead case agent for the investigation, Carpenter occupied a position of trust that he abused in a manner that allowed him to convert the government money."

Despite the government's recommendation that Carpenter not be sent to prison, the judge ruled that the disgraced former federal agent had received sufficient leniency, sentencing him to ninety days. It wasn't lost on Blazer that Carpenter had once told him that he didn't want to spend even two days in a federal prison, such were the degrading realities of life behind bars.

"I wasn't surprised when I learned the details of Scott's case—the drinking and gambling," Blazer said. "I saw the trouble coming as I watched Scott and Jeff DeAngelo get caught up in the money and glamour and celebrity. It is intoxicating. The same thing had happened to me. I got caught up, and I became addicted to feeling like I was above everyone else—like the rules didn't apply to me. I felt sorry for Scott, but it could happen to anyone—and does more often than is commonly appreciated."

In the years after Operation Ballerz, events have continued to cascade catastrophically for the NCAA. In quick succession, a patchwork of state laws officially outlawed the practice of amateurism. In late 2023, a class action lawsuit was filed in California by a collection of college student-athletes—football and basketball players—seeking more than $4 billion in damages and back pay for the years their names, images, and likenesses had been used during television broadcasts. The *House* case, as it is known, promises to be only one of many such lawsuits, seemingly inevitably leading to a new financial structure for college sports far from the illusory conceits of amateurism.

As the NCAA forlornly seeks an antitrust exemption from Congress, with little hope of success, the National Labor Relations Board began to hold hearings in late 2023 on the question of student-athletes in fact being employees of the colleges. This was the outcome the NCAA most dreaded, as it required the athletes to be paid and receive benefits like health care—thus potentially requiring the billions generated by the NCAA to be more equitably distributed. In desperation, at the same time, the new president of the NCAA issued a directive permitting schools to directly pay athletes a limited amount—a move that best resembled a Hail Mary pass. The seemingly inevitable implosion of the NCAA was caused, in many ways, by a chain reaction triggered by the curious case of a middle-aged financial adviser to NFL players in Pittsburgh who went undercover for the FBI.

Marty Blazer now lives a quiet suburban life, working in the tech industry, and with Trish, helps guide their three kids through college and into their own lives. Blazer can't bring himself to watch college or NFL football, and the entire experience has humbled him in many ways. But the character, Blaze, is still part of his life. Late at night, when there are guests over and he's had a scotch or two, Blazer will start to tell stories to his friends and neighbors about his days hanging out with NFL players in clubs and bars, and the time he went undercover for the FBI. To his listeners, there is an element of disbelief when Blazer starts holding court—but here's the thing about his stories: they are true.

Blazer still feels like the case he built with SA Scott Carpenter and AUSA Robert Boone was prematurely ended because of the government's unwillingness to truly go after one of America's most beloved—and disrespected—institutions. As much as Blazer stays away from college sports—he doesn't even watch games on the weekend—he believes that nothing has really changed.

"The government said they *had college basketball's playbook*, which was ridiculous," Blazer said. "The NCAA reforming itself is also ridiculous. NIL only made the student-athletes more vulnerable. If I used an alias and changed my name, I could go undercover again now, but this time it would be much bigger. All the elements are still there. The coach structure is genius. So are the connections to sneaker companies and the idea of keeping kids isolated in a money bubble. The nature of college sports in this country is all about the money. After all that I put my family through, I crave a quiet life, but the old Blaze is still inside me, lurking below the surface. I know the system inside and out now. Who knows?"

ACKNOWLEDGMENTS

As this book was going to press, as the final manuscript was about to be sent to the printer, Marty Blazer died suddenly of a heart attack on Monday, January 8, 2024. He'd had a heart attack years earlier, but he exercised regularly and showed no signs of any illness in the days leading up to his passing. He was only fifty-three years old. The shocking end to his life cruelly denied Marty the chance to see this book go into the world. Marty was excited about the book release, and he was primed to finally speak publicly about his experiences, some of which didn't make it into the final version. I am truly sorry that he never got the opportunity to know how his story would be received.

Marty's death is an awful tragedy for Trish and their children, Madison, Connor, and Ariana, his sudden departure leaving a gaping hole in the family he loved so dearly. It is my hope that this book provides some measure of consolation for the Blazers, a lasting testament to their husband and father and the way he fought to protect his family during his yearslong encounter with the justice system. In honor of Marty's memory, I want to thank Trish and the Blazer kids for their commitment to do all they can to ensure his story lives on.

Marty and I developed a real rapport over the years I was reporting and writing this book, and he tirelessly endeavored to make *Hot Dog Money* as complete and accurate as possible—precisely as he promised when we started to work together. I can think of no higher praise than to say that, in my experience, Marty was a man of his word. I am grateful that he trusted me to tell his story.

Publishing requires many hands and minds to fashion a finished book. It was a true pleasure to work with the smart and capable Laura Van der Veer of Little A. I hope I get the chance to work with her again, both professionally and personally. Associate publisher Carmen Johnson was a helpful sounding board and a great supporter of this project. Ellie Schaffer ably guided the publicity push, while Rachel Clark oversaw the excellent marketing effort. The striking cover was designed by Jack Smyth and overseen by talented art director Tree Abraham. Rachel Norfleet did a thorough copy edit, and Kellie Osborne and Jessica Poore attended to the vital proofreading details. Malika Whitley provided a cultural context read for the many racial and social issues that underscore this story. I would also like to thank those who aren't named here but added valuable contributions. It is a pleasure to see a book get better and better with each suggestion or tweak, so a heartfelt thank-you to you all.

My agent Robert Guinsler of Sterling Lord was a stalwart cheerleader for the book, as was my film and TV agent, Jody Hotchkiss of Hotchkiss and Associates. I also appreciated the vote of confidence in the project that came in the form of the acquisition of film rights by Smokehouse Pictures, and particularly the always-engaged president, Kerry Foster, and founders, George Clooney and Grant Heslov.

I leaned on many friends while writing this book, and I thank them all, but I would like to acknowledge my walking buddy Barry Berman for putting up with me. Likewise, my beautiful and kind wife, Maya, patiently learned more about corruption in college sports than she surely ever anticipated. My sweet twin daughters, Lucy and Anna, graduated from high school and moved off to university during the time I was working on this book. All three of the women in my life provide a support system that I rely on every day as they selflessly give me inspiration and love. Maya, Lucy, and Anna—my gratitude and love are forever yours.

ABOUT THE AUTHOR

Photo © 2024 Karen Pearson

Guy Lawson is the *New York Times* bestselling author of *War Dogs*, which was made into a feature film, as well as *The Brotherhoods* and *Octopus*. An award-winning investigative journalist, he has written articles on war, crime, culture, and sports for the *New York Times Magazine*, *Rolling Stone*, *GQ*, *Harper's*, and many other publications.